THE KING'S LOOT

THE KING'S LOOT

The Greatest Royal Jewellery Heist in History

RICHARD WALLACE

First published 2024

The History Press
97 St George's Place, Cheltenham,
Gloucestershire, GL50 3QB
www.thehistorypress.co.uk

British Library Cataloguing in Publication Data.
A catalogue record for this book is available from the British Library.

ISBN 978 1 80399 438 3

Typesetting and origination by The History Press
Printed and bound in Great Britain by TJ Books Limited, Padstow, Cornwall.

Trees for LYfe

For Ally, who always knew.

Contents

Prologue

The Duchess of Windsor's Jewels

There is pleasure and pain in irritating the sores of old wounds.

Lermontov, *A Hero of Our Time*

The staid and conservative Swiss city of Geneva had never seen anything like it. All the best restaurants, Il Lago at the Hotel des Bergues, Les Armures, Le Gruyérien, and even the Hotel President Wilson's trio of chic establishments were booked out for weeks and all the best rooms in the best hotels were changing hands on the black market for unremembered favours and fabulous sums of black money.

Limousines were driven in from Bern, Zurich, Lyon, even Turin, to meet the exorbitant demands of the hoards of incoming celebrities and their entourages, minor eastern aristocracy, assorted Eurotrash and truckloads of new money disguised in restrained Savile Row suits and severe Chanel dresses. The services of hairdressers, spa attendants and dry cleaners were stretched to breaking point. Dexedrine, Dextrostat, Desoxyn, ProCentra and Vyvanse, as well as Benzedrine supplied by hotel waiters, were being consumed in vast quantities to prop up the relentlessly ticking Swiss economy. Caviar, truffles and foie gras were in short supply and the great champagne houses of Rheims were releasing unprecedented amounts of restricted vintages at ridiculous prices to make a quick killing.

And then there was the cheese. The Swiss consume an estimated 22kg of cheese a year and Geneva is especially renowned for its cheese fondues, a special melange of Jarlsberg, Emmenthaler and Gruyère mixed with wine and kirsch. Most foreigners never reach the bottom of a Swiss fondue pot, but every Swiss native knows the bottom is the best part because that's where the rich, crispy, cheesy bits live.

Like everything Swiss, fondue comes with a civic responsibility: you are required to ensure your fork never touches the melty cheese, only your bread, and you must make sure your mouth does not inadvertently make contact with your fork.

Yes, the Swiss are deadly serious about cheese, which is why, despite all the inconveniences imposed on the clean and clinical city of Geneva's 230,000 inhabitants during the last weeks of March 1987, the greatest imposition was the sudden and unexpected deterioration of cheese stocks reported by the city's best cheese store, La Fromagerie Bruand.

The situation was said to be so bad it rapidly became the principal point of conversation across the dinner table, and the city's state councillors were constantly pestered about the obvious solution: a requirement for purchasers to present Swiss papers when ordering their cheese provisions. Or was this just an apocryphal story dreamt up by the local media intent on cashing in on all the transitory international attention? Probably, but one thing was for sure: it certainly *felt* as if the entire bling universe had descended upon the stolid Swiss burghers of Geneva, wrecking their ordered and calm lives with an arrogance bordering on occupation.

The culprit was Sotheby's, the venerable English auction house. It was offering 306 lots of the deceased Duchess of Windsor's jewellery and other Windsor items to the highest bidders at the prestigious Hotel Beau-Rivage, perched on the southern tip of Geneva's Lac Léman.[1] According to the hastily written, unreliable catalogue of the sale, eighty-seven of the lots consisted of Cartier pieces with twenty-three from Van Cleef & Arpels.[2]

The auction, set to run for two days starting on Thursday, 2 April, and Friday, 3 April, at 9 p.m. precisely, was being conducted under a couple of circus tents that had been stitched together to house 1,500 guests, plus amenities for the well-heeled to bolster their resolve for the bidding wars to come. Another 700 people were due to watch the proceedings on the Hotel Beau-Rivage's closed-circuit television in the ballroom, with satellite links beaming the event to similar venues in New York and London.

Then there were the reporters (over 250 of them) and seventeen international television crews reporting the sale live. They surrounded the tent and hotel, pens poised, flashbulbs popping, microphones jutting, wine quaffing. It was the most vulgar and daunting event Geneva had ever consented to host and a fitting testament to the tortuous, scintillating route it took the Windsor jewels to get there.

The whole extravaganza had taken a toll on everyone's nerves, including Sotheby's legendary English jewellery expert and auction architect, the debonair Nicholas Rayner. But even he, as he drew aside the curtains that Thursday morning in the pokey little room he occupied at the Hotel De La Paix (after releasing his sumptuous suite at the Beau-Rivage as a favour to an old client with deep pockets) and gazed at the majestic saw-toothed, snow-capped Alps in the distance, *must* have realised that this was likely to be *the* most incredible event in the lives of a lot of people.

The signs were already there: the unprecedented attention the jewels had received from international media; the lines of people waiting to brazen the cold and the rain as they snaked around the preview venues; the selling out of the first print run of 15,000 catalogues practically overnight (another 10,000 copies were printed and snapped up – it was estimated Sotheby's made £600,000 before the sale even started);[3] and the enormous number of requests Rayner received for private 'interviews' from the rich and notorious hoping for some kind of inside running on the lots in question. These were proof enough of the tremendous worldwide interest.

And then, of course, there was all the commotion and excitement in Geneva itself once the entire travelling circus had hit town, something which he hoped might happen after moving the Sotheby's office from the relatively hyper business environment of Zurich a short while ago. As he told his bosses after convincing them of the need to make the move, the international language of jewellery is French not German. However much money there was in German-speaking Zurich, Sotheby's fine jewellery business was unlikely to flourish there unless it relocated to a more international and cosmopolitan hub.

It says something of the charm of the man (described by one observer as a 'member of European glitterati')[4] that he was able to clinch the move by telling Sotheby's new chief, Al Taubman, that Geneva also had the best Indian restaurant of the two cities (Rayner was a frequent visitor to the country and its jewel encrusted maharajahs), something which appealed to the portly and avuncular American's sense of English eccentricity.

However, at this moment, on the morning of the great auction, the erudite old-Etonian was close to exhaustion. He had been kept mostly vertical by copious amounts of stimulants and cigarettes during the whirlwind pre-auction publicity tour of America, Monaco and Geneva. The pre-auction negotiations with the formidable Maître Suzanne Blum, *exécuteur testamentaire* of the Windsor estate and self-styled defender of the moral rights and financial interests of the Duchess of Windsor, were also a source of extreme stress.

According to Sotheby's, when the public exhibition opened in their Manhattan showrooms between 17 and 22 March 1987, the lines to view the jewels grew so long that people were turned away and the police were called out to assess the situation.[5] They determined that viewings should be limited to fifteen minutes per person in order to move the crowds through the stuffy building without incident. Similar scenes occurred in Palm Springs at the Montsorrel Mansion. One thousand people were invited to the reception and 2,000 showed up.[6]

Despite the incessant demands on his time, Rayner was sure there was some lucrative compensation in store for him once the madness had dissipated and things had returned to the routine normality of life in Geneva; like the huge bonus he was due to receive in the event things went spectacularly haywire, auction wise, and the particular cachet that attached itself to helming the biggest and most notorious jewellery auction of the twentieth century so far. Yes, this could very well be his year. This was even though Nicholas Rayner had been leading a spectacularly full and varied life for a while now.

This latest escapade was simply another knot in the rich tapestry of his life, albeit the most famous and dangerous one yet. Dangerous because he was still unsure whether he could get away with the ruse he and Sotheby's had perpetrated at the very heart of the auction itself. This was, of course, in addition to what historian Peter Watson called the prevailing 'unorthodox practices inside Sotheby's' during the late 1980s where the 'supposedly open and clean process of auctioneering was manipulated beneath the surface'.[7]

The biggest test of these practices was about to begin, and, ironically, it involved auctioning items connected with another entity who had devoted his life to the single pristine aim of getting away with whatever took his fancy: King Edward VIII of England, later His Royal Highness Prince Edward, the Duke of Windsor.

There have been sixty-three monarchs of England spread over approximately 1,200 years, going back to Egbert, the first monarch to be recognised by the title *Bretwalda* (Anglo-Saxon for 'ruler of the British'). Crucial to this story of royal deceit, greed and arrogance is the incredible fact that no English monarch's personal possessions, or indeed those designated Crown possessions, have been publicly audited or forensically examined to the extent that Henry VIII's were in 1547 (the list of these Crown possessions is documented in the British Library as Harley MS 1419).

Public scrutiny of the sovereign's personal wealth on such a scale is not likely to ever be repeated in the future, for reasons that will become apparent in this book.

Since the death of Prince Albert in 1861, the British royal family have shrouded their personal wealth, gifts and accoutrements in an impenetrable fog of discretionary secrecy. They are perfectly within their current rights to do so, of course, rights which even extend to their ownership of the Crown Jewels and other items in the Royal Collection.

These rights are often referred to as inalienable (cannot be surrendered or removed) by legal scholars such as Professor Vernon Bogdanor, with the added caveat that they are transferable from monarch to monarch in perpetuity (i.e. forever).[8] Another legal scholar, Ronald Lightbown, also cites a key ruling by the seventeenth-century jurist Sir Edward Coke that overwhelmingly enforces Crown ownership of palaces, artefacts and jewels in favour of the royal family with an additional devastating exception that allows a monarch to dispose of these items whenever he or she wants to: 'The ancient jewels of the crown are heirloomes and shall descend to the next successor and are not devisable by testament.'[9] Coke's ruling was reinforced 300 years later by Iain Sproat, former Secretary of State for National Heritage, when he confidently stated the sale, gifting or transfer of the Royal Collection and the Crown Jewels was 'entirely a matter for the Queen'.[10]

The Crown Jewels are merely the tip of an enormous iceberg of royal treasure that no one other than the current monarch and a few trusted members of the royal household is conversant with its true size and shape. So, the whole question of what jewels, gems and jewellery the present royal family has will never really be solved without their co-operation and a full independent inventory taken, like the one accorded to Henry VIII's personal possessions after his death. And, as already stated, there's little chance of that happening.

Which makes the 'relocation' of some of these incredible items in the royal family's collection, especially in the early days of the twentieth century when they were primitively secured, so plausible and unsurprising ... and inviting. Even so, in the historical ebb and flow of royal jewellery and the rogues gallery of individuals involved in its loss, destruction, disposal and theft, the Duke and Duchess of Windsor merit serious consideration for inclusion.

The grand extent of their larceny was only halted by the abdication of a king. And then, when the chance arose for an extension of these acts after the Second World War, it was greedily accepted.

But this isn't a book about the abdication of King Edward VIII. Neither is it a book about the Windsors' Nazi connections, sexual preferences, sexual practices or romantic peccadilloes. Those seeking information about that and Wallis Simpson's expertise with 'The Singapore Grip' will need to look elsewhere. This is a book about deceit and a series of outrageous deceptions committed by people with ample means, opportunity and motive to commit them.

In UK law, a crime is a deliberate act that causes physical or psychological harm, damage to or loss of property, which is against the law. *The Cambridge English Dictionary* calls it an action or activity that is against the law, or illegal activity generally. *The Oxford Dictionary of Sociology* defines crime as an offence which goes beyond the personal and into the public sphere, breaking prohibitory rules or laws, to which legitimate punishments or sanctions are attached and which requires the intervention of a public authority.

A crime is therefore something that is wrong, that can be punished by judicial laws, if proven.

Proof is structured around what *The Oxford Companion to Crime and Mystery Writing* calls the categorical trinity: means, motive, opportunity. Motive is the reason for committing the crime, means are the tools or methods used to commit the crime and opportunity is the occasion that presents itself to allow the crime to take place. For someone to become a suspect in a criminal investigation, all three must be established.

But this isn't a stuffy book about the law, the definition of crime or how it is proven. This is a book about how a series of wilful, premeditated and deceitful acts committed by certain reputable people succeeded, sometimes with the tacit approval of unimpeachable figures in authority. Were they wilful and premeditated? Or were they the result of something more mundane such as ignorance, misunderstanding and lethargy?

In the case of King Edward VIII/the Duke of Windsor, such nagging doubts about his behaviour persist, echoing the approach Winston Churchill used in framing disagreements with Charles de Gaulle in letters to King George VI: 'His insolence ... may be founded on stupidity rather than malice.'[11]

Whatever side of the argument you lean towards is up to you. But for any kind of deceitful behaviour to succeed at all (whether stupidly or maliciously), a person needs to be skilled at manipulating four psychological factors in tandem with the standard legal troika of means, opportunity and motive. They are credibility, chaos, chance and conviction.

What do I mean by these things? In the context of this book, I define credibility as the authority, reputation or status a person asserts to influence an outcome; by chaos, I mean an environment where confusion, secrecy, instability, fear and disunity is rampant. Chance is the ability to manipulate an unexpected set of circumstances to one's advantage; and by conviction, I mean a person's unwavering intention to continue a course of action despite the risk of scandal and retribution because they truly believe in the legitimacy of their actions.

Exploring how each of these facets in isolation and in combination made the greatest royal jewellery heist in history possible is the purpose of this book. That and how a royal jewellery collection fraudulently amassed over a period of fifty years came to be auctioned off so credibly and spectacularly on the shores of Lake Geneva in 1987.

The applicable crime or crimes associated with these events, and whether they were wilfully or accidentally intended, is for you to decide.

1

Hatless from the Air

My husband never was heir conditioned.

Duchess of Windsor

As His Royal Highness, Prince Edward, the Duke of Windsor lay dying in 1972 from throat cancer after decades of relentless smoking, each day was a kind of resurrection for his devoted staff involving rites and rituals worthy of the most elaborate coronation ceremony. First, he was gently awakened every morning, carefully washed and then stripped of the previous day's bedclothes by his night nurse, Baltimore-born Juliana Chatard Alexander.

While his favourite dog, Black Diamond, was removed from the foot of his bed and led away by a footman to be exercised and fed, the duke's drip was changed and cleaned, his gums, ears and nose swabbed, and his arms and legs massaged with ointment. Finally, he was turned over to prevent bedsores and his back was rubbed with medicated cream that tingled as it was applied. When the nurse had finished, his valet, Sydney Johnson (dressed in red and gold livery), helped him into a set of crisp Charles Dillon pyjamas embroidered with the duke's cypher in gold thread.

Now he was ready to begin the day, and Johnson returned with a beautiful poached pear in a crystal bowl sitting on a silver salver. The duke, as he always did, waved it away, and a few minutes later the valet came back with the same silver salver holding a single cigarette and the faithful Black Diamond, who resumed his position unbidden at the foot of the bed.

The duke's body had been falling apart since the mid-1960s. His left eye was completely closed. He limped and walked with a stick. In February 1972, he entered the American Hospital in Neuilly, Paris and the malignant nature of the throat cancer that was first detected in November 1971 was disclosed. On 10 May 1972, he suffered a cardiac arrest and was connected to a drip wherever he went but still managed to receive Queen Elizabeth II when she came to pay her final respects a few days later. From 25 May until he passed away, he was unable to leave his bed and was a frail and delicate figure of a man, his 5ft 7in frame shrivelled to skeletal proportions. All he had left was his identity, his memories and his personal effects that were displayed over a suite of four rooms that constituted his private quarters on the first floor of the manse at the edge of the Bois de Boulogne.

According to Alexander, the duke's relationship with the duchess was distant. 'She hardly ever came in to see him,' she told the Baltimore Sun. 'I saw her in his room on the first night, and then again the night he died. I was there from 7 pm to 7 am for about three weeks, and during that time, she didn't come in and eat with her husband.'[1]

The duke's quarters were separated from the duchess's on the first floor by the great armorial Order of the Garter banner belonging to his grandfather, Edward VII, which was pinned to a wall. In addition, a sumptuous heraldic banner on a pole bearing the ancient arms of the Prince of Wales in painted and appliquéd scarlet, yellow and blue taffeta, edged with a golden metal fringe, which was presented to the duke in 1911 and which once hung in St George's Chapel Windsor, now guarded the entrance to his rooms as if to denote the special royal presence that occupied them.

For the duke's passionate attachment to his royal pedigree vied with his obsession with the duchess and his love of money as the most significant driving elements of his life. The manse at 4 route du Champ d'Entraînement illustrated these facets of his character in all their gory, brazen detail.

The house was literally crammed with royal artefacts and heirlooms that had been either passed down to him by his forebears or simply taken from royal residences at Balmoral, Sandringham and Buckingham Palace, loaded into an army truck at Fort Belvedere and stowed in the hold of HMS *Fury* the morning of his exit from the throne, or stored at Frogmore. He had everything in Paris to make him feel like a king: from the imperial cypher-embroidered towels and nécessaires in his bathroom, to the linen in his bedroom, the notepaper, scrapbooks, cufflinks, desk accoutrements, Dunhill cigarette boxes, crystal dinnerware, leather wastepaper baskets, Cartier clocks, shirts, underwear, dressing gowns, Peal & Co. slippers, handkerchiefs, Goyard luggage, throw rugs, Aubusson carpets with Prince of Wales feathers woven in silver, Hermès photo frames, wall lights and walking sticks. Everywhere one moved, without exception, was tattooed with cyphers and insignia and coats of arms bearing either his or her or both Windsor initials, stylised or entwined, embossed or stitched, stamped or etched, all redolent of antique royal ownership.

It should be said that the Villa Windsor at the time of the duke's death in May 1972 was at the zenith of its opulence and upkeep, a fitting stage for all the paraphernalia the Windsors had accumulated over a lifetime of receiving, taking and commissioning. They had a staff of thirty servants, including separate chauffeurs to drive them on shopping expeditions, chefs, washers-up, scullery maids and seven liveried footmen.

The duchess was meticulous. When the last guest arrived at a Windsor party, the butler discreetly notified her as she put the finishing touches to her costume in her room. She would then appear marvellously at the top of the stairs, like a queen. The staircase was lined with hundreds of orchids and guests nibbled on 5lb of beluga caviar while they witnessed the spectacle.

At dinner, the duchess kept a tiny gold pencil beside her plate and a discreet notepad where she would jot down her thoughts on the meal, what worked and what didn't. In later years, the notepad became a tiny gold book linked to her wrist by a gold chain. The servants christened it the 'grumble book'.

The day-to-day routine at the Villa was strict. The sheets were ironed every night and changed every other day; equally, the duchess's money had to be crisp, either new from the bank or ironed by a servant. The water in the numerous crystal vases was always to be crystal clear. The floral decorations on the table were sprayed with Diorissimo to give them added fragrance and the footmen wore royal livery. It was 'non-U' to serve a tomato that contained a pip, candles were always lit at eye level and gold jewellery was never worn in the evening – it had to be platinum.

The beloved Windsor pugs, Trooper, Disraeli and Black Diamond, received their meals from solid silver bowls on the lawn in summer and on the terrace in winter. They were groomed every morning and smothered in Dior perfume. Their menu was printed in French and usually contained such delicacies as breast of capon. Fresh dog biscuits were baked every day by the chef.

Originally named Château Le Bois, the Villa at 4 route du Champ d'Entraînement was built around 1860 as a summer home for Georges-Eugène Haussmann, the controversial and frequently hated French official chosen by Emperor Napoleon III to carry out the massive urban renewal programme of new boulevards, parks and public works in Paris. The French government sequestered the property after the Second World War and Charles de Gaulle occupied the house in the late 1940s.

The Villa was subsequently leased to the Windsors by the City of Paris at a nominal rent from 1952. Maison Jansen, a Parisian interior-decorating firm, refashioned the home under the supervision of the duchess. The firm's president, Stéphane Boudin, is best known for being asked by Jackie Kennedy to assist in the renovation and restoration of the White House from 1961 to 1963 after Boudin impressed the First Lady with his work on the Red and Blue rooms.

Boudin decorated the Italian-styled hall with idyllic frescoes, lurid tapestries and a Japanese screen, supposedly donated by the Emperor

Hirohito. Duck blue walls and lush Louis XV upholstery gave the sitting room an anglicised French feel and illuminated the most significant item in the house: the Chippendale mahogany table where, at 10.30 a.m. on 10 December 1936, King Edward VIII signed the Instrument of Abdication.

Elsewhere, the autocratic Boudin allowed the library to be dominated by two paintings by well-known British artists: a tame portrait of the duchess by Gerald Brockhurst, which hung above the fireplace, and an equally idealised equestrian portrait by Alfred Munnings, featuring the duke as Prince of Wales. There were books on military and naval history, political biographies and sports, the most prominently displayed were assorted editions of the duke's autobiography, *A King's Story* and the duchess's memoir, *The Heart Has Its Reasons*.

Horst P. Horst was commissioned by *Vogue* to photograph the Villa in 1963 and told *The Architectural Digest*:

> It is hard to believe that there can ever have been an interior more surpassingly clean, where crystal was more genuinely scintillating and porcelain more luminous, or where wood and leather, polished to the consistency of precious stone, could more truly be said to shine.[2]

A later edition of *The Architectural Digest* had a snappier take on Chez Windsor:

> Chez Windsor – with green and yellow faux marble, silver and gold glints, and rich colors like sunflower-yellow and dahlia-red – Buckingham Palace met Versailles with a Café Society chaser.[3]

The most prominent feature of the duke's bedroom was another wall hanging bearing the arms of the Prince of Wales that once hung above his Fort Belvedere bed. A matching bedcover, the centre of which was embroidered with the badge of the Prince of Wales, consisting of an angular EP initial within a blue garter band, was another relic of a previous life.

Scattered between this room, his private study, drawing room, dressing room and bathroom was a treasure trove of royal family pieces he'd managed to squirrel away. These included a set of silver dishes engraved with the cypher of George III; a desk seal mounted with a bust of George IV; a set of silver ashtrays from Queen Victoria's royal yacht; a portrait of his mother, Queen Mary, by Sir William Llewellyn; and gold snuff boxes belonging to his father, George V. There was also a remarkable collection of over 12,000 royal photographs dating back to the mid-nineteenth century, many carrying personal inscriptions, which the Windsors' chauffeur of twenty years, Gregoire Martin, and his wife, Maria, had stashed in the duke's claw-footed bath tub to keep them from prying eyes during the duchess's fourteen-year widowhood following the duke's death (the duke preferred using an American shower for his daily ablutions).

Perversely, all this reverence for royal things was seen by many of his pre-abdication employees and friends as somewhat ironic given that he treated his lineage with a nonchalance bordering on contempt during his time as Prince of Wales and later as king. It was only when he abdicated that his sweeping veneration of status and rank really took off, though his greedy, acquisitive nature was a trait that ran in the family like a greyhound dashing after a decoy.

But then Edward was an obsessive man, prone to infatuations. He was stubborn, nervous and difficult to read, unsure of his purpose. A man who, most of the time, didn't know who he was, what made him happy or what he wanted most in life. Until, of course, he met Mrs Simpson.

Some of this antipathy for his situation and his determination to take what he could from it was probably a psychological reaction to the stultifying formality, coldness and sheer unpleasantness of his upbringing. From the very beginning, his relationship with his parents was associated with pain.

As a child, he and his brother Bertie were regularly abused by their demented nanny, Mary Peters, who would pinch Edward on the arms and hurt him in other ways, particularly when the boys were being prepared to see their parents, the Duke and Duchess of York, for their daily visit.[4] As a result, these became unpleasant experiences for everyone, the boys crying, screaming and red-faced, and their parents exasperated and pained at the unruly deportment of their royal children.

Aside from Mary Peters, the two princes were brought up by Frederick Finch, the dour nursery footman whose father had once been in the service of the Duke of Wellington (and who later became Edward's valet and butler), and Henry Hansell, their hapless tutor.

Their education was poor. Tommy Lascelles, Edward's future assistant private secretary, commented on their 'astounding ignorance of English literature' and a distinct aversion to books and reading of any kind which they maintained for the rest of their lives.[5] However, he thought this was a symptom of a deeper, profounder defect:

> … for some hereditary or physiological reason his normal mental development stopped dead when he reached adolescence [...] his mental, moral and aesthetic development, which, broadly-speaking, remained that of a boy of seventeen [... and this] immaturity persisted into middle age.[6]

Later, as Duke of Windsor, Edward confided to friends that his 'father had a most horrible temper. He was foully rude to my mother.'[7] He dreaded being punished, which was frequent and nerve-wracking. 'No words that I was ever to hear could be so disconcerting to the spirit as the summons, usually delivered by a footman, that "His Royal Highness wishes to see you in the Library".'[8]

During these ordeals in his father's tiny study, lined in military red cloth, he could not count on his mother, Queen Mary, for much help. James Pope-Hennessy, in his 1959 biography *Queen Mary*, has her saying of these moments, 'I always have to remember that their father is also their King'.[9] Mary Peters was eventually dismissed after several years of mistreatment but permanent, unredeemable damage had been done.

Edward's father and mother were a mystery, even to their closest staff and friends. They did not interact with their children on anything other than the most mundane, general matters. There was zero parental warmth. Personal matters were frowned upon. Expressions of love, feelings, spontaneity and emotion were subsumed by control, reservation and reflection.

This emotional gulf meant they never really knew what they had produced, other than a series of well-groomed, healthy, petrified bodies able to procreate the royal line. Naturally, this also meant their children could never confide in them and had to seek comfort and solace elsewhere.

Within the family, this source of warmth came from Edward's grandparents, King Edward VII and Queen Alexandra. For Edward, the bond he forged with Queen Alex during these boyish years was to have fantastic consequences in the years to come. At the end of his life, he still had the little silver child's knife and spoon set she gave him. 'For my little Grandson on his First Birthday from Granny', the inscription read. He was her favourite and she indulged him, much to the chagrin of her son, the Duke of York.

Generally, Edward's father was a boring but kind man, content to keep a low profile and, like his brother and father, was more comfortable on a shoot than in the drawing room. But when it came to his children, particularly the two eldest boys, Edward (known as David in the family) and Bertie, he was also known to be a brute. He had rigid ideas about punctuality, deportment and dress, and Edward was treated like a midshipman, constantly on parade.

Randolph Churchill claimed George V once remarked to the Earl of Derby that his Victorian approach to parenting was based on precedence, 'My father was frightened of his mother, I was frightened of my father, and I am damned well going to see to it that my children are frightened of me'.[10] Although probably an apocryphal quote, Edward was more diplomatic, 'I have often felt that despite his undoubted affection for all of us, my father preferred children in the abstract'.[11] To his authorial assistant, Charles Murphy, Edward was more direct, 'I had a *wretched* childhood! […] Of course there were short periods of happiness but I remember it chiefly for the miserableness,' he said.[12]

But although Edward could bear the brunt of his father's onslaughts with a rapidly developing talent for nonchalance and wilful carelessness, his brother Bertie could not. It is little wonder that Bertie developed the stammer that was to manacle his happiness forever, especially when it was well known in the royal household that his father thought the best way of dealing with it was by mimicking and laughing at him. In other words, by shaming and ridiculing an already sensitive and abused boy (poor Bertie, he even had the misfortune to be born on 14 December, Mausoleum Day, when Queen Victoria and the entire family gathered at Prince Albert's tomb at Frogmore like a murder of crows to pay their respects).

Edward's mother was an equal disaster. Another of her biographers, David Duff, described her as being 'out of touch with the human side of life'.[13] Even her aunt, the Empress Frederick of Germany, described her as cold, stiff and completely unmaternal. She had little time for motherhood, though she bore six children. She had no passion for them. She did not kiss, cuddle or hug them. Her youngest child, John, born severely disabled and epileptic, was kept away from his family, hidden in a cottage on the Sandringham Estate with devoted caregivers until his death at 14.

Edward expressed a commonly held view when he commented, 'My mother was a cold woman, a cold woman'.[14] In Brendon and Whitehead's *The Windsors: A Dynasty Revealed*, he was said to have remarked spitefully when she died from lung cancer in 1953, 'I somehow feel that the fluids in her veins must always have been as icy-cold as they now are in death'.[15]

There was, however, one massive trait Edward took from his mother that he wholeheartedly embraced for the rest of his life: a love of money and rank and all the entitlements it could buy or demand or access. Queen Mary, to put it kindly, was the royal magpie of the royal family of Windsor. And she never forgot where she came from.

She was born the daughter of two Continental royals who were constantly in debt. Though brought up in straitened circumstances and overshadowed by her ebullient mother, the Duchess of Teck, Mary became a stoic, serious young woman. She had to be, as the family were constantly on the move to escape their creditors, eventually ending up in Italy. Her father, the Duke of Teck, died insane (she once saw her father hurl a plate across the table at her mother's head). Even worse, her paternal grandfather had contracted a morganatic marriage to a commoner, Countess Claudine Rhédey von Kis-Rhéde (though she was an aristocrat herself), which excluded his son and grandchildren from the Württemberg succession, wrecking the Tecks' fortunes forever, it seemed.

Returning to England, they were thrown a lifeline by Queen Victoria who was looking for a suitable spouse for her grandson, the Duke of Clarence, Prince Albert Victor. Mary was selected. But when 'Eddy' died in 1892, it seemed at first that the cosmic bad luck of the Tecks had returned. Miraculously, though, Mary was given to the new Duke of York, Prince George, who was instructed by his grandmother to take her.

When Mary became queen in 1911 she was so appalled by the extent to which family pieces from the Royal Collection had passed into private hands as gifts or were sold that she was determined to retrieve them. She was an avaricious and ruthless collector. The apogee of her relentless desire to make up for what had been lost included the work of Peter Carl Fabergé, and she purchased three of the famous Fabergé eggs in the tragic aftermath of the Russian Revolutions of 1917 for a song. Indian art and antiquities were also on her radar. A Delhi dealer marvelled at how quick she was to seize Jaipur enamels and jade elephants for the Royal Collection when they were dispatched to her at Windsor.

James Pope-Hennessy wrote about her passion for collecting and preserving royal history in the following terms, 'She was constantly adding to the Royal Collection pictures and objects of family interest bought out of her own private purse'.[16] But this unrestrained mania, bordering on addiction, for all manner of bewildering purchases of things of dubious value exasperated her children. Lord Claud Hamilton told Pope-Hennessy, 'She bought family things chiefly and insisted on saddling her third son the Duke of Gloucester with a vast and impossible silver tea urn because it had belonged to Queen Victoria's uncle the Duke of Cumberland.'[17]

She cut a swathe through the auction houses and stately homes of her adopted country. Nor did the unseemly provenance of certain 'royal' mementoes faze her. One Christmas, the Honourable Mrs George Keppel gave a sumptuous and sexually charged Fabergé cigarette case featuring a coiled serpent to her lover Bertie, Prince of Wales. Mrs Keppel was the prince's temptress, '*La Favorita*', his 'little Mrs George'.

Ten years later, when Bertie died as King Edward VII, his widow Queen Alexandra promptly returned the cigarette case to her with undisguised relish. Not to be outdone, in 1936, Mrs Keppel offered it to Queen Mary as a gift. It was swiftly accepted and remains part of the permanent royal collection of Fabergé.

Queen Mary expected antique dealers, jewellers and estate owners who had items that interested her to render them up without hesitation. This irresistible sense of entitlement gave her hosts and unlucky proprietors no choice but to hand these items over with feigned alacrity.

But one day, according to royal folklore, Queen Mary almost met her equal in determination. Taking tea one late afternoon with Lady Hudson, her absent-minded gaze settled on a set of beautiful chairs painted by the artist Angelica Kauffman. The queen casually suggested, to no one in particular, that Lady Hudson's chairs would complement the Kauffman table she already owned.

Lady Hudson said nothing. The clock ticked on. Queen Mary continued to sip her tea. The sun went down. Queen Mary remained seated, endlessly chatting. More time passed. As the mantle clock struck nine o'clock, a drained Lady Hudson finally capitulated. She was an old woman, and she was exhausted, beaten. The chairs were stowed in the royal Daimler and the queen drove off at the end of another productive day.[18] At least on this occasion the transaction was socially transparent. On other visits, she just went ahead and took what she wanted.

Apart from her avaricious nature, she was also frugal and would recycle flowers from her vases to use as gifts when she visited her friends.

The Marchioness of Cambridge revealed, 'She would go round picking them out of vases in her rooms, so that often they were dead the day after she gave them.'[19]

It was her passion for jewellery that defined her exterior appearance. Her subjects, particularly her colonial subjects, indulged her to the max. None more so than in India, where the maharajahs handed out jewels like blackberries. She sought to outdazzle everyone around her, projecting such a fantastic image of imperial majesty that for many mere mortals she ceased to be human. There's the story that she was so decorated and gem-encrusted at Lord Harewood's wedding that a myopic and over-whelmed E.M. Forster felt obliged to bow to the iced and many-tiered wedding cake under the impression that it was Queen Mary.[20]

When full mourning for Edward VII ended in May 1911, Queen Mary also began to keep a book entitled 'The Gowns and Jewels Worn By Her Majesty at Important Functions', a leatherbound volume stamped with ostrich feathers. The jewels and orders that she wore were precisely recorded, in far greater detail than the gowns. As the historian Jane Ridley noted:

> This was a queen who measured her self-worth in diamonds, for whom the semiotics and dynastic narrative of jewellery mattered far more than the ephemeral, sexualised world of fashion [...] Encased in diamonds and ermine, wearing some of the most valuable diamonds in the world pinned to her sleeves, Queen Mary was a living icon of Empire.[21]

Her eldest son carried this obsession with glittering prizes into his adult life, along with an estrangement from family and an undisguised non-chalance. An incident in 1934 that Victor Meldrew would have been proud of hilariously illustrated his intolerance and boredom with the entire royal edifice. At the Westminster Abbey marriage of his brother, the Duke of Kent, to Princess Marina of Greece, he absent-mindedly pulled out a cigarette and lit it with a candle held by a priest. There is no record of the king's reaction, but he must have seethed with incredulity.

For years, ever since he could remember, Edward had especially hated Sandringham, where (in echoes of Villa Windsor) the intense claustrophobia of royal life had turned the place into a morgue: family faces were everywhere – painted, drawn or photographed. At Sandringham the king was often at his worst.

Alden Hatch, writing in *The Mountbattens*, described an occasion when Edward entered his father's study to ask him for a favour. The king looked him up and down and then thundered, 'You dress like a cad. You act like a cad. You are a cad. Get out!'[22]

He began to avoid family gatherings knowing full well they served only as opportunities for his father to interrogate everyone on what they were doing and why, with longer sessions devoted to a dressing down of the heir to the throne. Edward was obliged to keep conventional trousers in his luggage to wear in front of his father on these occasions as his fashionable turn-ups were always greeted with a scathing remark. Once Edward and his brothers were in their thirties, the king had them followed by agents who reported back to Buckingham Palace their associations and indiscretions.[23]

It is clear that Edward was hellbent on escaping from his family well before the abdication of 1936. They seemingly had nothing in common and were poles apart when it came to what he considered more important and sustaining than the dreary atmosphere of court. His lifestyle was incomprehensible to them, rising leisurely as he did on most weekdays at eleven, following this with a couple of easy official engagements, a round of golf and then various turns at dinner parties and nightclubs.

The king and queen did not venture into society but dined at home in their private apartments, he in a tailcoat and Garter sash and she in a tiara. It was more than a generational gap.

Perhaps worn out by the Great War, the king would say to everyone at family dinners, 'We won't talk, will we?'[24] Edward later referred to it as his father's 'private war with the twentieth century'.[25]

The only respite seemed to be Royal Ascot Week, which ran from Tuesday to Friday in June, but even here, the same dreary routine persisted year after year. The royal party entertained the good and the great every evening at Windsor Castle during the festival of racing.

Shortly before 8.30 p.m. the king and queen and members of the royal family in residence would set off for the Green Drawing Room. At the door they were met by the Master of the Household, who bowed and backed into the room, heralding their arrival to the other guests who were arranged in two quarter-circles, men on one side and women on the other.

The king, his sons and members of the royal household wore the Windsor uniform: a tailcoat of dark blue with scarlet collar and cuffs, worn over a single-breasted white waistcoat and plain black trousers. The other men in the party wore black tailcoats and knee breeches. Women were dressed in evening gowns and jewels.

Queen Mary moved along the line shaking hands with the men while George V did the same with the women. Moving into the dining room, the group was serenaded by a Guards string band, annexed out of sight in a small chamber and wearing tightly buttoned tunics drenched in sweat.

Each course was served by liveried footmen in scarlet. The meal lasted no more than an hour. When it was over, the queen took the women back to the Green Drawing Room and George V spent twenty minutes with the men over coffee, port and liqueurs and then abruptly stood up and led them out to join the ladies. Punctually at 11 p.m. the entire company reassembled into two quadrants, the royal family bid them good night, and then left the room. The evening was over.

In *A King's Story*, Edward recalled such evenings, 'Nothing was lacking but gaiety.'[26] One night, he and his brothers determined to enliven the atmosphere for the younger members of the party and arranged for the Guards band to stay behind after their parents had gone to bed. They rolled back the carpet in the Green Drawing Room and held an impromptu dance. But the bemused musicians could only manage some outdated foxtrots. It was a failure. 'The ancient walls seemed to exude disapproval. We never tried it again.'[27]

John Betjeman aptly described the incomprehensible gulf shared by the two sides and the arrival of a new breed of monarch when he wrote 'On the Death of George V':

Spirit of well-shot woodcock, partridge, snipe
Flutter and bear him up the Norfolk sky:
In that red house in a red mahogany book-case
The stamp collection waits with mounts long dry.

The big blue eyes are shut which saw wrong clothing
And favourite fields and coverts from a horse;
Old men in country houses hear clocks ticking
Over thick carpets with a deadened force;

Old men who never cheated, never doubted,
Communicated monthly, sit and stare
At the new suburb stretched beyond the runway
Where a young man lands hatless from the air.[28]

In 1920, Edward moved into York House, a suite of seventy-five rooms occupying a portion of St James's Palace, and acquired a household of his own, including the man who was to play a principal role in his life as both guide and thorn, Alan 'Tommy' Lascelles.

Lascelles was to serve the young prince, off and on, for some sixteen years and was a controversial figure in royal circles. It would be true to say Tommy never really 'got' what was going on in the young prince's mind, much less lifestyle.

After a disastrous series of match-making efforts by his parents, depressed and exasperated, Edward realised he had to base himself somewhere independent of them once and for all. Fort Belvedere, a castellated curiosity on the edge of Windsor Great Park, would do the trick nicely. It was the antithesis of his family's royal residences and a place where Edward could cut loose and freely spend the vast amounts of money he regularly received on himself and his mistresses without the prying attention of his boring, unimaginative and moribund family.

The money had been piling up since his 16th birthday in 1910 when, as Prince of Wales, he automatically inherited the Duchy of Cornwall. Established by Edward III in 1337, the estates of the Duchy produced enormous revenues for the young prince, comprising valuable property in London, twenty-three counties and huge estates in the West Country. The treasurer of the Duchy of Cornwall (at that time Walter Peacock) estimated that by the time he turned 21, his cash savings probably amounted to £400,000. Added to this was the tax-free annual £90,000 the Duchy generated in personal income, which went straight into his Coutts account. In fact, the prince had so much money sloshing around in his bank account that he lent his father £90,000 in 1915 to buy additional land at Sandringham.

The Fort was the most obvious place where Edward could pour all this easy money. The place had been built by the third son of George II, the Duke of Cumberland, and was then taken up by George IV, who had it extended and enhanced with Gothic embellishments. It lay abandoned until Edward saw it in 1929 and asked his father for it, who was surprised 'that queer old place' had attracted his eldest son's interest.[29]

Approached through Windsor Great Park, the Fort lay at the end of a narrow gravel drive that snaked through thick clusters of beech and evergreen trees before one arrived at the top of a low hill. The light stone walls were covered with creeping ivy and flowering wisteria. Lady Diana Cooper called it a 'Walt Disney coloured symphony toy'.[30]

Though it was old-fashioned and slightly creepy when he moved in, Edward opted for a light (for the day), modern style of interior decoration. A small hallway burst into an octagonal hall with a black-and-white marble floor, furnished with eight yellow leather chairs that were propped against plain white walls. The drawing room was panelled in natural pine with Chippendale furniture and several Canalettos in ornately carved and gilded frames. The dining room was similarly panelled in pine and hung with equestrian paintings by Stubbs.

A small library, by contrast, was filled with Queen Anne furniture. Upstairs were six bedrooms and as many modern bathrooms as Edward could fit in. There was also a steam bath in the basement, where he'd disappear every evening to complement the latest fad diet he had recently embraced to save his 5ft 7in body and 29in waist from going to fat (he was especially self-conscious about his legs).

But it was the garden on which he lavished most of his time. From the front terrace the land sloped away to Virginia Water, a long lake fringed by groves of thick trees. The Cedar Walk led into thick dells of rhododendron and azalea. Descending terraces were winged with stone battlements and eighteenth-century Belgian cannon.

There was a grass tennis court and a swimming pool but Edward, generally clad in baggy plus fours and a thick sweater, often corralled his male guests into the forests to cut down the flowering laurel with machetes. It may have been a robust distraction that conveniently took the place of other physical pursuits such as point-to-point and hunting, but it was also a place where Edward could relax and indulge himself, speak freely, and share things with a coterie of pals and confidants.

The Fort became a personal warehouse of sorts. From 1929 until he left for the last time in December 1936, Edward managed to stuff it to bursting with royal knick-knacks that, like his mother, he had requisitioned without asking. Because there was so much, it took years for the contents to find its way back to the exiled duke and duchess across the Channel. The army truck that followed the royal Buick to Portsmouth naval base immediately after the abdication speech in 1936 was hastily requisitioned and the merchandise it contained barely scratched the surface of the duke's possessions.

Then there were the jewels he had been amassing since his early twenties and which brought an added lustre to his most eligible bachelor status. He was a habitual devotee of the great jewellery houses. In 1925, he was drawn by the French cartoonist Sem being mobbed by Parisian women on his way to Cartier as 'Le Prince Charming de la rue de la Paix'.[31] Along with the *haute joailliers* of Paris, Edward also frequented the London jeweller Hennells, where he made substantial orders well before he met Mrs Simpson (he was known by a succession of girlfriends as a fountainhead of gems).

So where did all these jewels come from? He certainly had the money and access to the secret troves that were controlled by his family. But then, he really didn't need to tap into these resources if he didn't feel like it. Most, if not all, of the jewels and gems that Edward scattered among his friends had been gifts lavished on him because of his status, as they had been regularly lavished on his family for close to a century, since the days of his grandmother, Queen Victoria (or 'Gangan' as Edward called her when he was growing up).

In 1921, when the duke toured India as Prince of Wales, extravagant gifts were bestowed on him as he travelled through sixteen states. At Jodhpur, he sat on a solid silver throne watching parades of bejewelled elephants and bullocks with horns covered in silver leaf. At Baroda, he was garlanded in a heavy gold chain that dropped nearly to his feet and was taken into the jewel room where £3 million worth of diamonds and pearls were displayed. In a sapphire blue velvet book with a silver crest, printed as a limited-edition record of the trip, there is a tantalising glimpse of the scale and enormity of the jewels that were showered on him as *nazars*, or princely tributes.

At a public reception, the Taluqdars of Oudh presented him with 'a beautiful garland, made of gold and set with emeralds, rubies and pearls'.[32] There is no record or hint of this gift in any British newspaper reports about the reception nor in the *Times of India*. Suzy Menkes, writing in *The Royal Jewels*, comments, 'The garland is not in the list of crown property of the British Royal Family nor has anything answering to its unique description ever been seen by anyone connected with royal jewels.'[33]

One can only guess what other jewels, presented to the British royal family during their numerous tours of the Empire, like endless platters of crystallised fruit, were similarly given the secret treatment.

To be clear, such behaviour was perfectly within the legal parameters of royal discretion. Other gems, jewels and pieces of jewellery obtained later (including official gifts) might also be added to the Royal Collection at the sole discretion of the monarch. Which means they could also not be added to the Royal Collection or taken out of the Royal Collection at the whim of the monarch. This is the conundrum at the heart of the House of Windsor's jewellery collection and which the duke, as Prince of Wales and king, unashamedly exploited as part of his exit strategy, as we shall see in later chapters. As Suzy Menkes notes in *The Royal Jewels*, the essential question is 'which is the jewellery belonging to the Crown [...] and what is personal and private property?'[34]

The consensus view is that the monarch is the sole arbiter of what is in and what is out. Which means we will probably never know the full extent of the Windsors' personal jewellery collections because not only is the answer protected by personal discretion, it's also shrouded in decades of non-disclosure.

The practical application of this royal discretion was confirmed by Queen Elizabeth II's former lord chamberlain Lord Cobbold, who told a parliamentary select committee in 1971:

> There is a clear understanding, accepted by Her Majesty [...] that the Royal Collection is regarded as covering all pictures and works of art purchased or acquired by all Sovereigns up to the death of Queen Victoria and also certain property acquired since then at the discretion of subsequent monarchs.[35]

He went on to say that the Royal Collection was 'in no sense at her private disposal'.[36] Lord Cobbold did, however, refer to items, especially jewellery, which, he said, were 'regarded by Her Majesty as Heirlooms'.[37]

The term 'heirlooms' creates another grey area because the Crown has never specified what these might be. Since most of what it owns was inherited or given as a present, and will one day be bequeathed, the term 'heirlooms' could cover quite a lot. In Iain Sproat's (former Secretary of State for National Heritage) 1995 opinion, the disposal of objects from the Royal Collection was 'entirely a matter for the Queen',[38] as has already been noted. And in a 2000 television interview, the Duke of Edinburgh confidently expressed the view the monarch was 'technically, perfectly at liberty to sell them'.[39]

This secrecy is also substantiated by other legal devices known as 'closing' and 'sealing', which excludes the public from seeing the contents of royal wills. In his seminal book, *Royal Wills in Britain from 1509 to 2008*, Michael L. Nash writes how the death of Prince Albert in 1861 ushered in a new and altogether different phase of royal will making.[40] Until this date, the wills of sovereigns had been readily accessible, at least to scholars and historians. They were stored in well-known places and various copies were made. But, on the death of Albert, the whole question of his will was complicated by other issues, especially the mania of his wife Queen Victoria for secrecy. She was, writes Nash, extremely proprietorial and *sui generis* – a law unto herself.

To begin with, the will of Prince Albert was not lodged at Somerset House, which in those days all wills had to be, except those of the sovereign. What legal device did Queen Victoria use to keep Prince Albert's will from public knowledge? There are several possibilities. Nash suggests she could simply have used the royal prerogative, convincing herself that in such matters the public had no right to know. But most likely, Queen Victoria simply used the *Hausgesetze*, or laws of the dynasty, which closed such matters to everyone.

Queen Victoria's reticence in allowing a royal will to be made public created a precedent that was used by subsequent monarchs, including the Duke of Windsor. Nash ruefully concludes that determining what is in a royal will can only be achieved by looking at the evidence surrounding it. Regarding the will of Queen Victoria herself, it is known it was signed on 25 October 1897, but nothing was published as to the size of her fortune or to whom it was left, only that it did not go to her heir. The same reticence was observed with the wills of King Edward VII, George V and VI, and (mostly importantly for this story) Queen Alexandra, who died without making one.

Though royal wills are protected, the public scrutiny surrounding a royal death is not. Even for an ex-king like Edward VIII, who had managed to escape the stultifying conventions of royalty, there were rituals to observe and submit to.

Cocooned by his royal paraphernalia, trophies and souvenirs that had been gifted, collected and purloined over a lifetime, the duke's end at the Villa Windsor was as composed as his beginning, seventy-eight years earlier at York Lodge. One of his carers (though not the designated night nurse, Juliana Chatard Alexander) recalled that in the early hours of 26 May 1972, the corbeaux, or ravens, that had made the Villa their domain, kept hitting the duke's bathroom window with their beaks and claws as if ominously trying to get in.

By the 27th, a Saturday, the duke's continued deterioration prompted the duchess to ask the Windsors' American physician Dr Arthur Antonucci to fly to Paris from New York to review the duke's condition. With Dr Antonucci confirming the inevitable, Sydney Johnson, the duke's valet, and Oonagh Shanley, his principal carer, kept vigil and prayed at the foot of his bed where Black Diamond lay dozing. After Antonucci had left, Edward apparently asked Shanley, 'Am I dying?' to which she briskly replied, 'You're quite intelligent enough to decide that for yourself.'[41]

On the 28th, he asked Johnson to take him to his desk so he could write some letters, but his hands shook so much he couldn't hold the pen. Johnson suggested he eat something, perhaps his favourite Finnan haddock and scrambled eggs? The duke declined but then thought he might manage some peaches and cream. Johnson spoon-fed him and afterwards sponged him and put him to bed with the curtains drawn. It was the last time he saw him alive. That evening he woke up and requested stewed peaches, a favourite from nursery days, then lapsed into a coma before they arrived.

At 2.25 a.m. on Sunday, 28 May, the duke died peacefully in his sleep. The duchess was woken by Shanley and led into the bedroom, where she leaned over her dead husband and kissed his forehead. Cupping his head, she whispered, 'My David, my David ... you look so lovely.'[42] Black Diamond had meanwhile quietly and unobtrusively left his master's room never to return.[43]

Later that morning, the French coroner arrived to certify the death. There would be no autopsy. After he had left, the duchess's favourite hairdresser, Alexandre, visited her and then French couturier Hubert de Givenchy was admitted to her bedroom to fit her for a black dress and coat for the funeral.[44] De Givenchy told Suzy Menkes that he found the duchess dishevelled and devastated, her face ravaged by months of despair at the impending denouement. She drank vodka out of a silver mug.

Meanwhile, Sydney Johnson carefully washed the duke's body and laid him out on his bed, covering him with an immaculate Union Jack up to the neck. He then surrounded the corpse with banks of white lilies, roses, chrysanthemums and orchids.

'I remember they came to embalm him,'[45] Johnson later told the *New York Times*, 'and I picked a suit for him to wear. But they said, no, he'll be wearing nothing.'[46] Johnson was appalled. The duchess told him to leave the embalmers to their task. 'Just brush his hair the way he does it and leave him,' she told him.[47] The embalmers wanted to remove the Union Jack and cover the duke with a simple satin sheet, but Johnson was adamant it should stay. They gave in. 'The rule is, as he comes, so he goes,' they told Johnson. 'He came in with nothing and will leave with nothing.'[48]

Not quite with nothing – he arrived in the world as a royal prince of the blood with all the privileges and sense of entitlement that birth right entails, and he exited it a royal duke with additional privileges that were negotiated and uniquely bestowed (however grudgingly) on an ex-king. Then, of course, there were the fantastic material advantages his birth provided for, which he was able to tap into with only the flimsiest of restraints.

During the duke's lifetime, the wealth of the British royal family reached stratospheric heights due in no small part to the mind-blowing generosity of colonies keen to exploit the diplomatic advantages of regal gifting. After decades of largesse, there were so many gems, jewels and items of jewellery in the royal vaults it compelled Edward's mother, Queen Mary, to compile the first inventory of the family's personal collection to ensure the lax practices of the past, when these things were nonchalantly given away, was never repeated in the future.

Despite these loose safeguards, Edward was lucky he had not been born 100 years earlier into the comparatively impoverished, and none too clever, Hanoverian line. His acquisitive opportunities would have been severely restricted by the sheer financial incompetency of that dynasty.

It was George III who, in 1760, handed over the surplus revenue from the Crown Estate to the government of the day in return for an annual stipend known as the Civil List, a colossal mistake from which the Crown has never recovered. The loss is still acutely felt to this day and is reflected in the introduction to the royal household's 2011 statement concerning royal public finances. It notes that government aid totalled £32.1 million. It adds, pointedly, that Crown Estate income, described as 'surrendered', was £210 million. Not only were the Hanoverians incompetent, but they lost things, and when they had the good fortune to hang on to things they were given because of their rank, privilege and perceived influence, they became averse to passing them on to their adopted country as Crown property.

In 1785, the Nizam of Hyderabad, Ali Khan, decided to give a 101-carat diamond as a gift to curry favour with his new ally against the French, King George III. The Nizam's mistake was selecting Warren Hastings as his go-between in presenting the impressive stone to the king at a time when the former British Governor General was on trial in England for so-called 'irregularities' while in power. The diamond's arrival in England in 1786 immediately followed a crucial judicial vote in the matter of Hastings' ongoing political problems. To gain favour with his king, Hastings, upon presenting the diamond to King George, omitted the fact that it was a gift from Nizam Ali Khan, leaving the impression that it was a personal gift from him.

The British media of the day seized on Hastings' glaring omission and presented the whole affair as King George III accepting the diamond as a bribe from Hastings to use his influence to secure a positive verdict. Rather than setting the record straight, Hastings backed away from the firestorm and took no action to defend his king. The luckless George was reduced to the role of Hastings' patsy.

Coming a few years after England's loss of the American colonies, the British monarch was now forced to endure additional public ridicule. Much of it came from cartoons displayed in shop windows. Using an advertisement poster for a popular contemporary street performer named 'The Greatest Stone Eater', protesters altered the image, replacing the juggling Stone Eater standing next to a pile of stones with King George III, holding a diamond in his mouth with a pile of diamonds located nearby. Meanwhile, the Hastings Diamond (as it was now known), the core ingredient of this unseemly constitutional melee, simply disappeared and was never seen again.

Unfortunately for the Crown, this episode followed another suspect 'bribe' when, in 1777, the Nawab of Arcot gave George's consort, Queen Charlotte, five large diamonds totalling over 130 carats to ward off the British East India Company's plans to control his southern province. Charlotte regarded all the diamonds as her personal property and gave instructions that on her death the 'Arcots' were to be sold and the proceeds divided among her four daughters.

Her son George IV ignored her wishes and set two of the Arcots in his coronation crown. They also appeared in the regalia for William IV's coronation. In 1837, the year of Victoria's coronation, the Hanoverians finally got their wish and the Arcots left the British Crown and were snapped up by the 1st Marquis of Westminster at auction for £11,000. In 1959, they were sold again for £110,000 (then a record price for jewellery) by the 3rd Duke of Westminster to pay death duties. Harry Winston of New York was the lucky buyer, who recast them in individual rings. One of the larger stones was reset by Van Cleef & Arpels and sold at auction by Christie's in 1993 as a pendant to a diamond necklace.

Edward had his great-grandmother, 'Gangan', to thank for the Crown's spectacular reversal of fortune and good sense during her long reign. But first, the new dynasty had to accommodate the morbid insecurities and capricious nature of the house matriarch herself to refill its coffers.

2

Gangan & Co.

Everybody likes flattery; and, when you come to royalty, you should
lay it on with a trowel.

Benjamin Disraeli to Matthew Arnold.

Her Majesty Queen Victoria breakfasted alone at Osborne House on
soft-boiled eggs, eaten with a golden spoon from a solid-gold eggcup,
with a kilted Scots retainer at the door and two liveried Indian servants in scarlet and gold behind her chair. Porridge, marmalade on toast,
'fancy breads', tea and 'finnan haddies' (a kind of gently smoked haddock) followed the eggs and was delivered by stony-faced footmen in
Balmoral green coats.[1]

The queen, however, was not at all amused that morning. In fact, she
was boiling with indignation. But this was hardly surprising. Since the
death of Prince Albert, her stern, beloved husband, fourteen years earlier
in 1861, Queen Victoria's temperament had taken a turn for the worse.
And now, this latest missive from the two principal sources of irritation
and annoyance in her life had once again conspired to reopen the old
wounds of the past. It was too much!

Behind her back, it seemed, and despite her vetoing the idea when
it was first suggested by the Council of India in 1875, Lord Salisbury,

her Secretary of State for India, had resurrected the plan for the Prince of Wales, the feckless Albert Edward, to tour India. What annoyed her even more than this flagrant disregard of her wishes was the fact it was announced to her without due consultation in a routine government communication. The audacity of the man!

She felt personally affronted. After breakfast she wrote to Salisbury to convey her displeasure, citing among other things the delicacy of the prince's health (Albert Edward had survived a bout of typhoid fever in 1871, the disease that likely killed his father) and how she was anxious about his endurance and fatigue. This was despite his experience travelling to North America in 1860 and then to Jerusalem, Cairo and Constantinople in 1862.

The queen's simmering resentment would not abate. Two months later, she explained in a letter to Lord Northbrook, the Viceroy of India, that she had given 'a very unwilling consent' and 'she had expected it […] would have been very carefully considered and weighed in the Cabinet before being announced to the Viceroy'.[2] Clearly irritated by her exclusion from the planning process, she did everything she could to scupper the whole thing, complaining privately to Salisbury that she had personally received no information from the Secretary of State about the tour arrangements, even though the newspapers were full of them.

One can see the queen throwing the morning newspapers on the floor before tucking into her breakfast at Osborne House. Victoria demanded, in terms that watered the eyes of her privy councillors, that she be accurately informed on every point of the tour and that her sanction was obtained before anything was decided. And, as an afterthought, she also insisted the Prince of Wales was to travel to India as 'first subject' rather than as her representative.

Poor Albert Edward. His misfortune seems to have been that he wasn't his father. That he was his father's opposite quickly made him a lost cause in the eyes of his parents, who much preferred his older sister Victoria, and later, his brothers. He found his father's rules, morals and rigorous educational programme (promulgated by the Prince Consort's confidant and House of Saxe-Coburg-Gotha's resident 'fixer', the conniving Baron Stockmar) stifling and his expectations unachievable. With all this over-bearing German influence, it is little wonder that Bertie (Albert Edward's family name), although a good linguist in French and German, never learned to speak English without a German accent.

Albert Edward was neither trusted nor taken seriously (it wasn't until he was 10 that Bertie came to realise that it was he, and not his clev-erer sister, Vicky, who was set to inherit the throne) and consequently became a louche playboy, an unemployed youth, with no obvious role in life other than waiting to be king. His mother complained of his 'systematic idleness and laziness',[3] which she deemed 'enough to break one's heart'.[4]

When his father died after a confrontation with Bertie concerning his dalliance with the actress Nellie Clifton, his mother blamed him, his shenanigans and trouble-making for Albert's death. In a letter to her eldest daughter Vicky, she was more explicit, 'I never can, or shall, look at him without a shudder'.[5]

He also became her rival when she withdrew from public life fol-lowing Prince Albert's death. Albert Edward may have been successful as a royal ambassador in Canada and the Middle East, but he was never trusted to perform the queen's public duties, despite Victoria's own refusal to perform them. Like her granddaughter-in-law, Mary of Teck, Victoria was never maternal despite the carefully crafted fiction of her marriage.

The other source of her chafing irritation was the growing consti-tutional clout of her government. She had never forgiven Viscount Melbourne's government (despite her personal affection for Melbourne) for refusing to amend parliamentary laws that prevented her new hus-band from becoming king on the couple's marriage in 1840. The queen's sniffy government were obviously reacting to Albert's inferior status as the second son of a relatively obscure and minor German duke (Coburg is smaller than the Isle of Wight). They had no doubt noted that the queen's choice for a husband (the two also happened to be first cousins) was a mere Serene Highness, the lowest grade in royal hierarchy. It was just enough to give the German an entry-level pass into the most esteemed and revered royal family in Europe. Anything more would have been overly generous and unwarranted.

The British government was never going to elevate the prince to a position that would outrank the reigning monarch and give him a primacy they felt was not appropriate given his status and distance from the Crown. This defiance of her wishes continued as a point of resentment between the queen and successive governments, which became inflamed in the years after Prince Albert's death as the grievance grew.

Despite the queen's conniving, planning for the Prince of Wales' tour of India in 1875 continued, whether the authorities had her approval or not. Which was just as well, for the mountain of precious stones and gold he received on that visit marked the third significant turning point in the Crown's acquisition of fabulous jewels.

The first occurred with Victoria's coronation in 1837 and the second in 1850, when the East India Company confiscated the contents of the Lahore Treasury and an orphaned 11-year-old Indian prince named Duleep Singh was ordered to surrender the famed Koh-i-noor diamond to Queen Victoria in a contrived spectacle to show Indian submission to British rule. The Koh-i-noor was the most fabulous addition to the Crown jewels for over two centuries and together with the Timur Ruby (another gift from the East India Company), the Black Prince's Ruby (a spinel) and the St Edward's Sapphire, it was the second-largest gem in the Royal Collection at 186 carats.

Along with many other things, Victoria's passion for gems and jewellery had waned in the years following Albert's death. When he was alive, they collaborated on the acquisition and design of many pieces, incorporating gifts from the East India Company and recycling jewels from older Hanoverian settings. The confidence and tone of the new Victorian era was set with her coronation regalia. Prior to Victoria, English monarchs had the annoying habit of either losing (John, James II) or pawning their royal regalia to fund their wars (i.e. Richard I, Edward III, Henry V, Charles I) and Parliament was loath to vote them money for their coronations as a result of this profligacy.

The court jewellers at the time of Victoria's ascension, Rundell, Bridge & Rundell, located at the edge of the City of London, had done well out of the impecunious Hanoverians over the years, hiring out collection upon collection of costly gems for their coronations and then stripping the crowns bare and leaving them as skeletal frames between each coronation. George IV paid them the enormous sum of £6,525 for the loan of precious stones for his sumptuous crowning, which cost Parliament, and therefore the British people, an extraordinary £240,000. William IV's coronation came in at a more modest £30,000. For Victoria, Parliament sought a compromise and gave her a budget of £70,000.[6]

She started by ordering her own gem-set crown but, unlike her Hanoverian predecessors, she instructed Rundell, Bridge & Rundell to permanently solder the diamonds, precious stones, brilliants, pearls and sapphires into the new crown along with the Black Prince's ruby and St Edward's sapphire. Resetting these old gems cost £1,000, according to the Lord Chamberlain's accounts, and it was the first of a raft of new regalia comprising suites of sapphires, diamonds and her favourite blood-red rubies. Rundell, Bridge and Rundell's last commission for the new queen, before she switched to Messrs Garrard & Company located in Haymarket, was to make her new ruby coronation ring which she found difficult to take off after the ceremony and had to sleep with it before the jewellers assisted her in separating it from her finger. Victoria had a fetish for rings and wore one, sometimes two, on each of her fingers.

Garrard & Co. was granted the title of Crown Jeweller in 1843 and over the sixty-year period of her reign, Victoria spent £158,887 with them. Garrard's ledger of these transactions, a crumbling mustard leather-bound volume with a brass clasp and marbled endpapers, still exists and records a virtual river of commissions that chronicled the blossoming nature of her marriage to Prince Albert: £1,200 on a large emerald and diamond necklace, £1,400 on a suite of diamonds and rubies, a very fine suite of opals at £1,056 17s.[7]

The list goes on and on, until things really took off with the East India Company's annexation of the Lahore Treasury in 1849. In flowing copperplate, the ledger records the very first setting of the Koh-i-noor diamond in 1852 when the old Duke of Wellington trotted up to the door of Garrard's at No. 25 Haymarket on his white charger and deposited the newly cut stone to be set in a new tiara for the queen with over 2,000 other diamonds. This tiara became a mine of gems for future generations of Windsors and is still being mined today.

Apart from the Koh-i-noor, the Lahore stash also contained the fabulous 361-carat Timur ruby, known as the 'Tribute to the World', presented to Queen Victoria in 1851 and set in a necklace of smaller Lahore rubies by Garrard's in 1853. An extraordinary piece (it is now classified as a spinel), it has not been worn since 1911 and remains virtually intact in the royal strongroom today.

Between April and November 1853, Queen Victoria spent the enormous sum of £6,030 2s 3d at Garrard's on jewellery founded on the contents of the Lahore Treasury, gifted by the East India Company for political gain.[8] Many years later, at Windsor, decked out in a huge gold crown and splashes of Indian jewels, she was asked by her favourite prime minister, Disraeli, whether she had any more Indian jewels, whereupon she signalled to her Indian servants to bring out three large portmanteaux from the castle's strongroom.

Midway through this spree, she suffered a setback from which she never fully recovered emotionally. The ongoing struggle with her uncle, King Ernst-August of Hanover, over which Crown Jewels belonged to the British queen, and which belonged to the King of Hanover, was finally resolved by a commission set up by the British Parliament in 1857. The claim, made by the late King of Hanover (formerly the Duke of Cumberland), was that nearly all the jewels worn on state occasions by the English sovereign had been taken to England by George I and so belonged inalienably to the Crown of Hanover. Not only that, but the remainder of the English regalia had been purchased by George III out of his privy purse and had been left by his wife, Queen Charlotte, to the royal family of Hanover.

To everyone's surprise, the commission, headed by three English judges, found in the House of Hanover's favour. The returned jewels included Queen Charlotte's small diamond nuptial crown and some exceptionally fine and historic pieces such as a necklace of thirty-seven lustrous stones worn by Mary, Queen of Scots and purchased from her by Elizabeth I, given by James I to his daughter, Elizabeth of Bohemia, and then passed by inheritance to the House of Hanover and so on to the British Crown. Among a quantity of other jewels was the Cumberland diamond, presented to the Duke of Cumberland after the Battle of Culloden, which had already been set in a tiara by Garrard & Co. in 1853.

Such was the queen's dismay at the ruling of the 1857 parliamentary commission that she did not give up the last of the disputed jewels until 1866. But by then, she probably didn't care or had misplaced her obligation to fulfil the commission's findings. After Albert's death on 14 December 1861 (known within the family as Mausoleum Day), things changed, and all the colour was drained out of the queen's life and her interest in jewellery.

Ensconced in perpetual black mourning dress, simply adorned with the sapphire and diamond brooch her husband had given her on their wedding day, together with his blue Garter ribbon and its diamond star, the diminutive 4ft 11in monarch's jewellery commissions were mostly concentrated on trinkets, family keepsakes and macabre memento mori of her dead husband. She slept under a gold-framed photograph of Albert's death mask and had Garrard & Co. set the minutiae of their life together, such as the pebbles he put in his pocket from their first visit to Balmoral, in silver-gilt frames or cases edged with onyx. For the first few years after his death, his Windsor apartments were maintained as if he were still there, and a royal footman knocked at the doors every day with a pitcher of hot water for the absent Prince Consort's morning shave.

Her Christmas present to her 6-year-old daughter Beatrice, that first Christmas without Prince Albert, was a bracelet with a model of her dead father's eye. It is little wonder the Prince of Wales wanted to escape the claustrophobia of court life for some fresh air and adventure and why his mother was so intent on denying him the enjoyment she thought he did not deserve, while she had to endure the extreme torment of marital separation. The court was a morgue and royal life at the House of Saxe-Coburg-Gotha had atrophied to the point of social rigor mortis.

He was also keen to undertake the tour for purely personal reasons. The 1870s had not been kind to him or Princess Alexandra, his wife. Apart from contracting typhus and nearly dying, he was consistently overdrawn on his personal expenses (sometimes to the tune of £20,000) and had to be bailed out and was frequently harangued by his mother, sometimes in public. There was the indignity of the Mordaunt case in 1870 when the Prince of Wales was called into the witness box and acquitted of committing adultery with the young Lady Mordaunt, followed soon after by another sex scandal involving Daisy Brooke, later Countess of Warwick. Then the heartbreaking death of the Wales' premature son, Alexander John, in 1871 at just one day old.

So, it was a relieved, inwardly ecstatic Prince of Wales who embarked on a passage to India in October 1875 by first boarding a train at Charing Cross Station and then rendezvousing with HMS *Serapis* at Portsmouth for the six-month round trip. Armed with the £112,000 that Parliament had reluctantly voted to pay for the tour's logistical expenses and a further £30,000 from the government of India to cover his personal expenses, he and his fifty-man tour party (there were no women in the group) were due to visit more than twenty-one towns and cities in modern-day India, Pakistan, Nepal and Sri Lanka, and to be the principal guests at more than ninety royal courts.

Chosen to record the visit were the prince's Honorary Private Secretary, William Howard Russell, who reported on it for the *Times*, and the artist Sydney P. Hall, who was responsible for the illustrations in Russell's subsequent book about it.[9] It included travelling by train from Calcutta to Delhi, excursions to Gwalior (where Bertie bathed in a solid-silver bathtub and slept in a solid-gold bed) and Jaipur, and a hunting expedition in Nepal Terai in February 1876.

In Jumoo, painted elephants swayed towards him with gold anklets and gold and silver howdahs on their backs, while he was shielded from the sun by a gold umbrella. In balmy Bombay, he celebrated his thirty-fourth birthday with a two-hour carriage drive through streets lined with sentinels of soft lamps and banners proclaiming, 'Tell Mamma we are happy'.[10]

The sublime also abutted the absurd, such as in Kandy, where naked Hindu urchins were whitewashed so they could appear with gilt coronets and white wands as Victorian angels, or the performance of the prince's favourite farce, *My Old Dad*, using native actors, which he attended following an investiture of Indian princes on New Year's Day, 1876. The whole country was galvanised in a festival of extravagance and fantasy that would only be eclipsed by the visit of King George V and Queen Mary as Emperor and Empress of India in 1911.

The leading native princes, drenched in diamonds, emeralds and rubies, were obviously keen to outdo one another in terms of the opulence they could conjure up to dazzle and amaze the genial troop of travelling British aristocrats. Sir Jung Bahadur, Maharajah of Lamjung and Kaski and the autocratic ruler of Nepal, received the prince and his party wearing a magnificent headdress encrusted with emeralds, the top of the turban studded with an awesome and terrifying ruby. A present from the Empress of China, it was said to be worth six times the value of the Koh-i-noor or the equivalent of a fine estate in Buckinghamshire.

Not to be outdone, in Calcutta, the Maharajah of Patiala paraded before the British the magnificent crown jewels of France belonging to the chic Empress Eugénie, wife of Napoleon III (he had purchased them for the eye-watering sum of £300,000 when they were sold off by the French Republic in the 1870s). He wore around his neck a great collar of diamonds set in platinum along with five other massive necklaces of diamonds and emeralds plus another necklace of diamonds around his waist.

But even this show of unworldly opulence was outdone by a set of demure Buddhist priests in Kandy, who permitted the prince to view their holiest of treasures: a bell-shaped casket studded with gems containing the largest emerald in the world, 4in long and 2in deep, carved into the likeness of the Buddha.

Prior to the tour, the Viceroy of India, Lord Northbrook, tried to tone down the natural generosity of the princes by suggesting to them that gifts given to the Prince of Wales should be limited to 'curiosities, ancient arms, and specimens of local manufacture'.[11] This was universally ignored and Prince Albert Edward was loaded up with more than 2,000 precious articles, some of which went on display after he returned home in May 1876 (in its opening week, 30,000 visitors flocked to the Crown's Indian Exhibition in London). In fact, there were so many gifts and tributes that another ship, HMS *Osborne*, had to be pressed into service to accommodate the extra cargo of Indian booty and accompany *Serapis* home.

This extra cargo also included a menagerie of animals, both dead and alive. *Serapis*, where the prince's party were lodged in chubby Edwardian splendour (the ship's gun room was converted into a library where Edward could indulge his habit of smoking twenty cigarettes and twelve cigars a day with his cronies), was reserved for the skins, skeletons, heads, horns and hoofs of animals shot or given as presents. But lurking within *Osborne*'s murky lower decks, in straw-strewn cages, stomped two young elephants, a quartet of spotted deer, prowling leopards and cheetahs, small bullocks, chattering monkeys, a petite pony and a collection of Himalayan singing birds. The stars of the collection, however, were two handsome young tigers that sent shivers down the spines of seamen whenever they pierced the night air with their stately growling.

Aside from exotic animals, ceremonial weapons and courtly knick-knacks, the prince was showered with tribal gold and jewels, some of which made their way into the Royal Collection, but most of which disappeared into the family strongroom at Osborne House on the Isle of Wight, where it was stored (with unused pieces from the Lahore Treasury) in five large Morocco leather trunks lined with white silk velvet and fitted with Chubb patent locks.

Among the gifts was a lavish ten-piece gold dinner service given by the Maharajah of Mysore:

Commonly referred to as a Service of State, the stunning set consists of plates, trays, perfume holders, betel-nut boxes and rosewater sprinklers [...] Perfume was used at the beginning of meetings to freshen up after long journeys; paan, or betel-nut, was brought out later to politely signify the end of the session.[12]

This set was accompanied by, among other things, gigantic tusks; a magnificent silver palanquin picked out in gold and lined with gold embroidery; a large double bedstead of solid silver with a canopy and bed of red satin from the Maharajah of Behar; a massive gold crown hung with limpid emerald drops from the province of Oudh; an enamelled gold and jewel-encrusted crown presented by the Taluqdars of Awadh; a turban ornament from Udaipur with three large emeralds, bordered by bands of bright red enamel; a crown from Lucknow composed of magnificently embroidered velvet and liberally sprinkled with diamonds and pearls; an ornamented dagger and scabbard presented by the Maharajah of Alwar, featuring an enamelled and bejewelled handle and a scabbard (the blade was filled with loose seed pearls); from the Gaekwar of Baroda, two shields crafted from rhinoceros hide and decorated with bosses shaped as curled-up cheetahs, a pearl necklace with a huge emerald pendant, plus a diamond ring and brooch; a silver and gold perfume holder in the form of a lotus bud presented by Jaswant Singh II, Maharajah of Jodhpur; and a wonderful ornamental gold articulated fish featuring ruby eyes and an emerald set into the head, presented by Waghji II Rawaji, Thakur Sahib of Morvi.

But it was the three weighty trunks that housed the secret piles of uncut gems and locally wrought pieces of jewellery, that had been presented to the prince on arrival at towns and palaces, which represented the real treasure of the tour. James Allingham, in his book *Five Months with the Prince in India*, wrote after inspecting the jewel-studded crown presented to the prince at Indore, diamonds 'seem to be as plentiful in India as blackberries in England'.[13]

The prince's Honorary Private Secretary, William Howard Russell, duly published an entertaining official account of the visit titled

The Prince of Wales' tour: a diary in India; with some account of the visits of His Royal Highness to the courts of Greece, Egypt, Spain and Portugal, which was careful not to challenge the primacy of Queen Victoria in the imperial hierarchy.

Russell and the newspaper reporters who accompanied the tour were also careful not to highlight the disparity between the gifts the prince received and those he gave his hosts. This was so immediately and embarrassingly apparent that, soon after they arrived, they stopped listing the native offerings, noting only the prince's gifts, which they dressed up with breathless hyperbole, stating that the prince received presents of equivalent value. James Allingham repeated the official line that the presents received by the prince did not exceed £40,000 and the value of the gifts he gave amounted to nearly £40,000.

Not only was the value of the gifts problematic, so too was their appropriateness in some cases. The *Daily Telegraph* correspondent, in his book *From Pall Mall to the Punjab*, noted the towering sword given to the Gaekwar of Baroda that was bigger than he was, and the bewildering assortment of riding whips, field glasses and flagons given to the 13-year-old Maharajah of Mysore.

The *Times of India* listed, more or less accurately, the presents given by both sides, but in a deliberate act, repeated for a visit by another Prince of Wales fifty years later in 1925, it carefully omitted some of the more extraordinary, personally retained items. Suzy Menkes, in *The Royal Jewels*, attempted to list these, drawing from many different sources and contemporary accounts, and arrived at the following:

A diamond necklace with two large emerald pendants, a pair of diamond bracelets, a pearl necklace with emeralds inserted (from the Prince and Maharajah Holkar of Indore).

A massive virgin gold belt with figures of Hindu deities for the Princess of Wales (from the states of Madure and Trichinopoly).

A necklace of fourteen large diamonds set off by emeralds, pearls and ruby drops (from Maharajah Scindiah of Gwalior).

A bracelet set with precious stones (from the Maharajah of Mysore).

A crown made of diamonds and pearls with emerald drops, HRH coat of arms and feathers on front (from the Taluqdars of Lucknow and Dewan Mathura Dass).

A ruby necklace with eleven large rubies (from Sir Jung Bahadore of Nepal).

A pearl necklace with emerald pendant, a diamond ring, a diamond brooch (from the Gaekwar and Renee of Baroda).[14]

According to Menkes, these major Indian jewels have never been worn in public by any monarch or consort as they were originally presented.

Most likely, they were prised out of their ethnic settings and reset by Garrard & Co., Cartier, Van Cleef & Arpels and other favoured jewellers, or simply stored in one of the Windsors' many strongrooms. In 1901, for instance, Pierre Cartier was summoned to Buckingham Palace to create a new necklace for Queen Alexandra using seventeen pearls, thirteen cabochon rubies, and ninety-four emeralds from the family stockpile. Three years later, nine massive emeralds, nine rubies and 141 carats' worth of diamonds went to Cartier's workrooms to emerge as a *collier résille* for Queen Alexandra. Interestingly, the nine emeralds and rubies were returned to the family as surplus to requirements. Presumably, they went back into storage.

It was a jaunty, carefree Prince of Wales who rolled down the gang-plank of *Serapis* at Portsmouth in the spring of 1876, cigar in hand, secure in the knowledge he had a torrent of gifts and splendours to dazzle the nation, placate his mother and (most importantly) pacify his wife. To popularise his success, the prince cleverly orchestrated select displays of the vast hoard throughout most of England and Scotland. More than 2 million people saw them.[15]

Disraeli, who was prime minster at the time, also came to the rescue with his mother by finally caving in to his monarch's pining for an imperial title, introducing a Royal Titles Bill to Parliament while Bertie was away. Victoria was ruffled that Tsar Alexander II, as an emperor, outranked her in status and she was similarly appalled that her daughter Vicky, the Prussian crown princess, would also be elevated above her when Vicky's husband ascended his throne. The title 'Empress of India' had been used loosely but affectionately by officials and family for a while, but in view of her errant son's conquest of that land, she now pressed her government to have the title formally bestowed on her.

Disraeli eventually brought the Bill to a vote in the Commons, where it passed with a majority of seventy-five. Before the Bill was formally enacted, on May Day 1876, Victoria was proclaimed Empress of India (*Victoria Regina Et Imperatrix*) in Delhi and began signing her letters 'Victoria R & I'. Although he was rewarded by being created Earl of Beaconsfield, championing the Bill blunted Disraeli's already razor-thin authority in the House of Commons forever. The Prince of Wales was merely irritated by the whole saga but eventually saw it as another bauble for his mother to play with along with the other gifts he had in store, much like a preying tiger is thrown a bone to gnaw as a distraction from pursuing a juicier target.

His wife was another matter. Alexandra, Princess of Wales, was devastated and never forgave 'Tum-tum' (the cheeky nickname she gave her husband and shared with her ladies-in-waiting) for excluding her from going to India in the first place. It was a wound that never healed.

But her notoriously unfaithful and profligate Bertie had the perfect antidote. Upon reuniting with his family at Marlborough House, the prince slipped into the princess's hand a velvet sack containing a pot-pourri of randomly selected gems from the three weighty trunks of jewels that had been specially unloaded from *Serapis* and transported by train in the same carriage as the prince himself.

It did the trick. The princess did not make a fuss and resumed her duties as the radiant, composed wife of the future king. Meanwhile, the gems and jewels continued to roll in, mostly diamonds as big as ice cubes.

Victoria's Golden Jubilee of 1887 and Diamond Jubilee, ten years later, brought in so many tributes that Garrard & Co. charged a fee of £3 for writing new entries into the inventory of Victoria's jewellery collection which they had begun in 1896. For this task, a royal-red Levant Morocco-bound book with silk facings was purchased and a Mr Linton of Garrard & Co. spent ten days at Osborne House listing all the jewels and gems. The family felt this was necessary following the deluge of gifts she received when, on 23 September 1896, she surpassed King George III as Britain's longest-reigning monarch.

The Diamond Jubilee celebrations were delayed, however, at her request, until June 1897, the sixtieth anniversary of Gangan's coronation. Even then, she was disinclined to make any fuss, dreading the incoming 'royal mob' (as she called them) and the necessarily lavish accommodation her extended family warranted, plus the inevitable intrusions upon her quiet, sedentary life. Overweight, lethargic and wracked with excruciating arthritis and cataracts in both eyes, she had to be persuaded by the Princess of Wales that it was worth the bother, if not for her family then for the nation.

What followed was a jaw-dropping display of British imperialism, wealth and clout that could only be matched at the time by possibly the Russian imperial court (after a visit to Balmoral in 1896 Tsar 'Nicky' left a £1,000 tip for the queen's servants). After a family thanksgiving service at Windsor Castle on Sunday, 20 June 1897, the queen returned to London to find it dusted with thousands of Union Jacks draped from house balconies. She was inexplicably touched. Later that night at Buckingham Palace, Victoria sat next to Archduke Franz Ferdinand (whose 1914 assassination would spark the start of the First World War) at a state banquet saturated in diamonds, including the Lahore diamond suspended in a pendant from her necklace.

The next day had been declared a public holiday and hundreds of thousands of people crowded the London pavements in anticipation of sighting their empress. They were not to be disappointed.

A glittering seventeen-carriage convoy carried the royal family and leaders of Britain's dominions towards St Paul's Cathedral for another thanksgiving service. The empress herself was pulled by eight cream horses in an open carriage. Wracked by severe arthritis, the 78-year-old monarch's ability to climb the cathedral steps was not entertained and the service was held at the foot of St Paul's west steps. The empress, dressed in her widow's weeds, remained in her coach, shading herself with a parasol.

Returning to Buckingham Palace for a quiet luncheon, the empress unleashed herself at the final excruciating dinner banquet, gorging on her favourite soups, fish, various cold-boiled poultry, haunches of roast beef, desserts and fruits including pineapples grown specially for the royal household. This twilight bacchanalian generosity was also extended to the masses: the pubs remained open until the special time of 2.30 a.m.

In a quirky book that was published before her death, entitled *The Private Life of the Queen by a Member of the Royal Household*, it was claimed that 'Her Majesty confesses to a great weakness for potatoes, which are cooked for her in every conceivable way'. She also had a sweet tooth, with a great appetite for:

> … chocolate sponges, plain sponges, wafers of two or three different shapes, *langues de chat*, biscuits and drop cakes of all kinds, tablets, *petit fours*, princess and rice cakes, pralines, almond sweets, and a large variety of mixed sweets. [...] Her Majesty is very fond of all kinds of pies, and a cranberry tart with cream is one of her favourite dishes.[16]

In terms of alcohol, she especially enjoyed a glass of Atholl Brose (a syrupy mixture of whisky and honey).

In her journal, Victoria described her joy that:

> No one ever I believe, has met with such an ovation as was given to me, passing through those six miles of streets [...] The crowds were quite indescribable and their enthusiasm truly marvellous and deeply touching. The cheering was quite deafening, and every face seemed to be filled with real joy. I was much moved and gratified.[17]

Four years later, in 1901, the Victorian era came to an end. The signs were apparent to her household, but her family were in denial. On

17 January, the queen's health took a severe turn for the worse. She had already lost half her body weight during the past few weeks and was listless, sometimes rambling. At 6.30 p.m. on 22 January she died, surrounded by her distraught family at Osborne House.

After a few days, her personal physician, Dr Reid:

> … carefully placed the items she had requested in the bottom of her coffin: Albert's dressing gown; a plaster cast of Albert's hand. When that was done, her body was lifted into the coffin with the help of her son Albert Edward, her grandson Wilhelm (the German Kaiser), and her son Arthur (the Duke of Connaught). Then, as instructed, Dr. Reid placed Queen Victoria's wedding veil over her face and, once the others had departed, placed a picture of her favourite personal attendant John Brown in her right hand, which he covered with flowers. When all was ready, the coffin was closed and then carried to the dining room where it was covered with the Union Jack.[18]

During the funeral procession the coffin displayed the small, diamond-encrusted Imperial Crown she had specially made by Garrard & Co. in March 1870 containing 1,162 brilliant-cut and 138 rose-cut diamonds, weighing 132 carats, and the collar of the Garter along with other regalia: two orbs and the sceptre. It was a far cry from what she had inherited all those years ago in 1837, and a mere pinch compared to the five trunks of unused gems and jewels stored at Osborne House along with a set of Crown regalia that was the envy of Europe.

Much of her jewellery was secured as property of the Crown and held in trust for English queens. But there were still boxes and boxes of purple Morocco leather lined with white velvet bearing the queen's cypher, which housed the remainder of her jewels bequeathed to family, with the lion's share going to her daughter-in-law, Princess Alexandra.

3

Rubies as Big as a Pigeon's Egg

My eyes pierce the inmost recesses of the earth, and are dazzled at the sight of so much riches.

Alexandre Dumas, *The Count of Monte Cristo*

Alexandra had followed the traditional route into the British royal family: that of minor, impoverished European nobility headhunted by the sovereign as a suitable match for his or her children. Dubbed 'The Sea King's daughter from over the sea' by the poet Tennyson, Princess Alexandra was, however, not the most suitable candidate for the hand of the Prince of Wales due to the poor reputation of her family.[1] Victoria and Albert eventually settled on her because, in a limited field, she was 'the only one to be chosen'.[2]

Although Alix, as her immediate family called her, and her brothers and sisters were born into royalty, she and her family lived a relatively normal life. Like her future daughter-in-law, she was too royal to marry a 'subject' and not royal enough to marry a royal prince. Her father, Prince Christian, existed on a modest income of £800 a year from an army commission.

Alix shared an attic room and a zinc bathtub in the Danish Yellow Palace, an eighteenth-century town house in Copenhagen, with her sister Dagmar, who went on to become the formidable Empress Marie Feodorovna of Russia. When Alix's father became King Christian IX, the family moved into the monarch's official residence, the Bernstorff Palace.

Alix was never properly educated, made her own clothes and waited at table with her sisters. She was also handicapped by a limp (after an attack of rheumatic fever) and had a scar on her neck that she covered throughout her life with choker necklaces. But she had a sweet, gracious temperament that the queen and her eldest daughter (who had married the heir to the German Kaiser) thought might temper the boorish extremes of the hopeless Prince of Wales. And besides, the Russian royal family were sniffing around the Danish court and the English were determined this 'jewel' was not lost to them.

And so, the deal was sealed after the 21-year-old Alix passed her initiation test, spending six weeks incarcerated with Queen Victoria at Osborne House. She became Princess of Wales in 1863 and queen at the age of 57, when she at last had access to the royal jewellery.

To compensate for this denial and his numerous affairs, her husband showered her with jewellery, and she pioneered the fashion for the opulent display of these treasures that some society luminaries considered too overwhelming for her slight figure. Some have suggested she used these lavish trappings to barricade herself from the flagrant infidelities of her husband, which reached its peak at their 1902 coronation when she noted the 'loose box' of his past and current mistresses witnessing the formalities at Westminster Abbey.[3]

Whatever the psychological need, her voracious passion for jewellery is important to this story for two reasons: her fondness for paste (fake jewels that are exact replicas of the real thing) and dying intestate (without a will) on 20 November 1925, after suffering a fatal heart attack at Sandringham House in Norfolk.

The most interesting example of her fondness for paste exists in the form of the glittering crown made for her coronation by the jewellers Carrington, featuring the Koh-i-noor set in a platinum frame. Apparently, Alexandra found the Crown Jewels too heavy for her personal use and had her friend, Gladys, Lady de Grey, bring back quantities of paste from Paris to use instead, including fake strands of pearls and other gems.

The Carrington crown still exists but it is composed entirely of paste, including the replica of the Koh-i-noor itself. Presumably the queen was crowned in 1902 wearing this crown of paste, but it's very intriguing to wonder what other historic jewels were replaced and stored within her personal collection.

It is significant because when she died intestate, her personal jewels were split among her surviving children. On Saturday, 9 January 1926, King George V and Queen Mary with two of Alix's daughters, her spinster helpmate, Princess 'Toria', and the king's sister, Princess Maud, gathered at Sandringham to divide up the jewels. The queen and king took the jewels that had been given to Queen Alexandra as wedding gifts together with significant gifts from civic bodies as their share. This included an Indian necklace of diamonds and emeralds; the Dagmar necklace with pearls; a diamond necklace and earrings presented by the Corporation of the City of London; a diamond cross and pearl necklace presented by the Ladies of Liverpool; and Queen Victoria's Diamond Jubilee link-chain and bracelets.

Despite the absence of a will, Alexandra let it be known that specific pieces from her personal collection were earmarked for certain members of her family. Her daughter, Princess Victoria, received the magnificent Rundell tiara that she had mysteriously disposed of before her death. Princess Maud, her granddaughter, received an important diamond and amethyst tiara, a necklace composed of oval amethysts and a stupendous collar of sapphires and diamonds that was a silver wedding gift from Tsar Alexander III of Russia.

And what of her favourite, 'David', the Prince of Wales, in 1925? What was set aside for him? Was it the remains of the velvet sack of Indian gems his grandfather had pressed into his grandmother's hands on his return from India in 1876? Or did Queen Mary, his acquisitive mother, squirrel that away for safekeeping on her mother-in-law's death to ensure it did not become a tragic casualty of the careless practices of her dissolute son? And did David, on becoming King Edward VIII, extract it from the royal vaults as he was perfectly entitled to?

As Suzy Menkes observed:

> If she [Mary] allowed any major pieces to be given to her own children at this time, she would have been acting entirely out of character with the rest of her life and her attitude towards the acquisition of jewellery in the 1920s.[4]

Two revealing examples of this 'attitude' were the acquisition of the so-called Cambridge Emeralds and the spectacular Romanov jewels of the Grand-Duchess Marie Pavlovna and Dowager Empress Marie Feodorovna.

Prior to these episodes she had already built up a sizeable collection of jewellery in her own right, starting with wedding presents from her miraculous marriage to the newly created Duke of York. These included sapphire and diamond bracelets and an emerald and diamond brooch from the Russian tsar and tsarina; a cabochon sapphire and diamond brooch from Princess Alexandra's sister, Empress Marie Feodorovna; a delicate spiky diamond circlet from the Girls of Great Britain and Ireland; another diamond tiara from the County of Surrey; and a diamond bow pendant pearl from the inhabitants of Kensington.

The death of Edward VII in May 1910 brought Queen Mary unfettered access to all the Crown Jewellery, once that prerogative had been gently prised away from the dowager Queen Alexandra. Among the newly accessible pieces was a beautiful marquise diamond of 11¾ carats that was left over when the great Cullinan diamond was cleaved. She already had the rest of the Cullinan 'chips': six large brilliants and ninety-six smaller diamonds with which she adorned her generous bosom (the French called her 'Soutien-Georges', a pun on her support for her husband and on the French word for brassiere). There was also a batch of unpolished fragments which still exist in that form to this day (the two largest stones, the great Stars of Africa, were set at the top of the Sovereign's Sceptre with Cross which had to be redesigned in 1910 to accommodate it, and in the front of the Imperial State Crown below the Black Prince's Ruby).

She also began systematically sorting and categorising all the royal jewels, uncovering in the process seventeen historic royal rings which were dispatched to the strongroom at Windsor Castle. Many of the royal jewels in store today still bear labels in her precise writing, detailing their provenance and history. This supplemented the extensive notes on what jewellery and clothes she wore, plus when and where, which she and her elderly French maid, Tatry, recorded in her numerous maroon Morocco 'Dress Books', now preserved at Windsor Castle and dating from the time of her marriage.

But these trinkets almost paled in comparison to the spoils she received in 1911 when she and her husband, the King Emperor, were feted beyond belief by India's 135 ruling princes at the Delhi Durbar in December. The Persian word *Darbar* means, literally, a grand court, and the 1911 durbar was both a coronation celebration and an affirmation of British imperial power at its zenith. It was an extraordinary week of ceremonies, parades, military reviews, festivities, garden parties and polo matches that harnessed the attention of over 200,000 people in a vast canvas city stretched under the shadow of the Mughal's ancient Red Fort (the Maharajah of Kashmir's camp was a recreation of a Hindu temple in gleaming copper and gold with carved walnut interiors).

News of the impending apogee of imperial splendour had spread throughout the world, prompting many *haute joailliers* to send distinguished representatives to hand-deliver princely orders, seek new commissions and acquire incredible stones to satisfy the vast appetites of their Russian clientele. These included the spritely Jacques Cartier, head of Cartier's London branch, who made his first trip to the fabled subcontinent in a bowler hat. Laden with watches, carriage clocks and small items of *bijouterie* for his princely customers, Cartier was following in the footsteps of two of the firm's *grands vendeurs*, Jules Glaenzer and M. Prieur, who embarked in May 1909 on a seven-month speculative journey to Siam, Hong Kong, Singapore and India (Calcutta was hot and dirty, the prices of gems exorbitant, and the food uneatable). Garrard & Co., the Crown Jewellers, originally sold items to India through an alliance with local dealers like Hamilton & Co., but they established a showroom in Calcutta in time for the durbar, while the St Petersburg firm of Fabergé had been funding annual trips to India from 1908 until its demise in 1917.

The Indian princes were at Delhi to pay homage to their King Emperor, advancing in a procession of unimaginable splendour, festooned with jewels, to bow and smile at the royal couple who were protected from the glare of the sun by scarlet and gold umbrellas. The king himself was no slouch, sporting the new Imperial Crown of India, made up for the occasion by Garrard & Co. (the resident Crown Jewels are restrained by law from leaving Britain), with 6,000 diamonds, four enormous sapphires, four rubies and nine emeralds, costing £60,000 to be borne by the people of India. The princes were also there to compete among themselves on the most lavish personal displays of dress and jewels, and in the tributes, or *nazar*, they gifted to their alien visitors.

The Maharajah of Dewas Junior's daughter, Shashi Wallia, describes the scene as her father relayed it to her:

> First was the Nizam who gave the King a ruby necklace in which each ruby was as big as a pigeon's egg. Then the other princes followed – Baroda, Gwalior, Mysore, Kashmir – each presenting the King with other items of jewellery which must have been lying in their coffers for centuries [...]His Highness of Panna presented [...]an umbrella [...] which was at least twelve inches in diameter, carved out of a single piece of emerald from his emerald mines. Sir Tukoji Tao [Sir Tukoji Rao Holkar, Maharajah of Indore] dressed in gold and silver brocade clothes, walked up to the dais twirling a gold stick with jewelled engravings and with a hilt carved out of a single ruby. Unfortunately he slipped on the polished wooden floor, put his weight on the stick [...] and it shattered, so he was very put out.[5]

Even the Queen Empress got in on the act, presented with jewellery described by the *Statesman of India* as a 'large square of emeralds of historic interest engraved and set in diamonds, and a necklace and pendant of emeralds set in rosettes of diamonds' by a group of Indian ladies headed by the wife of the Maharajah of Patiala.[6] This was the same maharajah who had been befriended by Jacques Cartier at a garden party and persuaded to remodel his Crown Jewels in Paris, which included a delicate diamond, ruby, emerald and sapphire nose ring.

Again, no one knows exactly what was given by the princes to their royal visitors. Neither do we know what was transacted from this pile to the Crown and what was kept for personal family use, because there was no report of the presentation of gifts in the extensive newspaper coverage the durbar received both in England and India. It likely took place in private and as such, the details remain private. The only other eyewitness account of the durbar from the perspective of a jeweller was by Garrard's representative, William Bell. It is currently in the possession of Buckingham Palace and safely under lock and key.

Like the king, the Queen Empress also debuted something spectacular of her own at the durbar. In the early 1800s, the Duke and Duchess of Cambridge, Adolphus and Augusta, bought some raffle tickets for a state-sponsored charity lottery organised by the duchess's native Duchy of Hesse. Astonishingly (unbelievably is more likely), they won and received about forty globular green cabochon emeralds without the hint of a raised eyebrow.

The stones of various sizes became known as the Cambridge Emeralds. In 1837, the emeralds were incorporated into various pieces of jewellery including a five-pendant necklace and a pair of drop earrings. After Augusta's passing in 1889, her daughter, Mary Adelaide, Duchess of Teck, inherited her mother's custom-made jewellery and the remainder of the loose emeralds.

In 1897, Mary Adelaide died, but in a strange twist, her daughter Mary, Duchess of York, did not inherit the Cambridge Emeralds. Instead, they went to Prince Francis (Frank), Mary Adelaide's womanising, gambling, rakish third child. It was Frank who blew £10,000 in 1895 at Punchestown Racecourse in Ireland and who, after his sister, the Duchess of York, paid up and sent him off to India, wanted to send her a betting book as a Christmas present!

As one can imagine, the Duchess of York tried everything in her power to relieve Frank of his inheritance which, at this time, amounted to eight large cabochon emeralds set as a necklace (which was later embellished by the marquise pendant of the Cullinan diamond given to Queen Alexandra); emerald and diamond earrings; a brooch; a stomacher; two bracelets and some loose stones.

An opportunity arose in 1910 when Frank died after a nasal operation and Mary became queen. However, Frank had decided to leave the stones to his mistress, Nellie, the Countess of Kilmorey, the none-too-faithful wife of an Irish earl (and one of Edward VII's 'loose box' of royal mistresses at his coronation).

Of course, Queen Mary was furious and was not content to let a minor Irish aristocrat come between her and her impecunious family's only possession of any consequence. So, in the circumstances, she did what she was good at. She used the full power of her rank to bully the Countess of Kilmorey into submission.

As part of the deal, Frank's will was sealed and the beleaguered countess, exhausted by the queen's relentless clawing, received the emerald brooch from the Cambridge suite to keep her quiet. Queen Mary got her jewels and in 1911, for the Delhi Durbar, she commissioned Garrard & Co. to create a new set of Cambridge jewellery. The set would include a tiara, necklace, stomacher and a pair of earrings. An emerald brooch that Mary received at the durbar is often displayed with the set, but this, a choker necklace (later made famous by Diana, Princess of Wales) and a bracelet were given to Mary at the event.

This glut of fine jewels was supplemented in the 1920s by a truly staggering cache of royal Romanov jewellery. After the tsar's government fell in 1918 and all hope of a return to a constitutional monarchy was lost, Europe was flooded with Russian jewels, fuelled by the hastily gathered snatchings of fleeing émigrés and the mountainous hoard being unloaded by a nascent Bolshevik government starved of cash and on the verge of bankruptcy. This hoard included the Russian Imperial Crown, encrusted with 32,800 carats' worth of diamonds.

In 1919, the British government dispatched the warship HMS *Marlborough* to Yalta to rescue the king's aunt, the Dowager Empress Marie Feodorovna, her entourage and relatives. The ship left with over 350 packing cases on its deck containing the personal effects, mostly jewels, of its royal passengers.

Prince Felix Yusupov (Oxford-educated slayer of Rasputin) escaped with his wife and mother, two Rembrandts he'd cut from their frames and a small quantity of jewels, including the blue Sultan of Morocco diamond, the Polar Star diamond and a pair of diamond earrings that belonged to Marie Antoinette. The Bolsheviks had the lion's share of his fortune, discovering secret passages behind galleries at his Moika Palace, which led to five dungeons filled with treasure: 255 brooches, thirteen tiaras, forty-two bracelets, 210kg of jewelled ornaments, 1,147 paintings, Sèvres table sets and a precious collection of 128 violins that included the last violin made by Stradivari. At least Felix had the pleasure, on arrival at the Hôtel Vendôme in Paris, to be greeted by a local jeweller who returned a bag of diamonds Felix had left with him before the war.

Grand Duke Nicholas boarded *Marlborough* with over 200 packing cases containing gold, silver and diamonds. Amid the chaos of leaving, however, some fifty-four unidentified cases bearing the Romanov crest were left on the quayside and it was said that returning British sailors were offered diamond rings for as little as half a crown on the starving streets of Yalta and Sevastopol. The *Marlborough*, en route to depositing its cargo, human and otherwise, at Constantinople, Genoa and Malta, had its inventory taken. Currently at the Public Record Office in London, the manifest is strangely unavailable.

The Dowager Empress Marie Feodorovna and her daughters, Grand Duchess Xenia and Olga, had managed to save some of the family jewellery, though a part remained hidden at the Anichkov Palace in Petrograd. Felix Yusupov had also paid a visit to the Anichkov to retrieve them, but they had already been looted. They were later tracked down by agents and stored in Moscow, though that solution (owing to the parlous state of the country) was only a temporary one.

Still, Marie Feodorovna had managed to rescue a case of the choicest items, which contained (as described by her friend, Prince Chavchavadze) ropes of pearls; a steady stream of emeralds and sapphires; diamonds of the finest quality; rare Byzantine jewels and clusters of rubies; a tiara of rubies and diamonds; a flat band of diamonds and emeralds; plus, a set of twenty flawless pink diamond stars. Though well short of the collection that once covered two long walls of the imperial bedchamber, she felt confident the single casket would provide for her and her family in the days ahead.

Settling eventually in her native Denmark, in a villa washed by the sea at Hvidovre, which she and her sister, the Dowager Queen Alexandra had bought together as a holiday hideaway, Marie Feodorovna passed away in 1928 and the contents of her jewel box, though depleted through necessity and mismanagement, became the focus of much family interest and nefarious international attention. So much so that King George V dispatched his private secretary, Sir Frederick Ponsonby, and Peter Bark, the last tsarist Finance Minister, to Copenhagen to secure the Dowager Empress's jewel box for Olga and Xenia, with the guarantee he would personally supervise the sale of their mother's inheritance. The two sisters agreed to the king's proposal and Bark sealed the jewels in a portmanteau and had them transferred by special messenger to London, where they were received by the returning Ponsonby and stored at Buckingham Palace awaiting the presence of the two sisters.

It was six months before the heavy box, laboriously bound with tape, was opened, but this eventually took place at Windsor in the presence of the king, Queen Mary and Xenia on 22 May 1929. 'Some lovely things,' the king wrote in his diary.[7] Ponsonby, who was also present, wrote a more detailed description, 'Ropes of the most wonderful pearls were taken out, all graduated, the largest being the size of a big cherry. Cabochon emeralds and large rubies and sapphires were laid out.'[8] Ponsonby retired discreetly from the room while the royal group pored over this treasure trove.

A week later, at 10.30 a.m. Mr Hardy, the senior partner of Hennell &
Sons, the Bond Street jewellers, arrived at Windsor to make a provisional
valuation. A lot of ink has been spilt on what happened at this first
valuation, such as the amount of the estimate; how much was eventually raised from the sale of the seventy-six items in Marie Feodorovna's
jewellery box and then given to Xenia and Olga; and, most importantly,
how many jewels Queen Mary acquired and how much she paid for
them, if anything at all.

William Clarke in *The Lost Fortune of the Tsars* has managed to run the
saga to ground by consulting directly with the Hennell & Sons archives.[9]
He established that Queen Mary paid the going rate (this being five
months away from the stock-market crash of 29 October 1929) for all
the items she acquired and the £136,624 finally realised from the sale was
close to the final valuation of £159,000 arrived at by Mr Hardy.

It is undeniable that Queen Mary *did* use her privileged position to
snap up the choicest items of the collection but, given her history and
mania of acquisition, that is hardly surprising. It is also true that first
pick of the items was made by Xenia, who withdrew some £11,415
worth of jewellery from the sale for herself and her sister. So, the
choicest items, however, were not necessarily the most expensive or
those from the original inventory. But they were to Queen Mary's
taste. She spent under £10,000, with a pearl and diamond collar with a
sapphire and diamond clasp, at £6,000, being the most expensive. This
was well short of the £64,600 raised by the sale of just three Marie
Feodorovna pearl necklaces.

By 1933, the last of Queen Mary's Romanov jewellery purchases
(throughout the 1920s she regularly acquired items auctioned off by
the Soviet government such as Fabergé eggs and Sèvres snuff boxes) had
been added to the gigantic Windsor family collection, joining an earlier
purchase resulting from the 1920 death of another émigré in France.

Her Imperial Highness Grand Duchess Maria Pavlovna, former wife
of Grand Duke Vladimir Alexandrovich of Russia, was renowned
for her beauty and her jewels, though she once contemplated a coup
against her cousin, Tsar Nicholas II, in the winter of 1916–17 to force

his abdication. The idea was to replace 'Nicky' with the Tsarevich Alexei and install her eldest son, Grand Duke Nicholas Nikolaevich, as regent.

Marie's action was pure payback after the tsar's wife, the Empress Alexandra, had rebuffed the potential marriage between their eldest daughter, Grand Duchess Olga, and Marie's second son, Grand Duke Boris Vladimirovich. Alexandra wrote to her husband that she could not let 'a pure, fresh girl, 18 years his junior' marry a 'well used, half worn out, blasé young man'.[10]

Marie wouldn't let the snub go and remained in the war-torn Caucasus with her two younger sons throughout 1917 and 1918, still hoping to make her eldest son tsar. After sticking around for another two years she, and what was left of her family, boarded an Italian ship headed for Venice, the sad group making their way to Switzerland and then France, existing for seven weeks on black bread and soup on a refugee train.

Unluckily for the grand duchess, her jewels were walled up in the Vladimir Palace under the control of the Petrograd Soviet. Desperate for them and short of cash while holed up in Yalta, she was tempted to hire Crimean mercenaries to storm the palace and retrieve her only viable means of support. But luckily, an old friend of hers who had acted as a go-between between Tsar Nicholas II and George V got wind of her plight and offered to help.

Albert (Bertie) Stopford was an Englishman, a vicar's son from Titchmarsh, in Northamptonshire, who preferred to speak French rather than his native tongue. This served him well in tsarist Russia, where French was still the preferred way of communicating in all the smart salons and higher diplomatic circles. Bertie was a pal of Prince Felix Yusupov and Prince Serge Obolensky during their time at Oxford, where they were members of the Bullingdon Club and danced the fandango at wild undergraduate parties in pre-war London with prima ballerinas Anna Pavlova and Tamara Karsavina (he also had a hand in bringing Karsavina and Nijinsky to London in 1911).

In Russia, domiciled at the Grand Hotel Europe, Saint Petersburg, Bertie knew everyone who mattered and was soon recruited by British Intelligence as a courier. Though neither a soldier nor a diplomat, he was somehow free to move around wartime Russia rescuing jewels and other property for his aristocratic friends right from under the noses of the berserk, paranoid Bolsheviks. In this, he was very successful, and Obolensky estimated he had personally carried out millions of pounds' worth of valuables, including Obolenksy's own family jewels.

In April 1917, a cunning plan was hatched at Kislovodsk, a spa in the Northern Caucasus where the grand duchess was convalescing. Bettie had consulted his obligatory deck of tarot cards and had come up with the following idea: he and Marie Pavlovna's son Boris (the snubbed one), dressed as boiler-repair men, would enter the Vladimir Palace by the tradesmen's entrance (courtesy of a loyal caretaker), make their way to the grand duchess's boudoir and spring her jewels and cash, including the famous pearl-drop Vladimir tiara, from the safe. The duchess shrugged – why not?

The plan was subsequently carried out in August and worked beautifully. Bertie and Boris carried 244 jewels out of the palace in two battered Gladstone bags, the items wrapped in old newspapers masquerading as work tools. Bertie than transferred the loot to diplomatic bags he normally carried as an official courier and ferried them to London, where he stashed them in a safe-deposit box under the duchess's name. The cash he hid in his shoes and delivered separately to the grand duchess in Yalta.

Marie Pavlovna died in France in 1920 and, needing cash after their recent escape in a depressed, gem-flooded market, her children tried to get whatever they could for them to survive and pay off their debts. Her emeralds were left to Grand Duke Boris, the pearls to Grand Duke Nicholas, the rubies to Grand Duke Andrei and the Vladimir to her daughter Helen. They were disposed of discreetly, at knockdown prices, possibly by Bertie Stopford.

Queen Marie of Romania snapped up a sapphire tiara, the emeralds wound up in the New World, first with the Rockefellers and then with Woolworth heiress Barbara Hutton. The Vladimir was acquired by Queen Mary, who had the idea of using some of the Cambridge emeralds she had lying around mounted as alternatives to the pendant pearls.

As for Bertie Stopford, after stints in Belgravia and Italy before the war and Wormwood Scrubs after it, he lived out the rest of his life in Paris, with no visible means of support except lots of dinner invitations and the occasional commission from buying and selling antiques. In 1924, he was living at No. 31 rue de Valois, in the prestigious 1st arrondissement, according to the Fellows of the Zoological Society of London.

He was a gadfly and name-dropper *par excellence*, but when he died in 1939, his estate only ran to the cost of a thirty-year lease on a plot in Bagneux Cemetery. In 1970, the man who rescued the Vladimir tiara ended up in a communal grave. His world and his so-called friends had faded away. But his true wealth, of course, was in his memories as recorded in his *Russian Diary of an Englishman, Petrograd 1915–17*.[11]

As to the wealth of the Windsors in the late 1920s, thanks to the insane generosity of their dominions and the acquisitive nature of their queens, their strongrooms and jewellery caskets were overflowing with more diamonds, rubies, sapphires, emeralds, pearls, platinum, gold and silver than they could ever use or wear in several lifetimes. It was at this heady moment that Bessie Wallis Warfield Simpson made her first tentative forays into London society.

4

The Unimportance of Being Ernest

What win I, if I gain the thing I seek?
A dream, a breath, a froth of fleeting joy.
Who buys a minute's mirth to wail a week?
Or sells eternity to get a toy?
For one sweet grape who will the vine destroy?
Or what fond beggar, but to touch the crown,
Would with the sceptre straight be strucken down?

William Shakespeare, *The Rape of Lucrece*

Torrents of buttery yellow Touraine sunlight flooded the bedroom of Bessie Wallis Warfield on the morning of her wedding day, Thursday, 3 June 1937, at Château de Candé in the French countryside. And along with the sensuous sunlight came the first semi-conscious thoughts of the day.

Yes, she had come a long way. It had been a stunning achievement all round, although it wasn't *completely* unexpected. In her heart of hearts, she always believed she was destined for a special place in the world. Time and time again, considering the many twists and turns her life had taken, she had always managed to get what she really, really wanted. In the end.

But was this what she really, really wanted? It was certainly a kind of pinnacle, and it *had* taken a bit of doing this time around. But the jury was out on the prize, as the hard-boiled American pulp fiction she flicked through for distraction would have put it. Nevertheless, it was just spooky how things always worked themselves out, almost in a divine way, though she'd never call it anything so whacky in front of people, no matter how dissolute or illustrious they were (on the wall of a future country retreat, the Moulin de la Tuilerie, in Gif-sur-Yvette, south-west of Paris, she hung the inscription, 'I'm not the miller's daughter. But I've been through the mill.').

And yet here she was, in a fairy-tale castle, soon to be married to a royal prince, the richest man in Europe, with sacks of gems and jewellery in her luggage, racks of haute couture outfits, the imminent title of duchess, and enough personal cash to set herself up in Palm Beach, Palm Springs, Manhattan — wherever — for life. Not bad for someone many people considered to be a drab, ordinary-looking divorcee from Baltimore. And yet … and yet … why was she so unhappy and hard and cold? Why was she *so* ungrateful?

Because this time around, the whole palaver was more than what she really, really wanted — much, much more. She never wanted all this infamy. And to be trapped again. She really wanted less. She would have taken less. She would have taken everything except the marriage part. Yes, that part of the deal certainly took the gloss off everything else, in her mind.

But what could she do? What could she do to avert the avalanche that had swept her and everyone else connected with this whole ghastly mess towards the oblivion she now had to face on a daily basis? She'd tried, God knows, she'd tried, but that fool of a little man was hellbent on doing it his way and she, well she was powerless, it seemed, after all.

Fanciful as these early morning sentiments may seem to us now, almost sixty-three years later, on Wednesday, 2 March 2000, they were largely authenticated by the public release of King Edward's chief advisor and fixer, the barrister Walter Monckton's personal papers.[1] Monckton died in 1965 and many of his papers (probably copies of the duke's correspondence with his brother George VI) were dispatched to the Royal Archives at Windsor by his literary trustees in the early 1970s. This was in acknowledgement of a 3 December 1948 letter from Monckton to Buckingham Palace promising to deliver his 'abdication material' or copies of them.[2]

Historians and journalists who had gathered to read the ten boxes of embargoed papers at the Bodleian Library on that raw day in March 2000 were still expecting to unearth previously hidden nuggets of treasure. They soon discovered the most crucial personal papers had again been weeded from Monckton's archive and sealed until the year 2037.

And yet the boxes did, however, reveal confirmation of a handwritten note that was authored at the height of the abdication crisis in December 1936 and which slumbered among miscellaneous political papers belonging to the prime minister at the time, Stanley Baldwin. Signed by the future duchess (but written in pencil by Lord Brownlow, the courtier who accompanied her when she fled in 1936 to the Villa Lou Viei in Cannes), it declared, 'With the deepest personal sorrow Wallis Simpson wishes to announce that she has abandoned any intention to marry His Majesty'.[3]

Correspondence between Monckton and Alan Lascelles, the ex-king's private secretary, referring to this document was found in the released Bodleian cache in 2000. Its existence at that time certainly surprised Lascelles, who asked for copies of all Monckton's material on the abdication crisis.

The papers also backed up the future duchess's everlasting conviction that the whole affair was easier for Edward than it was for her because (as he always said) he'd never wanted 'it', by which he meant the Crown, the crushing, stultifying responsibility of centuries of tradition and obligation he was saddled with. He was bored and depressed by 'it', what his promiscuous pal Duff Cooper elsewhere called his 'intolerable honour'.[4]

In the papers, Monckton took the romantic view that there were two fundamental factors at play with Edward and Wallis. The first was:

[The] intensity and depth of the king's devotion [to her.] To him she was the perfect woman. It is a great mistake to assume that he was merely in love with her in an ordinary physical sense of the term. There was an intellectual companionship and there is no doubt that his lonely nature found in her a spiritual comradeship.[5]

Monckton believed the second factor was less generally recognised by the public. Edward had:

... remarkable determination, courage, and confidence in his own opinions and decisions [...] Once his mind was made up one felt he was like a death adder 'that stoppeth her ears and refuseth to hear the voice of the charmer' [...] For myself I am free to confess that I always underestimated the depth and strength of the king's devotion and of their united will.[6]

There was, however, an alternative to the 'mess', which the duchess tried to convince Edward to pursue – and which, coincidentally, his father also tried to persuade him to consider – but which Edward continually repulsed. Wallis quite liked the idea of being the king's mistress, the *maîtress-en-titre*, as the French would have it. She was perfectly fine with that arrangement. But no, it wasn't to be. To Wallis's eternal chagrin, Edward, the silly fool, wouldn't have it.

Wallis reminisced on that sunny morning in June 1937 how she'd cried, and cried, and cried after he'd then gone ahead and done it. Abdicated. Even after she'd told him not to – after she *specifically* told him not to. She was beside herself with frustration and anger and terror, later writing how she drained the dregs of that bitter cup of failure and defeat.[7] She even told him she wouldn't marry him if he went through with it but then he threatened her, the fool threatened her with his life. So, then what was she supposed to do with that and all the other death threats she kept receiving by the bucket load? Inhabit another planet? The papers reinforce the apparent helplessness of her situation and the almost fanatical romantic zeal of her lover.

Among the more fascinating documents in the collection are the drafts of Edward VIII's abdication speech. The final version, which in its raw and candid simplicity so affected the British people, bore little resemblance to the first attempts.

The tortured original, handwritten by Edward before heavy censoring and rewriting by Baldwin and more lengthy advice from Monckton and Winston Churchill, contained long passages devoted to Mrs Simpson and the taboo subject of marriage. After almost a dozen redrafts, the final version that was eventually delivered to the world excluded any mention of marriage. With a nod to propriety, it did contain a special tribute to the prime minister and a dutiful endorsement of the Duke of York.

But all that was in the past. Here she was at the Château de Candé, trapped yet again after she swore she'd never be trapped again. There was a price to pay for all this bewitching and, oh yes, she was paying it, but she also expected to be handsomely paid back in return. Today was the first step in that process, the payback for what she'd had to endure and what she knew she'd be forced to endure, now and forever more. She already had the cash, the clothes and the jewels. Now it was time for an injection of good old-fashioned status, the kind that only old, old money could buy.

The elegant Château de Candé, with its American millionaires and British aristocrats, was a world away from the Baltimore society that had shunned her and her mother (the proprietor of a Baltimore boarding house) when she was a little girl. Wallis's old home at No. 212 North Biddle Street, Baltimore, had been bought by a lawyer, Harry J. Green, who was planning on turning it into a museum, although none of the original furnishings or furniture were left. She didn't know whether to be flattered, horrified or compelled to sue him for breach of privacy.

But there were bigger things to be cross and indignant about. Such as the absurd model of herself in Madame Tussauds that was unveiled eleven days after the abdication. She complained to her lawyers and Monckton, writing, 'Is there any way you can have that appalling wax figure of me removed from Madame Tussauds – it really is too indecent and so awful to be there anyway'.[8]

But there was no legal way of forcing Madame Tussauds to remove the figure. She was certain she was being set up for ridicule, especially since it was being paraded, not with the rest of the royal family, but with figures like Rasputin, Marie Antoinette and Mary, Queen of Scots. Six months later, and it was still there, in the same nefarious company, a lightning rod for everyone's disgust and disappointment.

She had so many similar thoughts on that fateful morning. There were so many twists and turns.

While her maid, Mary Burke, fussed over the curtains and placed a new vase of fresh flowers on the corner of an ornate dressing table, Wallis stretched and yawned with a mouth as wide as a hyena and thought how this glorious, lemony morning was a world away from her arrival in the Touraine almost three months ago. What a contrast it had been: a stormy Wednesday afternoon in March, just two days after her fiancé was formally confirmed by Letters Patent as HRH the Duke of Windsor. It was the final stretch, she told herself, as the glistening black Buick limousine carefully crunched its way up the wet gravel drive of the chalk-white Renaissance château perched invitingly above the meandering River Indre.

The elopement to Candé had taken weeks of planning and extensive negotiation with its American owners, Charles and Fern Bedaux. It had been purchased in 1927 for $36,500 from Jean Drake del Castillo, and the Bedauxs had spent an enormous amount of money modernising it. New plumbing, electrical and central-heating systems were installed using 60 tons of new American pipes. The eight bedrooms were each equipped with an American bathroom and other indoor toilets were added. Bedaux installed a telephone at a cost of $16,000, which at the time was unique in French residences. Other embellishments included an eighteen-hole golf course, tennis court, gymnasium and solarium.

But Wallis wanted more if she and the ex-king were to stage the wedding of the century there. First, to pay for the prestige and notoriety of the occasion, the Bedauxs would have to pick up all the expenses.

Second, Wallis insisted on supplementing the twenty-four indoor staff already there with two nightwatchmen, accommodation for detectives from the Sûreté and Scotland Yard, rooms for her maid and chauffeur, a strongroom for her jewels, a pastry cook, sous-chef and scullery boy, a second butler and footman, four maids and two charwomen, five laundrywomen, an extra chauffeur and a telephonist to be on hand to work the telephone system at all times.[9] There were to be twice-weekly deposits of fresh flowers from the Paris markets and every weekend her favourite manicurist was to be ferried from Paris by train and car for a pedicure and manicure (using only the palest of nail varnishes so as not to draw attention to her ugly hands).

In the tense days leading to her scheduled arrival, Fern Bedaux was able to report that she had engaged Alphonse Diot, ex-chef to the Duke of Alba, for 2,000 francs a month (enticed perhaps by the gilded fresh-water fountain installed to preserve newly bought fish in the kitchen). And, of course, the Bedauxs agreed to foot this bill and every other expense for the Windsors' stay, estimated to total a colossal $60,000 for the three months they were there.[10]

Inside the Buick with Mrs Simpson (as she was known until May 1937, when she changed her name by deed poll to Warfield) were Mr and Mrs Herman Rogers, the American friends who had hosted her at their house, Villa Lou Viei, on the French Riviera, since December 1936. It was followed by another black saloon carrying servants and Mary Burke, plus two vans with sixteen trunks and thirty-six pieces of luggage including new jewellery from Van Cleef & Arpels, sixteen new costumes from the House of Schiaparelli, Paris, and thirteen from Captain Edward Molyneux's spring collection at Cannes.

On that day, the Buick had swept up the hill, scudded with low, gloomy clouds, to the château's immense arabesque doorway with its iron handles and patinaed grain. The chauffeur, Ladbroke, pulled the doorbell and the oak door creaked open to reveal a vast, glittering hallway lined by thirty-five members of staff, all of them uniformed, including James Hale, the English butler, impeccably dressed in a hand-tailored Savile Row suit. The liveried flunkeys wore royal blue and gold coats, black trousers and gold-buckled shoes. The maids were in floor-length black silk dresses with frilly caps and aprons and the housekeeper, tall, austere and sombre in a brushed charcoal tweed suit, was equipped with a large chatelaine of keys.

This army of servants, augmented by villagers from Monts, Les Montils, Chaumont-sur-Loire and Chambon-sur-Cisse, had spent the past week under the watchful eye of Fern Bedaux, dusting, scrubbing and repainting the ancient edifice from top to bottom. Completing the Agatha Christie tableau were crystal chandeliers glowing from the ceiling, furniture covered in eighteenth-century patterned linens that Mrs Bedaux had found unused in the attics, and 10,000 francs' worth of fresh flowers freighted by train from Paris.

After tea, Fern took Wallis on a tour of the château, through the drawing room with its oak panelling and pipe organ, a salon with panelled walls and Louis XV furnishings, the dining room with its massive, beamed ceiling, and her own bedroom with cream-coloured boiserie and tall windows overlooking the grounds that she had given over to Wallis. Wallis's bathroom had heated platinum-plated towel rails and an enormous tub equipped with massive gold taps.

When she was settled, Fern Bedaux informed her guest she would be leaving the château after a few days to ensure Wallis and her retinue had complete privacy and the necessary freedom to make themselves at home. The weeks of tetchy negotiations, the relentless requirements and ultimatums had evidently taken their toll on the elegant Mrs Bedaux. She exited as quickly as she could, joining her husband at one of their other properties as soon as her part of the deal was concluded.

Emptied by the journey, Wallis spent her first full day resting in her room, decorated in orchid silk and satin, overlooking the dripping woods and gunmetal-grey countryside. The château settled down to its routine, unpacking and hanging clothes, storing boxes and preparing for dinner.

After calling the duke several times in Vienna, Mrs Simpson tried to step outdoors for some fresh air at dusk, but the rain became so heavy that she returned. Despite the melancholy weather and the bad news the duke had relayed regarding the receding possibility of receiving any future money from the Civil List, she was glad to be out of the Riviera and away from the miserable experiences of the past four months.

Wallis learned a lot in the few days Fern Bedaux (a product of old money from Grand Rapids, Michigan) presided over the château and the effortless way she ran the household with strict adherence to formality, minute attention to detail, and a flair for discernment. A case in point were the arrangements for dinner. Two cloths were put on the dining table. The first layer was a cloth of gold, the second was fine Brussels lace, the gold shining through under the light of the candelabra when it was lit.

Meals were served by the butler, Hale, and flunkeys in livery. The monogrammed china and silver were of the finest quality. Individual menus were written in copperplate for each guest and placed on a tiny silver rest in front of them. Fish and meat were already filleted and offered to guests from silver platters served by Hale. Game birds and fowl, however, were brought to the table 'dressed' (with their feathers on) so everyone could see and feel them. Then they were taken away, cooked and served. Afterwards, there were dance music records and refreshments, all supervised by Hale and Mrs Bedaux. After Cannes, this was heaven.

Wallis had endured a wretched time since her long-distance telephone call to the Rogers' Villa Lou Viei on Saturday, 3 December 1936, when they had calmed her down and agreed to provide her with sanctuary from the madness that was enveloping the Crown, the British government and the British people. At that time, she was exhausted and depressed and had made up her mind to leave the country the previous day, telling the king at their last evening together at Fort Belvedere, as a fog crept towards them from Virginia Water, that she had instructed her staff to pack up her belongings in London.

He agreed it was probably for the best. The costly preparations for his coronation had been halted and, in a grim attempt at gallows humour, he related there had been a run on the special commemorative postage stamps issued for the event by thousands of people betting on their value increasing after his abdication. She tried to enter into the swing of things by suggesting that maybe he should snap them up as well. He already had, he laughed, but she could tell he was equally depressed and cringing at the thought of another stormy meeting with his prime minister scheduled for the evening of the 3rd at Buckingham Palace, followed by dinner with an increasingly hysterical Duke and Duchess of York.

The next day George Ladbroke was commandeered to drive her in the royal Buick from Fort Belvedere to Newhaven. By the afternoon, her nerves were shredded.

She was paranoid she would be assassinated or kidnapped and held to ransom en route and tried to divert those thoughts with a frenzy of last-minute activity. First, she increased her jewellery insurance (after the king gave her £100,000 worth of 'presents', which he insisted she take with her in the Buick).[11] Then she made a new will, leaving most of her possessions to her family confidante and companion, Aunt Bessie, two devoted maids and a few personal friends.[12] The king's solicitor, Sir George Allen, drew up the document on blue Fort Belvedere stationery.

She was desperate to get away and in the tense, hothouse atmosphere, the king arranged for her to be accompanied by Lord Peregrine Brownlow, a trusted friend, and Inspector Evans of Scotland Yard. There was no room for Slipper, the couple's favourite Cairn terrier. The king also gave her a ladybird bracelet charm with the message 'Fly Away Home' and other fabulous items to take away, concealed in luggage that was to travel separately with Mary Burke.

They were both shaking with emotion as the Buick idled on the gravel driveway. The king couldn't let her go. She eventually managed to break free and dived into the car wrapped in a new, three-quarter-length brown sable coat, insulating her against the fog and biting cold.

At Newhaven, she and Lord Brownlow were booked on the 10 p.m. Channel ferry to Dieppe under the names of Mr and Mrs Harris. During the crossing she pleaded with Brownlow to convince the king to stay on the throne and forget their marriage. Brownlow noted that, at this time, she still had intentions of returning to England after the king's coronation as his royal mistress.

In France, the next day they checked in to wretched rooms at the Hôtel de la Poste in Blois for a few hours, where she lay down and cried with primeval pain. On the 5th, Brownlow was alerted to an oncoming posse of reporters who had got wind of her flight to France and were descending en masse to intercept them. Ladbroke took a circuitous route south to avoid the onslaught.

At the Hôtellerie le Grand-Cerf in Evreux she spoke to the king by telephone, screaming through static down the line that he was not to abdicate. The Buick continued its journey through appalling weather of snow, sleet and driving winds. Adding to the discomfort, Brownlow had inadvertently smashed his glass hip flask of Scotch whisky and was drenched in it.

At Lyons, the press caught up with them and chased the Buick through the city streets like a scene from a gangster movie, engines screaming, tyres screeching. Finding sanctuary at Vienne in a private room at the Restaurant de la Pyramide, she managed to flee after lunch through a small window above the kitchen sink into a back alleyway and the waiting Buick.

They stopped again at Brignoles to buy medicine and then, at 2 a.m. on the 6th, drove through hundreds of spectators waiting in the rain before the wrought-iron gates of the Villa Lou Viei. Mrs Simpson was crouched on her knees on the car floor, concealed by a heavy rug.

On entering the Lou Viei, she immediately asked after Mary Burke and the sixteen trunks and thirty-six suitcases of luggage that were supposed to have arrived at Cannes by train the previous day. Assured the collection was safely installed in her suite upstairs, Wallis collapsed into a chair in front of a blazing log fire and covered her face with her hands.

That June morning at Candé, just the thought of those feverish, frenetic days last winter seemed to automatically compress her body into the foetal position. It was visceral and raw. But much worse had been to come in the shape of another of her solicitors, Theodore Goddard, who had visited her a few days after she arrived at the Lou Viei.

Goddard, the pompous 57-year-old solicitor from Serjeant's Inn, in the Temple area of London, had already been responsible for one farce in the duchess's life and now he was about to instigate a second. He had never been Wallis's first choice. Charles Russell, the first firm she consulted on her divorce, had declined. It was the king's solicitor, Sir George Allen, who recommended Goddard because he was well known in Establishment circles. Stanley Baldwin described him as 'a man of blameless reputation but extraordinary ingenuity [...] a man whom every crook in London employs by reason of his cleverness; everybody who gets into a mess applies immediately to Goddard, who gets them out at once'.[13]

The first farcical episode concerned the devious legal manoeuvrings (as described by many in the legal profession at the time) surrounding Wallis's controversial divorce from her second husband Ernest Simpson, a mid-level Anglo-American shipping executive and former officer in the Coldstream Guards, which in the eyes of the law allowed her to marry Edward VIII.

Devious and farcical because the decree nisi was initially defeated, according to a forty-seven-page private memoir of the affair penned by Robert Egerton, a junior solicitor with Theodore Goddard & Co.[14] As a solicitor, Egerton was 'well aware at the time of the humbug and sleaziness which inevitably result from divorce law' but even he was surprised at the 'judicial farce' that Goddard was enlisted to perform (for his trouble, Goddard was given the extremely generous fee of 100 guineas for his work).

In Egerton's view, the whole sordid caper tarnished 'the grandeur of the fact that a man renounced the world's greatest privileges and duties for love of a woman'. He was instructed by Goddard one Friday morning to cancel any arrangements he had for the weekend and pack a bag for a 'very good hotel'.

Their client's husband, Mr Simpson, had dutifully taken a room at the Hotel de Paris at Bray in Berkshire to commit the required adulterous act for a successful divorce petition. The first attempt by Goddard to expedite the divorce before the agonising self-imposed restraint of British newspapers evaporated (the UK blackout was courtesy of the powerful proprietor Lord Beaverbrook, but this was not the case in America where Wallis was hot property) was spectacularly thwarted because the hotel chosen for the staged adultery declined to provide the required details due to its exclusivity! But this proved only a temporary setback.

The Simpsons' contrived divorce proceedings began on the morning of 27 October 1936 at Ipswich Assize Court. Wallis arrived a few minutes early, accompanied by an embarrassed-looking detective, Goddard and her erudite counsel, Norman Birkett. The group were quickly herded through a side door before the police locked down the front of the building from the inside. When it was time, Theodore Goddard quietly shepherded Mrs Simpson to her seat near the witness box where she was flanked by Birkett and his assistant, Walter Frampton.[15] A guardsman, dressed in a scarlet tunic, then entered the room and startled everyone by heralding the arrival of the judge with a blast on a silver trumpet.

Memories of this very public appearance always made the future duchess cringe with embarrassment. Not only did she have to insist in open court that she had never misbehaved with another man, but she had to do it in the presence of a decidedly unsympathetic and dour judge. Even Egerton noticed the judge's evident disgust, writing:

He had not liked what he saw of Mrs. Simpson in the box, particularly, no doubt, her claim that the chance discovery of her husband's infidelity had driven her to write [a] legally concocted letter expelling him from their home.[16]

But Sir Anthony Hawke, the venerable 67-year-old High Court judge in question, was also visibly suffering on the morning of 27 October 1936 – from both from a wicked cold and extreme annoyance at the commotion that was taking place outside his courtroom.

Hawke was a short elderly man, almost completely hidden behind his crimson and ermine robes and long, white wig. Despite Goddard's elaborate arrangements, nobody had bothered to inform the tetchy Hawke of the unprecedented turmoil about to be unleashed on his court that day. Studying the nervous-looking middle-aged woman standing before him, and completely oblivious of her fame, Hawke expected to be assured unequivocally that the three Cs – connivance, collusion and condonation – were not involved in the case.

The few people allowed into the court were witnesses who were integral to the case along with about twenty smirking journalists. One reporter described Wallis as 'like [a] living portrait Whistler might have painted [... she was] a chick [sic] woman with chiselled delicate features'.[17]

Hawke sourly observed the flustered Wallis taking the witness box to be cross-examined by her counsel. She removed her white glove to take the oath. A chair had been provided for her, although it was customary for witnesses to stand. After fourteen minutes of testimony, she was allowed to leave the witness box. The corroborating evidence of Hotel de Paris witnesses was then heard, testifying that Mr Simpson was in bed with another woman, 'both of them occupied [...] it was a little bed'.[18] Birkett ended his address and asked for costs.

An irritated Sir Anthony Hawke hesitated for a moment, blew his runny, purple nose, and reluctantly granted the petition, awarding costs against Mr Simpson. Wallis left the icy court as quickly as she could, got into the chauffeured Buick once again and sped off to London with Goddard, quietly triumphant. The police had considerably blocked the road outside the court for their getaway, giving them a clear run before the inevitable pursuit began. It was a bittersweet memory.

Later that evening at Buckingham Palace, Edward surprised her during a private supper with a dazzling Cartier ring set with a 19.77-carat rectangular emerald flanked by diamond baguettes. It was engraved with the phrase 'We are ours now 27 x 36' inside the classic platinum band.

It was a strange choice of stone. Compared to a diamond, emeralds are soft, can scratch easily and generally don't respond well to everyday wear. And strange for another reason, as the king had recourse to plenty of uncut emeralds from his own collection and those belonging to the monarch.

However, in this case, so the story goes, he had been alerted to the availability of an exceptional stone by Jacques Cartier himself, who ran the London branch of the Place Vendôme jeweller. Legend has it the gem was one of two stones cut from an emerald as large as a bird's egg that once belonged to a Mughal emperor (although the king had plenty of Mughal stones from his 1921 four-month tour of India). Edward snapped it up from Cartier for £10,000.

For Edward to fork out so much of his own money when he had free alternatives is surprising. Maybe he swapped one of his for one of Cartier's and had them make it up as part of the deal. Jacques Arpels, from Cartier's Place Vendôme neighbours, Van Cleef & Arpels, remembered Edward being extremely involved in the design of jewellery and 'arriving with jewels' at the store, so the idea might not be so far-fetched.[19]

John Culme, writing in Sotheby's infamous 1987 Geneva Catalogue, stated:

> The magnificent emerald was first purchased by Cartier in the 1920s. One of the Cartier jewellers went to Baghdad to see a collection of gems. He sent back a messenger to say he needed a very large sum of money. The money was sent but when the representative came back, all he brought was a tiny pouch. Out of it tumbled a very large, almost unsaleable emerald.

Cartier's solution, in the limited market for such a stone of that size, was to divide the emerald in half and recut it. In 1957, to celebrate their twentieth anniversary, the Windsors had Cartier remount and redesign the ring with a more modern style consisting of a yellow gold band set with several new diamonds. This version was sold in the 1987 auction for $2.1 million. Wallis kept the original mounting her entire life. Sotheby's found it among the hoard of monogrammed red Morocco jewellery boxes stored at the Bank of France prior to the sale.

The skulduggery surrounding the Simpson divorce was not the end of Theodore Goddard's involvement with Wallis Simpson. The second farce he was about to inflict upon the future duchess concerned her jewels.

The ruse for this intervention (coming a few days before the abdication) was based on, first, mining the possibility that Mrs Simpson might persuade the king to withdraw his plan to abdicate and, second, on stirring up the perceived threat posed by a citizen's intervention concerning the legality and integrity of her divorce. Both ploys were calculated to intimidate Edward and Wallis and were couched in terms of the king's government taking every reasonable step to prevent the impending rupture to the monarchy.

Edward got wind of the intervention (but not its true purpose) on 7 December 1936. Versions differ as to whether Goddard was summoned by Edward and told not to fly to Cannes to see Wallis or whether Edward merely telephoned Wallis to warn her of the impending coercion to withdraw. It is certain that Goddard conferred with Prime Minister Stanley Baldwin at Downing Street and, owing to the urgency of the matter, an aeroplane was chartered with government money to fly him directly to Cannes.[20]

The ruse of sending Goddard to France was concocted by Baldwin, acting on an approach by the royal family, who had learned of the fabulous stash of jewels and uncut gems Edward had given Wallis on her exit from the Fort on Thursday, 3 December. The family were naturally alarmed (given Edward's overt habit of plundering royal assets for his mistresses' personal use) at the very real possibility that the stones might have been taken from the Royal Collection, which was under his guardianship and whose dispersal was at his sole discretion as monarch.[21] The problem was, no one knew whether the hoard was from his private heirloom collection, the Royal Collection or a mixture of both, given the secrecy that permeated the whole subject of royal jewels within the family. Not even Queen Mary herself, who had begun cataloguing the House of Windsor's trunk-loads of gems, was sure what they had in its entirety.

Unfortunately, Goddard had a weak heart and had never flown before. He asked Baldwin if he might take his doctor, William Kirkwood, with him as a precaution. Baldwin agreed, blithely unaware that Kirkwood was employed as a resident doctor at a maternity hospital. While

Goddard and Kirkwood were in the air the news leaked, with newspapers sensationally reporting the solicitor had flown to Mrs Simpson's bedside accompanied by both a gynaecologist and an anaesthetist, prompting speculation that Mrs Simpson was either pregnant or having an abortion. If that wasn't enough, one of the small plane's engines misfired, forcing it to land at Marseilles.

The frosty reception the shell-shocked Goddard and his entourage received at Villa Lou Viei at 2 a.m. on the 8th seemed hardly surprising, with the villa's owner Herman Rogers even barring the bewildered Kirkwood from crossing the threshold.

Goddard's papers were burned when his office was bombed during the Blitz, so we have no record of the success or not of his clandestine mission to rescue the royal jewels. But it must have been a tense and difficult time even for the resourceful Goddard, the confidant of crooks and crime lords. Did the subject ever come up? Did he try and persuade or threaten Wallis to give them up? Did he casually engage the servants in friendly banter, hoping to tease out some morsel of information that might lead him to where the loot was stashed? Did he case the joint during the wee small hours while everyone slept? The record does not show. But surely he was the most bizarre, underprepared, ill-equipped cat burglar of all time.

Oblivious to Goddard's true purpose in suddenly flying to the South of France, the Rogers household were nevertheless suspicious of his presence and resentful of the emotional impact he was having on the increasingly besieged and emotionally frayed Mrs Simpson. It was not the first time the king's family had tried to claw back what they imagined was rightfully theirs, and the next attempt was to take place eleven years later. In the meantime, Goddard and his crew took the train back to London empty-handed on all three counts.

On Thursday, 10 December 1936, in the presence of his brothers as witnesses, Edward signed six copies of the Act of Abdication at ten in the morning in the octagonal drawing room at Fort Belvedere. But he very nearly didn't. He hesitated, not because of the persuasive arguments of Baldwin, the royal family or his friends. He hesitated because (as everything of importance associated with Edward always was) there was still the question of what and how much money he was entitled to take with him.

On the morning of the 10th, as he was about to put pen to paper, Edward was informed that, unconnected to his inclusion on any future Civil List, he would be forgoing his substantial income from the Duchy of Cornwall upon abdicating the throne. A visibly distressed king bit his lip and surveyed the line of his three surviving brothers before him. It was a peculiar moment. The royal dukes thought he was overcome with the immensity of the moment.[22]

Wallis was unaware of this sliding-door moment occurring seven months earlier. Still in bed, and eschewing the customary breakfast tray that Mary Burke brought in, she wondered instead what would happen if she couldn't or just didn't get up? Was that petulance? Capitulation?

She'd often felt like doing such a radical thing in the past six months, refusing to surface, denying the world around her the opportunity of knocking her down or taking yet another pot-shot at her and her royal association. Not exactly hiding, just not exactly participating.

It was a tantalising proposition that she invariably stubbed out like one of her long, thin Dunhill cigarettes. She was made of sterner stuff and came from a long line of Warfields, bred to survive the worst that life could throw at them. She was damned if she'd give them the satisfaction. Besides, without her, the wedding of the century wouldn't be, would it?

Wallis rolled on to her back and blew out her cheeks as another maid informed her it was 8 a.m. and her hairdresser, Alexandre, had arrived to set her hair.

5

The Vast Shipwreck of My Life's Esteems

I am – yet what I am none cares or knows;
My friends forsake me like a memory lost:
I am the self-consumer of my woes –
They rise and vanish in oblivious host,
Like shadows in love's frenzied stifled throes
And yet I am, and live – like vapours tossed

Into the nothingness of scorn and noise,
Into the living sea of waking dreams,
Where there is neither sense of life or joys,
But the vast shipwreck of my life's esteems;
Even the dearest that I loved the best
Are strange – nay, rather, stranger than the rest.

John Clare (1848), 'I Am'

Directly across from Wallis's suite of rooms on the ground floor at the Château de Candé, her lover, the recently appointed Duke of Windsor, was in an equally sour mood that bright and sunny June morning. Not as luxurious as the rooms he occupied at the Schloss Enzesfeld 'safe house' after he escaped from the throne in 1936, the duke's living arrangements at Candé consisted of a double bedroom, sitting room and a bathroom that he shared with his best man. It wouldn't have mattered what the arrangements were. Like Enzesfeld, his life at Candé seemed to be an extension of the disappointments and calamities that had dogged him since his escape that wretchedly cold morning in December 1936.

Swapping the luxurious embraces of his hosts, the Rothschilds, at the *schloss* for the Bedauxs at Candé had made little difference, except the prince was able to play golf every day in the sun and scythe the 100 acres of meadows at the château for exercise, stripped to the waist, as he had done at the Fort. It seemed as if the tide of universal good fortune and goodwill that had washed over the little prince throughout his gilded life was suddenly cursed and compromised and there was nothing he could do about it except complain.

Osbert Sitwell captured the devastating turnaround in his fortunes during the aftermath of the abdication in *Rat Week*:

Where are the friends of yesterday
That fawned on Him
And flattered Her
Where are the friends of yesterday
Submitting to His every whim
Offering praise of Her as Myrrh
To him?

Built on a steep rock in the Triesting Valley, some 40km south of Vienna, the *schloss* had served as the duke's base while he endured five torturous months of waiting for the divorce of his mistress, Mrs Bessie Wallis Warfield (previously Simpson), to be duly formalised. Despite the luxurious suite of rooms put at his disposal by the baron's American wife (bedroom, drawing room, library, smoking room and bathroom), it was still a far cry from what he was used to. At Buckingham Palace, for example, the king's bathroom had three washbasins in a line. One was marked 'teeth', another 'hands' and the third, 'face'.[1]

Despite this downsizing, he mostly spent his time at the *schloss* watching Mickey Mouse movies, knitting, sightseeing, playing the drums very loudly to jazz records, losing badly at cards, drinking a lot and doing his famous imitation of Winston Churchill pleading with him not to abdicate.[2] He was guarded by a detachment of *gendarmes* from Baden. When he shopped, he sent the bills to the British Legation, who passed them back to his aide, Piers Legh, to pay out of Legh's own pocket.

But most of the time he spent on the telephone to Wallis, racking up enormous bills that staggered even the Rothschilds. When he and his hosts could no longer stand the situation, he left the *schloss* in March 1937 for a more private establishment near Ischl.

Their health wasn't the best during those early days of exile. He suffered from ear infections and headaches, seeking treatment from a Professor Neumann in Vienna. She was equally miserable. He sent her a mink cape; she sent him a possum coat. Neither gift seemed to dispel the gloom that surrounded them. The baron's dogs mauled Slipper within days of his arrival and the duke saw it as an apt metaphor of his treatment at the hands of former friends and the press.

The upheaval in his personal staff was another source of discomfort and annoyance. His equerry, John Aird, who had accompanied him on his 1936 escape aboard the warship HMS *Fury* and then the *Orient Express*, had been recalled back to London by the new king. The duke subsequently asked Sir Walford Selby, the British Ambassador, to release Dudley Forwood from the Embassy to take care of his needs. Forwood had skied with the ex-king and Wallis at Kitzbühel and Edward needed someone compatible to compensate for the stuffy incompatibility of his other aide, Sir Piers Legh, who had been getting on his nerves.

Legh was not at all sympathetic to Edward's plight, particularly his mooning obsession with Wallis. His take on Edward's wallowing-in-misery pose at snowbound Enzesfeld was to present the duke with a frozen, disapproving countenance. It was not an attitude the duke appreciated in the circumstances.

It must have been intolerable for the fastidious, highly strung, non-German-speaking Legh. He had never been a supporter of Edward's relationship with Mrs Simpson and as early as February 1936, he had warned Tommy Lascelles that plans were already afoot to 'liquidate' Wallis's second husband, Ernest Simpson (matrimonially speaking), and 'to set the Crown upon the leopardess's head'.[3] It was inevitable that Legh, finally capitulating to his deep-seated revulsion about the entire sorry business, gave up all pretence of equanimity. His Majesty's downward spiral from idolised monarch to exiled lovesick toy spaniel was just too much to take.

From the outset, Edward was hopeless. He was a mess, and his rooms were a mess: his clothes and starched monogrammed linen were everywhere – in bundles on the floor, flung over furniture and trays of food. He had over a dozen framed portraits of Wallis in his bedroom, which he had converted into a kind of shrine, and he was observed by staff constantly hugging a pillow of hers that was embroidered with her initials.[4]

The two doomed exiles spent hours on the phone every evening, which left Edward further depressed and nervous, her torturous mix of nit-picking and emotional bashing, cloying baby-talk and rock-steady common sense reducing the former king to an obsequious, supplicant wreck.

Legh was disgusted. Even visits from old friends such as former aide Edward 'Fruity' Metcalfe did nothing to elevate the patina of misery and dependency that surrounded him. Perry Brownlow thought the new duke was a 'pathological case' at Enzesfeld.[5] In Legh's view, the once-dashing young prince's life had disintegrated to a pathetic degree in the absence of Mrs Simpson. It was a pattern that was to last for the rest of his life.

A future secretary, Diana Wells Hood, commented on a feature of this morbid dependency:

His wife was constantly in his thoughts. If he went out alone he looked for her the moment he returned home. If she went out without him and remained away for any length of time, he became nervous and pre-occupied.[6]

Alexander Hardinge, formerly King Edward's private secretary, presaged the pattern during the early 1930s:

> As time went on it became clearer that every decision, big or small, was subordinate to her will [...] It was she who filled his thoughts at all times, she alone who mattered, before her the affairs of state sank into insignificance.[7]

Edward's nerves in those first few days alone in exile were further shredded when word reached him of a BBC broadcast made by his arch-enemy, the Archbishop of Canterbury, Cosmo Lang, who accused him of surrendering to a common craving for private happiness. Edward was incensed. He harangued the Palace, both Buckingham and Lambeth, raging at the insult on the phone, his voice steadily morphing into an incandescent, high-pitched scream.

His mood persisted for days and was not assuaged by supporters rallying round him in print, such as the crime novelist Gerald Butler (the English James M. Cain), who authored a widely circulated poem:

> My Lord, Archbishop, what a scold you are
> And when your man is down, how very bold you are
> Of Christian charity, how very scant you are
> You Auld Lang Swine, how full of cant you are

As if to infuriate Lang and former courtiers who had consistently failed to propel him to church on Sunday mornings while he was king, the duke reportedly volunteered to read the lesson at a Vienna church on Christmas Day, which he did loudly and enthusiastically.

Some things had not disintegrated, however. Despite the subsequent straitened arrangements of his exile, Edward still insisted on the royal treatment he had been accustomed to since birth. Of course, some things could not be translated to Schloss Enzesfeld or Château de Candé, but these omissions were supplanted by other fabricated rituals.

Generally, as Prince of Wales and king, he rarely woke before midday. If he had no appointments, Horace Jack Crisp, his valet, would poke his head around the door several times to make sure his master was awake before entering the room with a cup of Royal Blend (a tea created by Fortnum & Mason for his grandfather, Edward VII) on a silver tray with a freshly pressed linen napkin embossed with his royal cypher. After a casual look at the day's sporting papers and a conversation about the day's clothes, he took a quick shower (unlike most of his family, Edward was never a devotee of baths, preferring the American way of washing).

While this was going on, the first of five changes of clothes for the day were laid out for him. He did not shave. This only happened when he dressed for dinner and, even then, according to his assistant private secretary, Tommy Lascelles, he needn't have bothered. Lascelles mischievously wrote in his diary:

> I saw him constantly at all hours of the day and night, yet I never observed on his face the faintest indication of the bristles which normally appear, even in men as fair as he was, when one has passed many hours without shaving. Years ago, I mentioned this peculiarity to [Baron] Dawson of Penn, [the king's physician] who said at once that it was a common phenomenon in cases of arrested development.[8]

Breakfast was taken alone and generally involved his favourite smoked craster kippers, eggs, toasted bread and coffee. It was more brunch, in the American way, than breakfast and it was wolfed down. It enabled him to skip a meal, which complemented the fastidious devotion to his waistline that he pursued for the rest of his life. Like his family, he preferred brown eggs because he thought they tasted better.

After the death of his father, Edward rescinded the time-honoured tradition (dating back to his great-grandmother, Queen Victoria) of being serenaded by a lone bagpiper for precisely fifteen minutes following the completion of the monarch's breakfast at Buckingham Palace, Windsor, Holyrood House and Balmoral. It generally marked the start of the working day for the monarch's staff and, like so many 'innovations' he tried to introduce, it was met with disdain.

He had little time for official engagements and didn't like to waste his time on them. Crisp once proffered that his master could undress, bathe and 'be on the way downstairs in tails and Garter star within three minutes' and needed minimal attention from his manservants.[9]

The most boring and tedious part of his day as king theoretically began with the grind of going through the black boxes of official papers at his immaculate Chippendale desk. In practice, he timed himself on how quickly he could get through them, signing everything and reading nothing. To protect the king's privacy, the desk's blotting paper was traditionally black so no one could read what he had written by holding it up to a mirror. It was also replaced every day.

Without a proper valet at the *schloss* (Crisp, who had worked as valet and page to the former Prince of Wales and king from 1919 until Edward went into exile, had refused to accompany him), it was left to the urbane Dudley Forwood to supply a new one and serve as private secretary. It was an eye opener. Forwood was required to enter the duke's bedroom after his German valet had woken him and announce the order of business for the day. He was supposed to bow as he did so, and if he didn't, the duke quietly reprimanded him. It was as if the wretched ex-king was determined to remind everyone within his limited orbit that he was still a person of rank and was due the required signs of deference without fail:

> To the end of his life, he carried about him the aura of his royal birth, he never outgrew the habits and expectations of his youth, and, to everyone but his wife, he could be formidable.[10]

An exhausted Piers Legh, relieved of his duties by the emergence of Forwood, quietly left the *schloss* in a snowstorm.

Added to the series of surreal forces that seemed to be arrayed in front of him during those very early days at the *schloss* was news on 21 January that Sir Boyd Merriman, the President of the Divorce Court, had ordered the King's Proctor Thomas Barnes to formally investigate the intervention of an outraged Francis Stephenson, a solicitor with Thorp, Sanders & Thorp. Stephenson had brought an action on 9 December 1936 against the awarding of a final divorce decree to Wallis. Merriman had chosen not to ignore it, despite Stephenson having apparently withdrawn his action upon hearing the king's abdication speech. Wallis's solicitor, Goddard, thought it was largely a procedural matter, unaware that Barnes was conducting an extensive investigation to establish whether Wallis was guilty of adultery.[11]

Stephenson's action was based on having information (according to files released by the Public Record Office on 30 January 2003) 'that Mrs Simpson was aiming to be Queen of England and that it was the late King's wish that she should be so and that his infatuation for her was abnormal'. Stephenson had been told:

> Mrs Simpson was the King's mistress and that her husband was to be paid a large sum of money to let his wife divorce him. In one case I was told the sum to be paid to him was £100,000 and another sum mentioned was £150,000.

The action was eventually formally dismissed on 19 March when the small, round-shouldered, droopy-moustached Stephenson confirmed in court that he no longer had any reason for complaint.

The whole futile exercise was a source of malingering irritation while it dragged on because the threat of discovering the truth was real and imminent. Everyone knew the divorce was rigged but (as was the case with most of the Windsor conniving) no one could prove it. Miraculously, the Windsor wedding, roughly planned to follow the coronation of George VI, was still on track.

When he wasn't obsessing over Wallis or trying to preserve his royal aura at the *schloss*, Edward was fixated on his other passion: money. He had a pathological fear that he never had enough and in his dislocation from the source of his former wealth, the Crown, he probably rued the many opportunities he had as king to supplement the hoard he was planning to abscond with. Because, as king, he could do whatever he liked with the personal assets of the monarchy.

Walter Monckton wrote in a private note (collected in his papers at the Bodleian Archives) that the duke had told him that he'd made up his mind to marry Wallis Simpson in 1934 'and from that time onwards, his mind never wavered'. It can also be assumed, knowing his character and history, that he had also turned his mind at that point to what he could scrape together to facilitate this union, knowing full well his best chance of independence and escaping scot-free would be easier as Prince of Wales rather than as king. However, as we shall see, the death of his father in 1936 and the sobering reality of his personal inheritance quickened that pace considerably.

The most portable assets he could lay his hands on were obviously the monarch's jewels and it was crucial that he and Wallis never wavered in maintaining the pretence that prising them away from the royal vaults was not only offensive to them, but also unnecessary. In an interview she gave the barrister and freelance journalist Helena Normanton (a key figure in the Women's Suffrage Movement and a founder member of the Women's Freedom League), published in the *New York Times* days before the wedding, Wallis reiterated the party line under the headline, 'Mrs. Warfield Denies Rumours On Gems, Trousseau, Aid to Nazis':

> In the first place, Queen Alexandra's collection of jewellery was – for a Queen – none too remarkable. In the second, the Duke of Windsor never at any time in his life inherited any jewellery from any member of the Royal Family. Third, by no sort of route, through him or otherwise, has Wallis Warfield ever been in possession of any jewels ever owned by the late Queen Alexandra![12]

The campaign also drew in well-placed society gossips such as her new friend, Constance Crowninshield Coolidge, Comtesse de Jumilhac, who confided to her diary:

About those emeralds [...] Queen Alexandra never left any emeralds. The only emeralds in the royal family all belong to Queen Mary who bought them or acquired them from the Tzarina. She still has them. The Duke never had any jewels at all. He even had to buy his own silver when he went to Belvedere. The jewels that Wallis has are all new jewels he has bought for her here in Paris – some at Cartier's and mostly at Van Cleef and Arpels [...] She has several sets of jewels but they are all modern. After all she would have told me if they had come from the royal family. I asked her and she said no – none of them, that the Duke had not been left any jewels at all.[13]

The Anglo-American journalist and critic Alastair 'Ali' Forbes, whose unique prose style consisted of vast 100-word sentences delivered to long-suffering editors in longhand on yellow foolscap, was never more succinct when describing Edward's voracious appetite for money. Reviewing Frances Donaldson's biography of Edward VIII for the *Times Literary Supplement* in 1974, he wrote, 'Money was an obsession and he was obsessively mean about it. To the last this was a "royal" who counted his royalties'.[14]

In practice, this meant bombarding his brother, the new King George VI, with almost daily telephone calls on a whole range of money matters: the duke remaining on the Civil List (money appropriated annually by Parliament to pay the expenses of the sovereign and his or her household); the progress of monies owed to him on the sale of personal assets to the new king; the location of his impending wedding (the king agreed the Château de Candé near Tours would be better than the louche Château de la Croë at Cap d'Antibes on the Côte d'Azur and, no, the expense would be Edward's); the storage of his personal effects from Fort Belvedere; when he might return to his country (he required one of the royal houses and two aeroplanes for staff and luggage); the additional Crown-funded police needed to safeguard Wallis at Cannes; which of his brothers would be attending the wedding; the latest insult he'd received from one of the king's courtiers and so on, and on.

Finally, an exasperated and mentally exhausted king (who apparently spent most of his time painstakingly practising his new signature, George RI, with a peculiarly sad expression on his face) told him point-blank on the phone to stop.[15] Stop what? The telephone calls.

The duke felt slighted, embarrassed.[16] His paranoia regarding what he was owed went up several notches. This included the most precious thing after the jewels and cash he could bestow on his bride: her right to use the title of Her Royal Highness, which was only given to female members of the Royal family and he insisted on delivering.

At Candé that morning there was a knock at the door and his immaculately groomed best man, Fruity Metcalfe, still in his pyjamas and silk dressing gown, asked if he might use the bathroom. 'Go ahead, old man,' the duke responded, sitting up and lighting his first Piccadilly Number One cigarette of the day.

Tensions at the *schloss* reached a crescendo in February, forcing Baroness Kitty de Rothschild to leave. Edward didn't bother to say goodbye, such was the strained atmosphere.

His nerves were further eroded when his favourite brother, George, Duke of Kent, visited him on 24 February and gently advised him there was no prospect of getting money from the Civil List, despite Churchill's support in committee meetings. In a fit of pique and running short of cash, Edward threatened not to release Balmoral and Sandringham to the new king until he was fully paid for them (their sale was negotiated as part of his abdication package in December 1936). Kent was mortified by the callow, twitching wreck his shining brother had become. He left, distraught and sickened by his visit. Edward seemed to inhabit an alternate universe.

However, despite his ravaged state, the ex-king was still cosseted by the glamour of his previous life. When he advertised for a secretary, 800 women applied for the job.[17]

March brought a reunion of sorts with Lord Mountbatten, who volunteered to be Edward's best man (he would rescind the offer in early May when it became obvious he would disappoint the new king if he went through with it). It didn't matter, the duke was sure he would be supported by one of his brothers and imperiously declined Mountbatten's offer.

By the 28th, Edward couldn't stomach the situation any longer and left the *schloss* for Appesbach House, near St Wolfgang in the Salzkammergut lake district of Austria, accompanied by Schnuki, his new Cairn terrier. It was a fateful decision.

He had dispatched Slipper to Candé with Detective Storrier to comfort Wallis a few days earlier, but on 8 April the dog wandered on to the golf course, was attacked by a viper and died. The Windsors were poleaxed with grief.[18] The duke later memorialised the sad occasion with a small 14-carat gold, emerald and diamond pendant featuring a slipper and a paw print. This modest, emotionally charged disc sold at auction in 1987 for almost £50,000.

Finally, at the end of April 1937, the duke received some good news through Lord Wigram and Winston Churchill. His brother had agreed to personally guarantee the duke's income into the future, independent of his inclusion (or not) on the Civil List. The money pressure, at least with regard to an annual income, was relaxed a notch. Whether or not he made the list was now immaterial.

It was a huge piece of news. The duke was palpably relieved. And yet, there was the nagging doubt that it was all based on a brother's promise, relayed to him second-hand.

These were fickle times and Edward, more than most, knew how quickly things could change, especially when he was so far away from the epicentre of these decisions, unable to influence or exert any kind of first-hand pressure. It was beyond his control and for a royal used to getting his way, it was maddening and another unwelcome lesson in how his circumstances had changed irrevocably. But things were slowly coming round to his way.

On 3 May came the best news of all: Wallis's decree absolute had come through. She was now divorced and free to remarry. The duke was ecstatic and lost no time in leaving St Wolfgang and driving to Salzburg to rendezvous with the overnight *Orient Express*.

Boarding the train at 4.45 p.m. with two wrapped bouquets of edelweiss and alpine forget-me-nots, and his private car crammed with seventeen suitcases that he refused to store in the baggage van, the duke struggled for space with Detective Storrier, his equerry, Captain Greenacre, and a valet. It did not matter. The duke was jubilant. Even the publication of the Civil List that day with his name conspicuously absent from it did not dampen his mood. As he told himself, it was irrelevant, completely irrelevant.

Arriving at the small French town of Verneuil-l'Étang, near Paris, the next day (the train's diversion was organised by the British Ambassador Sir Eric Phipps), the duke bounded into a waiting car and sped off to the château escorted by a police car and two *gardes mobiles* on motorcycles.

It was quite the entrance. The entire village of Monts had turned out to greet the greatest celebrity they had ever seen, lining the road to the château's gates waving hats, scarves and paper kites. Even the pugnacious Charles Bedaux, newly arrived from New York, must have reckoned his investment was paying off in spades despite the escalating, eye-watering costs.

In commemoration of their reunion, Edward presented Wallis with an 18-carat yellow-gold Cartier ruby and sapphire dress ring in a turban design set with three tapered rows of cushion-shaped rubies and three similar bands of sapphires inscribed with the dates of their separation (3 December 1936–3 May 1937).

The May weather in the Touraine, after a terrible winter for Edward and Wallis, was fabulous that year: cool, clear nights, cold flagstones and crackling fires, followed by bright, buttery-yellow days interspersed now and then with quick bursts of percolating rain. The scent of new grass and succulent flowers permeated the air, lubricating the birdsong that serenaded the château's inhabitants as they woke from their well-fed and well-watered escapades during the night. It carried the promise of good things to come and a welcome relief from the body blows of the previous months.

It also heralded an eventful time for Edward and Wallis. But it inevitably started badly. The day after Edward arrived at the château, he received a letter from Mountbatten advising him that no member of the royal family nor any person who held office under the Crown would be allowed to attend his wedding. Edward was crushed and hit the telephone to try to reverse what he considered a vindictive and cowardly act instigated by a coven of 'English Bitches'.[19]

In his inimitable way, he bombarded the Palace, his family and friends throughout the month to convince them to overturn this cruel and unnecessary indictment of his honourable decision to abdicate. He never gave up. It was constantly on his mind. At the very least, couldn't his favourite brother, George, Duke of Kent, be spared to make the trip? He would be satisfied with that. It wasn't too much to ask, surely?

Events escalated in the meantime. In a clear signal to his adversaries that he could also play a fine game of one-upmanship, the date for the wedding was fixed for 3 June, the birth date of his father. On 11 May, Wallis and Edward announced their formal engagement. On 12 May, the duke's brother was finally crowned, bringing relief to the Court and government, some sixteen months after the previously anointed king's death. On the same day, Wallis changed her name from Simpson to Warfield by deed poll and on 18 May they concluded their formal marriage contract. Both parties agreed their property would be separate and that neither would make any claim on the other's personal possessions in the event of a divorce (thereby safeguarding Wallis's jewellery). On 25 May, the Mayor of Monts, Dr Charles Mercier, rehearsed the couple for the civil ceremony that would be held in the château's music room.

Letters and wedding gifts poured in and the phone rang incessantly. Representatives from Van Cleef & Arpels arrived from Paris with trays of jewellery and cases of gems. The gifts included an inscribed gold box from Hitler and flashy trinkets from Mussolini.[20]

The duke thought the worst was over now the coronation was done and dusted, but then he received official word from Buckingham Palace that not even George, his favourite brother, would be attending the wedding. The Palace also confirmed that no one else from the royal family would be coming. Edward attempted to cajole Dudley Forwood into convincing George VI to change his mind but the king this time was adamant that he wouldn't allow the family to participate in an 'illegal act'.[21]

Edward was astounded. As far as he and his bride were concerned, he had broken no laws and had acted wholly within the constitutional constructs of his country. Why was he being ostracised by those closest to him by blood and sentiment? Apart from the coven of 'English Bitches', he blamed his old foe, the Archbishop of Canterbury, Cosmo Lang, for pouring poison into the ears of his gullible, gutless family. He was incandescent with rage.

But then, just as quickly, he was reduced to tears and profound depression when on 27 May, Sir Ulick Alexander rang Candé to inform the ex-king that Letters Patent approved by his brother would only apply the title of 'Royal Highness' to Edward and not to his wife nor his descendants. Alexander added that Walter Monckton would be arriving within days to hand the duke a letter from the new king by way of a personal explanation.

Monckton arrived on the eve of the wedding and handed the letter to Edward in Forwood's presence. After reading it, Forwood remarked he had never seen a man so shattered by a solitary letter. The sense of a profound, deeply personal failure was palpable. A Fabergé box, a gift from the Kents that had arrived on the day of the wedding, was returned.

Even now, on the morning of perhaps the most iconic day of his life, the taste of that moment was still bitter in the duke's mouth and would continue to be for the rest of his days.

The duke rubbed out his third cigarette of the day and decided he'd better get out of bed. Doing so triggered his customary bout of early morning coughing. His valet knew better than to enquire after him during these prolonged phlegmy episodes, which could last as long as twenty to thirty minutes.

The duke knocked on the adjoining bathroom door and entered. Everything was as it should be following Fruity's occupation, with freshly laundered monogrammed towels in place and the whiff of quickly applied disinfectant just discernible. His ivory-handled toothbrush, prepared with a strip of toothpaste down the bristles, rested alongside a sterling-silver beaker of mouthwash and a starched-linen napkin. Edward faced himself in the mirror, watery-eyed and puffy from the previous evening's memorable dinner party. It was memorable for many reasons, not least because it was the last time Bessie Wallis Warfield had curtsied and addressed His Royal Highness Prince Edward as 'Sir', as she always did whenever she entered and left his presence.

It was time to dress and join the rest of his guests at breakfast. Before he was able to do so, he was intercepted by the Reverend R. Anderson Jardine, the eccentric vicar of St Paul's in Durham, who had defied his bishop to officiate at the Candé wedding, waiting to see him in the private sitting room.

Jardine, a cheery man with protruding teeth, had not only defied his boss and the Archbishop of Canterbury in volunteering his services to the duke, but he was also flying in the face of established Church practice. He always maintained it was an individual choice on his part, though it was made under immense pressure, having been told by his bishop over the telephone that he had no ecclesiastical standing in France and had no authority to act on behalf of the Anglican Church. His position in the ceremony would be equivalent to a private person who had been invited to say prayers. Obviously, he was not capable of legally solemnising a marriage.

Jardine was undeterred. He also knew there was no process of ecclesiastical law by which he could be restrained from doing what he or his host desired in a private house, because a private house was not within the territorial jurisdiction of a bishop of the Church of England. He told the press, who surrounded him when he arrived at Tours railway station, the day before the wedding, that he would not be persuaded from performing the ceremony. When asked how he knew the duke wished to have a religious ceremony and how he decided to make the offer to officiate, Jardine replied, 'It seemed to me unthinkable that any member of the Royal family could be married without the Church of England service'.[22]

The duke needed Jardine more than Jardine needed him and he received the vicar that morning with a sinking feeling that Jardine had come to tell him he was pulling out. Palpably relieved that this was not the case (Jardine had just wanted to wish him good luck before they were due to meet officially before the altar), the duke suddenly remembered something and fetched a prayer book given to him by his mother from a trunk in the corner of the room. As they went through it together, tears dropped from Edward's face on to the book's brittle paper.

Jardine was deeply moved by Edward's piety. At that moment, he received the assurance he secretly craved, that he had made the right decision to come to Edward's aid. The conviction sustained him during his darkest days after he returned to his parish as a pariah. Within a month, he and his wife had fled to America, where they opened a modest house of religion called the Windsor Cathedral of Los Angeles.

After a few moments, the duke dabbed his eyes with the sleeve of his dressing gown and announced he'd better get dressed. Jardine shook his hand and left.

6

Bride Stripped Bare

Society is a masked ball, where everyone hides his real character, and
reveals it by hiding.

Ralph Waldo Emerson

The Duke of Windsor's preferred style of dressing was what he later
described as 'soft'.[1] In practical terms, it represented a rejection of the
rigid, stuffy, starched dress conventions of his father and grandfather's
generation in favour of a looser, distinctly more casual and modern
approach. As King Edward VIII, he took this stylistic approach a step
further when he abolished the conventional frock coat as court attire,
requiring his courtiers to wear more sophisticated morning coats.

In the 1930s, Edward was one of the first men to wear unlined,
unstructured jackets made for him by Frederick Scholte, a Dutch-born,
London-based tailor who disapproved of any form of exaggeration in
the style of a jacket. As the duke wrote in *A Family Album*, his treatise
on style written in 1960, 'Scholte had rigid standards concerning the
perfect balance of proportions between shoulders and waist in the cut
of a coat to clothe the masculine torso'.[2] The sleeves of the duke's jackets
were usually fixed with four working buttons, and he preferred welted
pockets rather than pocket flaps.

Before the Second World War, Forster & Son of Bond Street in London tailored his trousers:

I never had a pair of trousers made by Scholte. I disliked the cut of them; they were made, as English trousers usually are, to be worn with braces high above the waist. So preferring as I did to wear a belt rather than braces with trousers, in the American style, I invariably had them made by another tailor.[3]

To avoid the necessity of wearing either a belt or braces to support the duke's trousers, Forster devised an internal elasticised girdle, which fastened at the centre front with a series of adjustable hooks and bars. To prevent gaping, two vertically positioned trouser hooks were set on either side and hooked over the tight-fitting girdle. For every jacket the duke had made, two pairs of trousers were produced. These he wore in strict rotation.

In 1934, along with his brother, the Duke of York, and his cousin, Lord Mountbatten, he replaced the conventional button flies with zip flies. As a heavy smoker, the duke instructed Forster & Son to make his trousers with a slightly wider left pocket with no fastening, allowing him easy access to his cigarette case, which he always carried in his left pocket. The duke preferred trousers with cuffs or turn-ups. With the adoption of rationing restrictions in Britain during the Second World War, which banned turn-ups, he placed all subsequent orders with H. Harris, a tailor based on East 59th Street, New York.

The Oxford Street firm of Peal & Co. made the duke's shoes; Lock & Co. of St James's made his hats; and Hawes & Curtis made his shirts and ties. He favoured shirts with soft, unstarched cuffs and collars, and wore his ties (which he ordered with thicker inner linings) with a wide 'four-in-hand' knot. Hawes & Curtis created the famous spread collar, designed specifically to accommodate this knot. He had a good relationship with founders Ralph Hawes and Freddie Curtis, and Curtis even attended the wedding in France (delivering a fresh batch of shirts to HRH).

Despite popular opinion, the Duke of Windsor did not, in fact, wear a style known as the Windsor knot. That knot, to which the Americans gave his name, was just a double knot in a narrow tie, a 'Slim Jim', as it was sometimes called.

Like his father, the duke was meticulous about his clothes and stipulated that gentlemen invited to the wedding should wear morning suits, even down to what colours would be appropriate, while proffering his own intended outfit as a guide.[4] He was, of course, counting on his guests to respect the formula that he and stalwarts like Cecil Beaton had painstakingly devised for their wearing. Aleksandar Cvetkovic described it this way:

> ... coats are cut close to the chest, much closer than a civilian suit coat of the period – which is necessary given the way that a morning's coat lacks a skirt at the front to keep it sitting flush to the figure. Tails reach exactly to the back of the knees, lapels are broad with some belly but never too wide and shoulders are clean and simple – without too much weighty padding [...] waistcoats for morning dress should be short, whether single or double-breasted. The coat's quarters are quite obviously cut-away from the waist downwards, revealing a good deal of torso and there's nothing less elegant than seeing two crumpled linen waistcoat tips protruding beneath, much better to see a pair of forward-facing trouser pleats flowing seamlessly from underneath instead. This means of course that your trouser rise will need to be relatively high and supported by silk braces to allow pleats to fall openly. Morning trousers suit a wider leg without turn-ups and should feature only the lightest of breaks. The colour of your coat will of course also impact upon the waistcoat. Plain linen or tropical worsted is the conventional cloth of choice for a contrasting waistcoat, dove grey is a safe option if a little pedestrian, but champagne, fawn, powder blue or dusty pink make for fun alternatives. A trouser featuring a dark grey morning stripe is conventional, but not mandatory [...] Shoes must remain black, and highly polished [...] Plain white or cream shirts are acceptable, but should one wear pale pink, lilac or blue, a white shirt collar

should not be forgone – it lends an added level of formality that is necessary to the harmony of the look […] Morning dress, above all, must be discreet. It should not be showy and it should never be gauche.[5]

The ensemble that was laid out for the duke by his valet that morning was made during his time as King Edward VIII. The duke had a sentimental attachment to the clothes he wore as Prince of Wales and King of England and, unable to part with them, he preferred to have the collars and cuffs replaced and the fabric patched and repaired. The cashmere black jacket, yellow linen waistcoat, charcoal striped trousers, silver checked tie and plain black shoes were accompanied by a new Hawes & Curtis blue and white pinstriped shirt with a white collar. The cuffs were fastened by double-sided cufflinks made by Cartier of London, featuring patterned 'E & W' brilliants, single and carré-cut diamonds. On the back, they were inscribed 'David 23/6/35, Wallis 19/6/35' (the 23rd was Edward's 41st birthday and the 19th was Wallis's 39th birthday).

The duke plucked a white carnation from a bunch in his sitting room, tucked a white silk hanky into his breast pocket and padded down the hall to where breakfast and champagne had been laid out for guests.

Wallis Warfield, meanwhile, attended by her Aunt Bessie and various maids, was still hard at work perfecting the look she had devised for the wedding day.

During the 1930s, she favoured the designers Mainbocher, Schiaparelli, and Vionnet, while after the Second World War she preferred Dior, Givenchy and Yves Saint Laurent. With these outfits, she wore shoes by Roger Vivier, who began working for the House of Dior in 1953. Her maxim was sobriety by day and fantasy at night.

Cecil Beaton described her as 'compact as a Vuitton traveling case, tidy, neat, immaculate'.[6] It was a look she maintained through strict adherence to a vigorous diet, adapted in part from self-described 'diet masseuse' Sylvia Ulback's 1931 *Hollywood Undressed*, a gossipy manual full of celebrity weight-loss secrets that became a sensation. Sometimes, Wallis existed for a whole day on one perfectly boiled egg and 2 litres of bottled water. When it came to their waistlines, both Wallis and Edward were fanatics.

Throughout the months of March and April 1937, Wallis had auditioned a plethora of couturiers at the château from Mainbocher, Schiaparelli, Vionnet, Chanel, the House of Patou and Lanvin. In May, Wallis chose Mainbocher to make her wedding ensemble. The trousseau of eighty dresses and forty hats was split between the unsuccessful fashion houses.

The wedding ensemble included a simple, floor-length dress of soft 'Wallis Blue' silk crepe (a shade between pastel and hyacinth blue) with a tight, buttoned, long-sleeved bodice draped into a heart shape; a tiny skull cap of 'Wallis Blue' straw with a turned-back halo brim of blue tulle, the base of which was a bandeau of blue and pale pink ostrich feathers by Caroline Reboux; crepe high-heeled openwork sandals by Georgette of Paris; and matching wrist-length gloves, the left-hand ring finger opened up to allow the placement of the wedding band. Wallis wore a piece of antique lace stitched into her lingerie as something old, a gold coin minted for the coronation of Edward VIII worn in the heel of her shoe as something new and a lace hanky from her Aunt Bessie as something borrowed. The 'Wallis Blue' colour was specially developed by Mainbocher to mimic Wallis's eyes.

Days after her marriage, copies of the 'Wally' dress were sold at American retailers in a variety of styles, colours and materials for a small fraction of the original's cost, from $25 at Bonwit Teller to a mere $8.90 at Klein's cash and carry.

At her throat, she had plumped for the tremendous art deco diamond and sapphire brooch made by Van Cleef & Arpels earlier that year from loose stones supplied by her. On her left wrist, she had fastened the glittering and treasured Cartier charm bracelet of spectacle-set brilliant-cut diamonds now adorned with seven crosses, the most recent added only that morning (the bracelet was eventually to feature nine charms). Set with calibre-cut sapphires and emeralds, with one ruby and one baguette diamond, the 'Wedding Cross' charm bore the inscription, 'Our Marriage Cross Wallis 3-VI-37 David'. The bracelet had begun life in November 1934 when the first cross made entirely of platinum was given to her with the inscription 'WE are too [*sic*] 25-XI-34'.

On her right wrist hung the fabulous sapphire and diamond *jarretière* bracelet, also by Van Cleef & Arpels and designed by René-Sim Lacaze. The duke had purchased it in May to commemorate the signing of their marriage contract and had it inscribed with the date. It was designed as a wide, flexible band of baguette and circular-cut diamonds, the clasp invisibly set with cushion-shaped sapphires and more baguette diamonds.

A little after 11 a.m., word came through to the ducal party that Wallis was ready and would make her entrance at 11.30 for the first of the two ceremonies. Dr Charles Mercier, the 46-year-old Mayor of Monts, had arrived for the civil ceremony exactly on time, wearing his *Tricolore* scarf of office with gold tassels. He waited behind a walnut table covered with a pink velvet cloth in the château's green-panelled music room. The table stood in a bay window framed in damask curtains overlooking the Lys Valley. On either side had been placed large vases of pink and white peonies.

There were flowers everywhere on that day: peonies on the mantelpiece of the gigantic stone fireplace, white and yellow Madonna lilies on window ledges, and more peonies around the various rooms. Someone had even tacked up strings of festive paper American flags. Society florist Constance Spry had spent two whole days prior to the event with her assistant, Val Pirie, decorating the château with mountains of flowers from the Paris markets, cramming them into a car they had hired for the purpose. (She also poignantly recorded how the bored ex-king spent hours on his knees pathetically reading old, damp copies of *The Times* she had brought with her and spread underneath her arrangements to preserve the priceless rugs and stone floors.)[7]

In front of the music room's walnut table were four armchairs. Dr Mercier was noticeably nervous, partly because he had forgotten to bring with him the *Livret de Famille*, the official handbook on how to raise a family that is the French Republic's official present to all marrying couples, and partly because of the occasion. Before officiating at Candé, Dr Mercier had attended to several of his patients in the surrounding villages. He was, however, anxious to discharge his duties as correctly as possible, without fuss or pomp.

Soon after 11.30 a.m., a small door in the panelling at the northern end of the room opened and the duke looked in. He hesitated for a moment, and then, accompanied by Major Metcalfe, advanced towards the chairs. After welcoming the mayor, the duke sat down. A minute or two later, Wallis came through the main doorway with Hermann Rogers.

Just before the ceremony began, a bouquet of red, white and blue flowers tied with a *Tricolore* ribbon, the gift of M. Blum, the French prime minister, was handed to Wallis by M. Vernet, prefect of the regional *département*. Major Metcalfe was on the duke's left, and Rogers sat beside Wallis; the other guests were seated in rows behind the couple.

It was a simple ceremony and brief – it opened at 11.35 a.m. and concluded at 11.47. The mayor read the relevant articles of the civil code under which married couples promise to be faithful and help each other. The husband must protect the wife and the wife must obey the husband and must live with him and follow him wherever he deems fit. The husband must maintain the wife in accordance with their status.

'By one of the chances of destiny,' Dr Mercier declared, 'the most moving idyll of all time takes place under the blue skies of France, amid the flowers and trees of the Chateau au de Candé. I salute your Royal Highness as a former sovereign of a most friendly nation.'[8] The mayor then explained that the wedding was held in the château by special permission of the prefect of the *département*.

Addressing the duke, using all his Christian names and titles, including those of Admiral of the Fleet, Field Marshal and Marshal of the

Air Force of Great Britain, he asked, 'If he took Mrs Wallis Warfield as his wife.'

The duke replied, '*Oui, Monsieur le Maire.*'

Dr Mercier repeated the question to Wallis, who replied, 'Oui', in a slightly unsteady voice.

The mayor then declared, 'In the name of the law, we declare you united in the bonds of matrimony.' Turning to the bride with a smile, he said, 'You may now sit down.'[9]

Dr Mercier concluded the ceremony with a short address. He said it was fitting that this wedding should be celebrated in the ancient province of Touraine, the land of poets, great writers and intellectuals, in which the best French was spoken. Thousands of Britons and Americans knew and loved it well and the Duke of Windsor had added fresh honour to the province by choosing it as the scene of his marriage.

The religious ceremony followed *tout suite*, as reported by *Time* magazine in the vernacular of the day (it was one of only five news outlets granted permission to witness the events):

In the music room an altar had been hastily improvised on an old oak chest on which stood a gold cross and two yellow tapers. By it in a clean white surplice stood the Rev. R. Anderson Jardine awaiting the greatest moment in his life. Hollow-eyed, the Duke of Windsor stepped in a moment later, accompanied by his elegantly groomed best man, Major Edward Dudley ('Fruity') Metcalfe. While Organist Dupré played the march from Handel's Judas Maccabeus, entered (Bessie) Wallis Warfield (Spencer) (Simpson) on the arm of the faithful Herman Rogers. She wore a dress that most U.S. department stores were soon to feature: soft blue crepe with a tight, buttoned bodice, a halo-shaped hat of the same color, shoes and gloves to match. At her throat was a tremendous diamond-&-sapphire brooch. Mrs. Warfield carried a prayer book, had no bouquet but wore a large lavender orchid at her waist.

Only two incidents disturbed the ceremony. When Vicar Jardine asked, 'Wilt thou love her, comfort her, honor and keep her?'

overwrought Edward cried 'I will!' in a shrill voice that was almost a scream. When he put on her finger the plain wedding ring of Welsh-mined gold that has become a tradition in the British Royal Family, the trembling of his hands was noticeable even to the farthest watchers.

Later there were champagne, salad and a few speeches. To tact-ful Herman Rogers, unofficial press minister of the affair, combined newshawks presented a gold fountain pen. His last official statement was a request: 'Please do not follow them.' The Duke & Duchess of Windsor climbed into their limousine, were driven by George Ladbrooke [sic], the Duke's chauffeur for 17 years, disappeared through the château gates. Ahead of them went 226 pieces of luggage, includ-ing 183 trunks.

Newshawks did not have to follow the honeymooners to a destin-ation everyone knew. But a few had secured compartments on the same Simplon–Orient express to which the ducal car had been attached and as the train rolled southeast across France they brought each other word that the private car contained one large double bed, covered with the usual Thomas Cook & Sons-Wagon Lits brown blanket – and a complete bathroom. Later reports announced that the Duke was going to bed in a pair of bright red pajamas [sic], that he had early tea alone, that both Duke & Duchess enjoyed a hearty bacon & egg breakfast.[10]

Behind the veneer of efficiency, glamour and sentiment, one guest saw the skull beneath the skin. Lady Alexandra 'Baba' Metcalfe, Fruity's wife, was the last surviving witness of the twenty or more guests who attended the Windsors' wedding and wrote a raw account of it in the form of an unpublished private diary.[11] Baba observed the 'pitiable and tragic'[12] scene at the Château de Candé with anguished sympathy, noting in her diary the once idolised ex-king's 'simple and dignified manner … so sure in his happiness that it gave the sad little service something which is hard to describe. He had tears running down his face.'[13] Wallis was rigid and 'could not have done it better'.[14]

After the ceremony, the duke and duchess received their guests in the salon:

… glasses of champagne were drunk in a toast to the bride and bridegroom, proposed by Major Metcalfe, who wished them many years of happiness. An emotional Duke replied: 'Ladies and gentlemen. We both want to thank you very feelingly for your kind and friendly attendance on this very important occasion for us. That is all I can say – thank you.'[15]

Then the bride and bridegroom chatted with guests before venturing to the front of the château, where five minutes was spent posing for press photographers.[16]

Outside the château, the *New York Times* reported that the old concierge, Madame Briault, 'to satisfy newsreel men in search of a picture, broke a bottle of champagne against the gate when the news that the wedding was over was flashed down by telephone to the lodge'.[17]

Madame Briault recalled that the last wedding held at the château was in 1907. It was conducted by an archbishop and hundreds of guests danced all night. She added sadly that there would be nothing like that today, those days were gone. 'She then carefully got out her brush and shovel and swept up the broken glass.'[18]

Baba also took photographs (Cecil Beaton had spent the afternoon of the 2nd taking pictures of Wallis and Edward in the grounds of the château but was not invited to the wedding) and wrote in her diary:

If she occasionally showed a glimmer of softness, took his arm, looked at him as though she loved him one would warm towards her, but her attitude is so correct. The effect is of a woman unmoved by the infatuated love of a younger man. Let's hope that she lets up in private with him otherwise it must be grim.[19]

After a buffet luncheon of lobster, salad, Chicken à la King and strawberries, washed down with 1921 Lanson champagne, Wallis cut the wedding cake, a six-tier, 3ft-high affair, until it was all gone. Every uneaten piece was subsequently placed in a cardboard box covered in white silk (signed on top by both the duke and duchess), tied up with white silk bows and sent later to friends and family who had been unable to attend. The Baron and Baroness Eugene de Rothschild, the last guests to arrive, were the first to leave.

After the Windsors' mountain of trunks had been safely loaded in hired vans, Wallis and Edward set off in the late afternoon with two valets, two footmen, two detectives, two dressers, various maids, a butler and three chauffeurs as well as the household comptroller, Monsieur James, and Dudley Forwood in a convoy of vehicles escorted by French *gendarmes* on motorcycles.

Monts, meanwhile, had been transformed into a carnival town, crowded with visitors. A holiday had been declared to celebrate the occasion and special *char-â-bancs* were run from many parts of France, bringing hundreds more to join the thousands of visitors already in the district. Interlaced British, American and French flags decorated the houses and arches of flowers spanned the streets.

Detachments of police, who had been in position since 7 a.m. along roads leading to the château, joined in the festivities as the two French air force aeroplanes assigned to patrol the grounds overhead peeled away and the camouflaged observation posts in the woods surrounding the château were abandoned by the guards. Similarly, those press representatives who had been allowed to witness the ceremonies were finally able to use the telephone and leave the château, but were prohibited from pursuing the departing ducal convoy by *gendarmes*.

Edward and Wallis had treated their time at Candé as an extended country-house weekend and their departure was no exception. (In polite circles between the wars, it was never referred to as a 'weekend', however, the accepted phrase being 'Saturday-to-Monday', and it was decidedly 'non-U' to call it anything else.)[20]

Scheduled to rendezvous with the *Orient Express* en route to their honeymoon destination of Schloss Wasserleonburg in Austria, the duke announced a few minutes into the journey that they would have a picnic before they boarded the train and exercise the dogs. But when Monsieur James opened the large picnic hampers, he found all they contained were peaches. Abandoning the idea after a few bites, everyone piled into the cars again and raced to meet the waiting *Orient Express* and its fuming passengers just outside the little village of Laroche-Migennes where a private *wagon-lits* carriage filled with yellow and red roses had been hitched to it.

Cramming 226 pieces of luggage into the train took time, with the duke insisting that fifty pieces of his private baggage (mostly cases of jewels, including his wedding gift of a new diamond tiara) were loaded into their private car. Finally at 6.30 p.m., after rescuing one of the Cairn terriers that had wandered off, the train resumed its journey to Venice carrying the newly minted duchess into the uncharted territory of a new life — a life that had been paid for and resourced eighteen months earlier.

7

An Iceberg Through the Heart

Nothing is ever settled until it's settled right.

Rudyard Kipling

Among the many pivotal moments of the Duke of Windsor's remarkable life, perhaps the most significant (in terms of an event that triggered the biggest crisis in his and the nation's life) was the reading of his father's will at Sandringham on Wednesday, 22 January 1936, at 2.30 p.m. Psychologically, it marked the beginning of the end of his reign, revoking any hope he might have had of legitimising his profound desire to make Wallis Simpson his queen, and throwing into chaos all the neat little schemes he had mapped out for the next few years. It also hardened his attitude towards his family, while clarifying his purpose and the means he had at his disposal to achieve it. To his wily assistant private secretary, Tommy Lascelles, 'It provoked incalculable disaster; it was, in fact, directly responsible for the first voluntary abdication of an English King.'[1]

His Majesty George V, by the Grace of God, of Great Britain, Ireland and the British Dominions beyond the Seas, King, Defender of the Faith and Emperor of India, had been unwell for some time. The emotional and physical setbacks of the past few months, the rising irritation of his heir's infatuation with Mrs Simpson, culminating in the death of Princess Victoria and the bronchial catarrh he had developed had all taken their toll. When Edward arrived at Sandringham for Christmas, he was shocked at how much he had deteriorated.

The old man was sometimes bent over double with wracking, coughing spasms and weeping, yellowy eyes, holding off all attempts at assistance with a firm, outstretched arm. Teams of physicians led by Lord Dawson of Penn were on hand and the whole place smelled and felt like a field hospital for invalids. There was a general sentiment pervading the gloomy house that the monarch was suffering the last few days of his reign, although Edward surprised everyone by pluckily insisting he would rally and that the worst was behind him.

Whether this was just another adorable sign of Edward's whacky grasp of reality or a symptom of a much deeper personal denial at the beckoning call of kingship, widespread panic among the royal household and his family had already set in, exacerbated no doubt by a dread of the incoming regime and its skew towards hedonism and hypocrisy.

For years, servants at Fort Belvedere, Balmoral, Sandringham and Buckingham Palace lived in hope the prince would drop Mrs Simpson and she would fall, as previous royal mistresses had fallen, into what Chips Channon described as 'the nothingness from whence she came'.[2] But, if anything, the Prince of Wales' dependency on his mistress had grown stronger with each passing year and the royal household faced the decidedly unpalatable but impending prospect of the unfettered reach of Mrs Simpson, and all that it entailed, now her man was king.

To say she was feared was to put it politely. The eggshells everyone was conditioned to skirting around in her presence had the potential to become as sharp as a knife edge on her ascension to the top job. The resulting gloom that descended on the Court was as thick and pernicious as the January fog that enveloped it.

Together with fear, there was also loathing. Several of the royal ladies-in-waiting, including the wife of Edward's private secretary, Alexander Hardinge, refused to shake her hand. When Wallis came up to one of them with her hand outstretched, they would drop a handbag and bend down to pick it up, leaving the American's arm frozen in the wind.[3]

Queen Mary was especially concerned, albeit for a different reason. Alarmed at the plethora of stories circulating among society hostesses and the Court in general about the glittering Mrs Simpson, 'dripped in new jewels and clothes',[4] she made discreet enquiries to the crown jeweller, Garrard & Co., about their provenance and funding.

Striking a dead end there, she was assured by senior members of the Prince of Wales' circle that the fantastic displays of jewels were, in fact, all paste or dressmakers' jewels. But the queen herself was not so sure. Wallis's jewellery was the talk of the top end of town and it was significant that the talk was not of the brazen manner of their display but the sheer volume and profligacy of her son's lavish endowment.

At the height of her husband's illness that January, she received more disturbing news that Edward had showered this inconsequential American divorcee with £50,000 worth of jewels at Christmas and a further £60,000 worth a week later to celebrate the New Year.[5] The speculation jolted her into action as it became immediately apparent that Edward 'might pass'[6] to Mrs Simpson the best pieces of Princess Victoria's jewellery collection which, on her death a month earlier, was now available to the greater family.

Queen Mary was so concerned about the possibility, given all the rumours and stories she'd heard, that she exercised the living monarch's discretion and divided the spoils between the Princess Royal and the Duchesses of York, Gloucester and Kent before the operation could be reversed.[7]

She was also fearful for the trunk-loads of uncut royal gems and loose, unset stones which were currently under the protection of her husband, the sovereign. She secretly consulted the king's lawyers, even his principal private secretary, Lord Wigram. But the looting had already begun, and she was powerless, it seemed, to stem the wave of princely removals she was sure would only accelerate once the old king had passed.

She even feared for the existence of Balmoral and Sandringham, given Edward's evident distaste for both establishments and the overbearing aura of stale sentimentality and cloying claustrophobia that he associated them with. It was a terrible prospect for everyone, it seemed, except its future guardian.

Determined to continue his daily schedule of shooting at Sandringham despite the cruel, bitterly cold weather, King George inevitably caught a chill to add to his chronic bronchitis and by 16 January was confined to his bedroom. Things were looking grim when Queen Mary wrote to Edward at Fort Belvedere suggesting he should spend the weekend at Sandringham. Edward found his father even thinner and frailer than before, seated in an old Tibetan robe, shivering before a blazing log fire. The reality of what Queen Mary most feared was cemented when the Duke of York arrived, and he and Edward were briefed by Wigram on the succession arrangements. Both royal princes drove to London to confer with Prime Minister Baldwin immediately afterwards.

On 20 January the king lapsed into a coma, and his sons drew up plans for the funeral after a morose family dinner. A coffin was ordered. There was some talk of a possible cremation but that was dropped as setting too much of a precedent and an obvious departure from accepted ways.

The recent burial of the corpulent Duke of Teck was on everyone's mind. During the funeral procession, his septic body had suddenly burst open with a loud clap of thunder resembling a gigantic explosion of bodily wind. Practically gritting their teeth and pinching their ears to avoid laughing at the macabre memory, the younger members of the family suggested embalming the body might work, before everyone trooped into the king's bedroom to witness the end.[8]

After 11 p.m., Lord Dawson, to ameliorate everyone's suffering, injected a fatal dose of three-quarters of a grain of morphine and one grain of cocaine into the king's distended jugular vein and he was pronounced dead at 11.55 p.m. Ironically, Dawson's private diary, unearthed after his death and made public in 1986, revealed the king's last words were a mumbled, 'God damn you!'[9]

Queen Mary rose from the deathbed and kissed Edward's hand, saying, 'The King is dead, long live the King.'

Edward's royal reserve immediately broke and he sobbed hysteric-
ally against the rigid, stoic shoulders of his embarrassed mother. It
was painful and spontaneous. He had never felt so distraught, alone
and utterly bereft of comfort in a place he hated surrounded by
people he felt no connection with other than a distorted filial bond.
He was inconsolable.

The Dowager Queen gently patted his back and led him out of the
silent room. She then left him in the hallway, making her way to her
own room and her own private grieving.

Edward immediately telephoned Wallis, still sobbing and in a fearful
state. She had just returned from a late dinner and a charity gala at a
London cinema. 'I am so very sorry,' she told the new king.[10] She put
the phone down after an interminable few minutes of crying. She was
tired. There was nothing she could do but patiently acknowledge his
emotional capitulation.

The king's 70-year-old body was embalmed the next day and taken to
the little church of St Mary Magdalene just outside the grounds of the
estate to await transportation to the capital. Lascelles wrote in his diary:

A dark and windy evening, with flurries of rain; there were not more
than a dozen of us, including the Queen and the family: the coffin was
on a little wheeled bier, flanked by a few towering Grenadiers from
the King's Company; somebody had an electric torch which was our
only light; Forsyth, the King's piper, led us playing a lament I did not
know [...] The guardsmen, with scarcely a sound, slung the coffin on
their shoulders and laid it before the altar; and there, after a very brief
service, we left it, to be watched for thirty six hours by the men of the
Sandringham Estate.[11]

The outpouring of national emotion at his passing seemed to mirror the
inexplicable heart-rending inner turmoil of his rattled heir. The English
always had a soft spot for their rather boring, dull king, who was cast
in the national psyche as a conservative English country gentleman pre-
occupied with country pursuits and sedentary hobbies. His moderating

role in the country's constitutional crisis of 1931 and his announcement in September of that year that he was surrendering £50,000 of his Civil List entitlement at a time of severe economic recession was welcomed by the population at large as further proof of his practical good sense.

The *Daily Worker*, however, was not so easily bought off by 'George Windsor' and his good intentions, noting:

> ... the straits to which the King will be reduced should bring a lump to the throat of the most callous. Now the royal housekeeper will have to make do on a mere £488,000 a year or £9,384 a week, [a sum] equal to a worker's dole for 225 years or about 90 years' pay for a miner.[12]

The king's Silver Jubilee, four years later in May 1935, was a cause for celebration, with Union Jacks and festive bunting seemingly adorning every lamppost and window in the land.

The news the king was dead, eight months later, barely days after his Christmas radio address, came as quite a shock. Vanessa Bell and her husband, Duncan Grant, drove by Buckingham Palace on 20 January, 'It was rather an amazing sight, crowds so thick we couldn't get near the railings to read the bulletins and cars parked all the way along the Mall'.[13]

Once his death was announced, the English press universally expressed the nation's grief, although the *New Statesman* also congratulated the dead king for not being particularly clever, which it claimed was 'an advantage in a country which distrusts cleverness in high places'.[14]

The frail Poet Laureate John Masefield, confined to bed with severe laryngitis, cabled a sonnet to *The Times* from Los Angeles (which he later apologised for, claiming it was written while he had a bad chest cold and had been scrawled out with his left hand because Californian hand shakers had disabled his right). Edward Blunden contributed an elegy and John Betjeman an ode. People donned black ties, black armbands and black ribbons in ritualised mourning that was predicted to outlast the London Season and encompass a black Ascot.

The royal focus was so universal that the king's death had completely overshadowed another venerable 70-year-old's passing. Rudyard Kipling had died on 18 January and was interred in Westminster Abbey without much fuss or commotion. The journalist Philip Gibbs expressed the chattering class's inner frustration when he declared, 'I am beginning to think that the death of the King is the greatest event in human history since the crucifixion'.[15]

In this vacuum of national mourning, Edward had been busy in the day following his emotional deathbed scene. He had calmed down sufficiently to fly with the Duke of York to London on 21 January (the first time a reigning monarch had flown) and appear nervously before the Accession Council at St James's Palace to be declared king. As soon as that was done, he returned to his apartments at York House and invited Wallis to attend his proclamation by the Garter King-of-Arms the next day.

In his wake, he had shocked the grieving royal household by first ordering the famous Sandringham clocks to reflect the correct time as opposed to Sandringham time (minus thirty minutes); instructing Frederick Corbitt, Deputy Comptroller of Supply at Buckingham Palace, that the royal lunch would no longer be served (as it had been for over a century) at 1 p.m. but whenever the mood suited him – usually at 2.30 p.m. – and that he wished to be served salads, fruit, fish and eggs in the American style of brunch rather than the stodgy, meaty mess of previous regimes; and ordering in person from Lendrum & Hartman in Mayfair an exact copy of the royal Buick (to be manufactured in Canada), complete with identical license plates and royal insignia for Wallis's exclusive use.

The proclamation took place at 10 a.m. in Friary Court, St James's Palace, on the bitterly cold morning of the 22nd. Four state trumpeters, dressed in tabards covered with gold lace, pierced the midwinter gloom like sparks flying from an anvil, walking onto a low, crimson-draped balcony followed by sergeants-at-arms holding aloft their gold maces. More sparks flew when a fanfare of trumpets announced the Garter King-of-Arms Sir Gerald Wollaston along with heralds and pursuivants dressed in gold braid and scarlet uniforms.

A cannon boomed across St James's Park, sending a volley for every year of the dead king's reign. As Wollaston solemnly proclaimed the accession of King Edward VIII in a hoarse voice, in a break with tradition, the king himself appeared at a window of the palace, illuminated by a dancing fire in the grate, and watched the ceremony with Mrs Simpson by his side. The ceremony ended with the regimental band in the courtyard striking up 'God Save the King'.

Mrs Simpson left for her flat at Bryanston Court via the royal Buick, with onlookers curtseying in the belief it was a member of the royal family. After a brief stop at Buckingham Palace to change clothes, Edward left for Sandringham and the most auspicious meeting of his life.

To the Court and royal household, the reading of the king's will was a mere administrative formality staged principally for the benefit of the immediate family. They were reassured by the dead king's rigorous approach to royal customs and processes in life that it contained no surprises and was governed by accepted practices and provisions. It was all very procedural and was the least important component of the machinery of succession. The only attendees were to be Edward, his mother, Lord Wigram and the royal solicitor, Sir Bernard Halsey-Bircham.

Confiding to his diary on 5 March 1943, Tommy Lascelles picked over the scab of what everyone thought at the time was just a benign, commonplace ritual:

> My impression is that the Prince of Wales was caught napping by his father's death; he expected the old man to last several years more, and he had, in all probability, already made up his mind to renounce his claim to the throne, and to marry Mrs S. The comparatively sudden death of George V upset any such plans. But I believe that even then, he would have clung to them (he always hated changing any scheme he had evolved himself) but for the provisions of his father's will.[16]

A blazing fire in the salon at Sandringham had been stoked for the occasion. Edward was late. He strode confidently towards the others, past the grand piano and plethora of potted plants. Everyone rose;

the king kissed his mother, winked at Wigram and shook hands with Halsey-Bircham.

Then it began – clause after interminable clause. Edward was amazed. Every so often he would quiz Halsey-Bircham with 'Where do I come in?'[17] At first it was a joke, but as the reading went on and on, Edward grew more restless and more agitated.

Finally, sensing the rising tide of tension in the little group, Wigram explained that although he had inherited both Balmoral and Sandringham and all its contents, the late king had assumed Edward had substantial reserves of cash income from the Duchy of Cornwall, estimated at over £1 million at his disposal. His father's father, King Edward VII, had also left a cashless bequest to his heir.

Edward sucked in a lungful of stale Sandringham air and lit a cigarette. Queen Mary was stony-faced. The absence of any cash was more galling to Edward because he was still owed the £90,000 he'd lent his father from Duchy revenues in 1915 to purchase more land around the detested Sandringham estate.

He was the odd one out. His brothers had each been left £750,000 in cash while he hadn't received a farthing – apart from the fact that the Duchy contributed £365,000 a year to his personal account, a further £425,000 from the Duchy of Lancaster and £2,355,000 from the Civil List. Sandringham and Balmoral with its contents could bring in a further £5–6 million if sold. Then there was the £10 million worth of gold plate, a collection of old masters' drawings and paintings valued conservatively at £5 million, plus trunk loads of fabulous jewels, gems and uncut stones in the vaults at Windsor, which were personally owned by the reigning sovereign.

There was, of course, much more, including a ranch in Canada with several hundred head of shorthorn cattle, the stamp collection and racehorses that he was precluded from converting into ready money (in the short term, at any rate), plus a very substantial stock portfolio put together by the Rothschilds.

The new king found it hard to contain his anger. In fact, he couldn't.

Wigram was pained by his extreme reaction, and in the days following this unpleasant scene, the 63-year-old tendered his resignation, effective after a generous transition period of six months.

Tommy Lascelles recounts the immediate aftermath:

… coming out of my office, I ran into him striding down the passage with a face blacker than any thunderstorm. He went straight to his room, and for a long time was glued to the telephone […] Money, and all the things that money buys, were the principal desiderata in Mrs Simpson's philosophy, if not in his, and when they found that they had been left the Crown without the cash, I am convinced that they agreed, in that interminable telephone conversation, to renounce their plans for a joint existence as private individuals, and to see what they could make out of the Kingship, with the subsidiary prospect of the Queenship for her later on.[18]

Philip Ziegler also attributed the 'painful shock', despite the immense wealth he had already accumulated and would continue to accumulate in the future, courtesy of the Civil List and Privy Purse, to the fact that Edward had:

… believed, and must have promised Mrs Simpson, that another huge fortune would soon be theirs; it was not to be, and the disappointment he felt for himself was a hundred times worse because it would distress and anger the woman he loved.[19]

Edward's setback and the tremendous strain it imposed on his royal mood was plain for everyone to see at the time of his father's funeral procession, two days later.

On 23 January, the body of George V was carried by gun carriage to Sandringham railway station with the royal brothers and the late king's shooting pony, Jock, walking behind. It had been prepared for four days of lying in state. Arriving at London King's Cross, it was carried on another bare gun carriage, draped with the Royal Standard, through the streets to Westminster Hall, accompanied by a cortège consisting of the plodding new king, his brothers, frozen regiments of soldiers and sailors, and various carriages of dignitaries.

Edward wore his dead father's heavy greatcoat lined with fur, the same coat he was to wear when he boarded HMS *Fury* and sailed into exile eleven months later. It remained with him throughout his life and was later auctioned off with his other clothes in 1998.

Wallis thought he looked grim, as if gritting his teeth, while his brothers were seemingly serene and expressionless. Other witnesses thought he looked exhausted and drawn. Harold Nicholson thought he was 'utterly done'.[20] Vanessa Bell found the procession unexpectedly lovely until the new king appeared, 'looking utterly miserable, very small, disreputable, patchy and debauched, and his hardly handsomer brothers'.[21]

At one point, as the gun carriage rumbled and rattled into New Palace Yard, the sapphire and diamond-encrusted Maltese cross atop the Imperial State Crown (sitting on the Royal Standard along with the Orb and Sceptre) wobbled loose, bounced on the edge of the coffin and fell into the gutter. In the blink of an eye, the Grenadier sergeant major in command of the bearer party, on seeing what had happened, swiftly bent down and, without missing a step, picked it up and slipped it into his greatcoat pocket.

Edward witnessed the gesture with a prickly desperation that had been maturing exponentially since the humiliation of his father's will, two days earlier. Such was his demeanour and mental condition that just before the lying-in-state procession, he had stormed into the offices of the Duchy of Cornwall demanding immediate reassurances that no portion of his income would be denied him as king.[22] The cross in the gutter incident seemed to unleash all his pent-up frustrations and financial quibbles. 'Christ! What will happen next?' he exclaimed loudly.[23]

Perhaps to make amends for his churlish behaviour, Edward proposed that he and his three brothers mount guard at each corner of the catafalque on the final night of his father's lying in state. Close to a million people filed past the coffin, guarded by officers of the Household Brigade, before it was taken by train to St George's Chapel Windsor for interment on 28 January.

Edward sneaked Wallis through a side door, where they were secretly filmed standing before the catafalque by a German agent. The film was later sent to Hitler.[24]

Five kings walked behind the bier when it arrived at Windsor. Representatives from numerous countries followed, including an emissary in full SS uniform from Nazi Germany.

People were glued to their wireless sets throughout its final journey. This time, everything went off without a hitch. On the same day, Hitler gave an elaborate memorial service for the dead king in Berlin and that night, the new king hosted the customary ceremonial dinner in the Gold Dining Room at Buckingham Palace.

After the tedious formalities were done and dusted, Edward reluctantly began moving offices to Buckingham Palace while continuing to maintain his residence at York House. The excuse was that he didn't want to disturb his mother, who still had apartments at the palace, but the truth was he abhorred the place and its constricted atmosphere and ritualised expectations. As he wrote later for an American newspaper:

> Being a Monarch [...] can surely be one of the most confining, the most frustrating, and over the duller stretches, the least stimulating jobs open to an educated, independent-minded person. Even a saint would on occasion find himself driven to exasperation by the taboos which invisibly and silently envelop a constitutional monarchy.[25]

It was a perfect storm of entrenched positions: the 'cold, serried resentment'[26] of the Court and royal household, and a king who did not want to be king, egged on by a resented mistress. The next few months were a complex tussle between these two diametrically opposing forces.

In later life, Edward wrote disingenuously about his needling and his undermining of the system he had inherited:

I brought to the Throne no ambitious blueprints for reform – no Royal counter-parts of the Five-Year-Plan. I had no desire to go down in history as Edward the reformer [... but] to open the windows a little and to let into the venerable institution some of the fresh air that I had become accustomed to breathe as Prince of Wales. My modest ambition was to broaden the base of the Monarchy a little: to make it a little more responsive to the changed circumstances of my times.[27]

To Court observers in those first few months, Edward's 'open window' was not intended to let in fresh air, but to facilitate the premeditated, wholesale ransacking of royal possessions and the liquidation of uneconomical paternal practices. This included old and ailing retainers and other 'cave dwellers'.[28]

Now that Edward was deprived of the cash he had expected, he was determined to economise in ways that freed up income that could be syphoned off to the benefit of Mrs Simpson. At least, that was how it appeared to courtiers like Tommy Lascelles:

The events of the next ten months bear out this supposition; for, throughout them, he devoted two hours to schemes, great and small, by which he could produce money to every one that he devoted to the business of the State. Indeed, his passion for 'economy' became something very near to mania, despite the fact that his private fortune, amassed while he was Prince of Wales, already amounted to nearly a million – which sum he took with him, of course, when he finally left the country. It was substantially increased by the considerable sums which his brother paid him for his life interest in the Sandringham and Balmoral estates, so that, by the time he married, having no encumbrances, no overhead charges and no taxes to pay, he was one of the richest men in Europe – if not the richest.[29]

In modern terms it was a PR disaster, a lesson in how *not* to progress transition during regime change. Queen Mary understood, 'It is always better to do such things very piano and with much reflection'.[30]

The staff tensions, which had been somewhat contained within the Prince of Wales' limited household, spread like a virus throughout the new king's various residences and the Court in general. Edward was not savvy enough to acknowledge the harm he was doing to himself or enlist help. His relentless, myopic pursuit of the overriding purpose of his life cast him as an iceberg through the heart of the establishment.

The 'reforms' in themselves were not overly contentious, and in later life, Edward believed the only two real innovations of his reign were the setting up of the King's Flight, for royal transport by air, and allowing the Yeomen of the Guard to remain clean-shaven if they wanted to.[31] Mixed among them, however, were displays of ostentation and deference to Mrs Simpson, which the royal household found hard to reconcile or excuse.

Anyone who was surplus to requirements was let go and the remaining staff served with a 10 per cent salary cut. (British civil servants had been required to take a similar cut four years earlier, but this precedent was lost in the general outrage.)

Staff reported to each other that Wallis, immaculate and cold, appeared without warning in underground kitchens, storerooms, cellars and food repositories on cursory inspections. Food purchases at each of the royal households were cut by a third and while this was mandated, it was also decided that the interior of Buckingham Palace would be redecorated and remodelled at vast expense in a modern style.

Sometime in late winter, Edward also settled on Wallis the enormous sum of £300,000, or one-third of his entire life savings, but, on reflection (perhaps the only instance when he rescinded a gift to her), he reduced it to £100,000.

To be fair, Buckingham Palace, like the Imperial State Crown and all the other royal residences, was falling to bits. The wonky Maltese cross incident was not so much an omen for the new reign as an emblem of the atrophy and torpor of the previous regime.

Although perhaps not in the Miss Havisham class, things had been allowed to stagnate and fall into genteel disrepair at an alarming rate. Marion 'Crawfie' Crawford, who became nanny to Princess Elizabeth and Princess Margaret, described living at Buckingham Palace in early 1937 as rather like camping in a museum, but a museum:

> … that's dropping to bits, with equipment three decades behind the times […] the palace had only recently had electricity installed, and with little thought to those who had to live there. My bedroom light, for instance, could only be turned on and off by a switch two yards outside in the passage. On top of that, when a housemaid came to draw my bedroom curtains, the whole lot – curtains, pelmet and heavy brass rods – came down with a clatter, narrowly missing my head. It became clear the Victorians considered no one needed sun in their bedrooms: every single one faced north.[32]

The first time she had tea with the new king and queen, she was invited to sit down on a magnificent pink and gold chair, 'Suddenly, I heard an ominous ripping sound. Within seconds the chair – which hadn't been re-caned since Queen Victoria's day – had dissolved.'[33]

The palace was considered too big and gloomy for modern living. Food had to come over half a mile from the kitchens at the Buckingham Palace Road end to the dining room at the Constitution Hill end. It was also infested with vermin and needed a vermin man, who fought an endless battle against mice using cardboard traps that had a lump of aniseed in the middle and treacle all around.

Balmoral was also antiquated and in need of refurbishment. Upstairs, almost everything was as Queen Victoria had left it at her death: tartan linoleum, tartan curtains and even little tartan hair ties hanging from mirrors. For washing, everyone had an old-fashioned basin and jug. Sandringham was the exception, owing to the late king's devotion to his hunting pursuits.

Windsor Castle was a fortress, not a home, with no central heating and a sinister labyrinth of beetle-infested dungeons and vaults. There were also caves that George III had built into a hillside near the castle, which were used as air-raid shelters during the Blitz.

The mouldy, dripping vaults, most of them unlit and unstable were still home to the fabulous personal jewellery collection of the monarch. But, as with many royal assets, this immense, priceless collection of jewellery, uncut stones and loose gems was still housed in the same iron and leather trunks that had been used since Queen Victoria's Diamond Jubilee. And despite the efforts of Queen Mary to catalogue the collection, nobody knew *exactly* what the trunks contained.

This eccentric method and attitude towards storage persisted through the years, well into the reign of Queen Elizabeth II. Crawfie describes an incident in the early days of the Second World War:

> One rainy day, the King's librarian, Sir Owen Morshead, let us explore the vaults under the castle. 'Would you like to see something interesting?' he asked. He took us to a stack of ordinary-looking hatboxes, which seemed merely to contain old newspapers. But when we examined them more closely, we were soon unwrapping the Crown Jewels – hidden there for the duration.[34]

In 1936, access to the jewels was similarly antiquated. An iron key, like a jailer's key, unlocked a heavy cast iron and wood door, and there they were: the vast jewellery hoard of the Windsors, propped on the dusty flagstone floor like the remnants of a pirate's treasure. The old key was traditionally kept by the king's librarian, probably in a desk drawer. All the king had to do was ask for it.

Today it is quite different and, after a fire raged for fifteen hours in Windsor Castle on 20 November 1992, destroying 115 rooms (including nine state rooms), efforts were made to revamp the paltry security and storage facilities. The monarch's jewellery collection was transferred to Buckingham Palace.

Equipped with sophisticated electronic security surveillance systems, the vault today is a well-lit showroom of 45m, accessed via a secure elevator that travels 12m below the palace foundations.[35] It is split into sections, with hundreds of tiaras, brooches, necklaces, earrings, uncut stones, gems and other jewels carefully stored and maintained in velvet pouches within their own digital safety box lined with pink fabric, some even trimmed with lace hand sewn by Queen Mary.

Apart from the Crown Jeweller, Mark Appleby, and his staff to assist when required, the only people cleared to access the room unaccompanied (though still constantly under surveillance) were the late queen and Angela Kelly, her long-time dresser.

8

The Whole Bag of Tricks

Darling, you must understand, you can't abdicate and eat it.

Wallis Simpson, November 1936[1]

As Queen Mary had feared, only a couple of months into the new reign, the servants at Buckingham Palace began complaining of loading cases of champagne, furniture and plate into trucks destined for Mrs Simpson's flat at Bryanston Court. It wasn't just the overt looting of royal goods and possessions the royal household objected to but also the seemingly abject devotion, some would say cringing slavery, the king persisted in exhibiting whenever Wallis was around.

Wallis had never been a 'hit' with royal servants and her brusque manner had largely been confined to Fort Belvedere, but now her casual arrogance seemed to know no bounds. An ex-footman who had served the king at Fort Belvedere told his new employer:

Well, Madam, the butler, Mr Osborne, sent me down to the swimming pool with two drinks. When I got there what did I see but His Majesty painting Mrs Simpson's toenails. My Sovereign painting a woman's toenails. It was a bit much Madam. I gave notice at once.[2]

The king's relentless economy drive was also exacting a heavy toll on staff morale at exactly the time he seemed to be lavishing gifts and perks on his mistress. Disgruntled staff called him a 'pincher'.[3]

By the end of April 1936, the financial secretary, Sir Ralph Harwood, reported the cost of household food had been reduced from £45,000 to £13,500. Drinks allowances for staff had also been lowered and livery compensation abolished. Though the cost of the royal aeroplane and pilot had been transferred to the Air Ministry, on several occasions during the spring and summer, it was on standby and used to transport Wallis and her friends to Paris for shopping sprees for which customs duty was never paid.[4]

Sandringham, that 'voracious white elephant',[5] was to be pared down to recoup some of the £50,000 used for the upkeep of the family mausoleum annually, and two farms, Flitcham and Anmer, were to be sold for cash (the contracts were awaiting Edward's signature at the time of the abdication) but were saved at the last minute by his brother, King George VI. Two other farms were also on the chopping block.

Dissatisfaction with the new king's priorities and fitness to serve extended beyond the confines of the household, sometimes to unintended comical effect. The library at Lambeth Palace holds the diaries of Alan Don (a future Dean of Westminster), who served as chaplain to both the Archbishop of Canterbury, Cosmo Lang, and the Speaker of the House of Commons. In 1,764 closely written pages, in volumes marked 'strictly confidential', Don shines a light on some of the significant and not so significant events surrounding the abdication and 'C.C.' (Cosmo Cantuar), Don's nickname for his boss Cosmo Lang.

Large sections of the Church were particularly non-committal when it came to the new sovereign, as this entry from Thursday, 30 January 1936, records:

The Speaker [Fitzroy] came to lunch – he wants a new Speaker's Chaplain, having induced Canon Carnegie to resign – the climax came on the occasion of the recent meeting of the House of Commons when the members assembled to swear allegiance to King Edward VIII

– Carnegie took the prayers as usual and prayed for King George and then for Edward Prince of Wales! The members were greatly annoyed. When the Speaker remonstrated with Carnegie, the latter excused himself by saying that he was 'thinking of something else' – that put the lid on and his resignation followed.[6]

So concerned was the royal household that Edward was not 'normal' in his gratification of Mrs Simpson's every wish and whim to the exclusion of his necessary kingly duties, they feared he would eventually go mad like King George III.[7] Some in his private office even went so far as to press the Baldwin government to pass the Regency Bill (a Bill to provide a regent in the event of the reigning monarch being incapacitated or a minor) as a matter of urgency.[8] The Bill eventually secured royal assent in March 1937.

There is no record of Edward getting wind of this action by some of his trusted advisors, but if he did, the betrayal would probably only confirm what he and Wallis already knew: they were cavorting on borrowed time. And there was precious little time to lose.

At a dinner at York House in March, Wallis's husband, Ernest, had brokered a deal with the king in the presence of Bernard Rickatson-Hatt, editor-in-chief at Reuters, whereby the Simpsons would divorce, and the king would take on Wallis's upkeep with a view to a future union as king and queen. Reports of the bombshell deal soon circulated among the king's inner circle of advisors with some fearing (and voicing) to sections of the government the potential for blackmail.[9]

Wallis always protested she had no knowledge of the deal and was physically upset at the thought she was being treated as a mere commodity to be handed over like a precious stone. This is despite Osborne, the butler at the Fort, reporting to a prominent member of Edward's staff (Ulick Alexander) that he had picked up a label in Wallis's handwriting in February, evidently attached to a present for the king. It read 'To our marriage'.[10]

The duplicity and deceit exercised by the king at this time towards his family, staff and the government also extended to the arrangements for his coronation. As Edward told his brother, the Duke of York, 'it was never in my scheme of things to be King of England',[11] so the thought of willingly going through an antiquated ceremony that would anoint him as king and emperor and seal his imprisonment forever was something he strenuously sought to avoid. He therefore connived various ruses to forestall the inevitable for as long as he could.

Though he was bored by the whole religious aspect of the ceremony, he tactically conceded to Cosmo Lang that he would follow the ritual laid down in the past two Westminster Abbey coronations (with one or two changes) after giving up trying to water the extravaganza down to a bare-bones service.[12] In fact, Edward had initially been reluctant to have a coronation at all, asking a shocked Archbishop of Canterbury whether it could be dispensed with.[13] His desire for a lower-key event led to the planned abandonment of the royal procession through London the following day, the thanksgiving service at St Paul's Cathedral and the dinner with London dignitaries.

Lang himself had mixed feelings about the whole thing. He wrote in his diary, 'The thought of my having to consecrate him as King weighed on me as a heavy burden [...] Indeed I considered whether I could bring myself to do so.'[14] Both men loathed each other, so it was perhaps mutually agreeable when Edward prevailed upon the Duke of York to attend most of the coronation committees in his place while he was away cruising the Mediterranean on the *Nahlin* with Wallis.

There were three of them: the Coronation Commission, the Coronation Committee of the Privy Council and the Coronation Joint Committee. After months of prevarication, the Coronation Committee met for the first time on 24 June 1936. Ramsay MacDonald, the Lord President of the Council, sat with the Duke of Norfolk, the Earl Marshal, to discuss the proceedings and agreed MacDonald would chair the overall Coronation Committee and the duke would chair the sub-executive committee. It was also announced the ceremony would finally take place on 12 May 1937.

Cosmo Lang remained the major driving force behind all the preparations and many of the decisions in respect of the order of service were made by or with him. He attended all the subsequent rehearsals and dealt with questions on how the service should be broadcast by the media.

By then Edward had lost interest and simply didn't care what Lang had authorised because he knew all Lang's planning would never amount to anything for him, so advanced were his plans for escape. A sense of history or anything that profound was not something that especially resonated with him, especially if it didn't include a special provision for his mistress. During discussions of a new Civil List, Edward focused his attention on special provisions to be made for a queen to the exclusion of all other matters, alarming his already tetchy advisors.[15]

Coronations have taken place at Westminster Abbey since Christmas Day 1066, when William the Conqueror was symbolically crowned with Edward the Confessor's crown using both Saxon and Norman rites with the bishops speaking English as well as French. Thirty-nine monarchs have been crowned there, together with fifteen separate coronations of consorts, the last being Anne Boleyn in 1533. Archbishop Dunstan devised the coronation rite for King Edgar in AD 973, which is basically the same rite used today.

A special book containing the English coronation service, the *Liber Regalis* or Royal Book, was introduced for the crowning of Edward II in 1308 and a copy of it in Westminster Abbey, made after the coronation of King Richard II and Queen Anne of Bohemia, dates from 1382. The illustrated pages, or illuminations, show a king alone, a queen alone, and a king and queen together. It was translated into English for James I (1603), discarded by James II in 1685, and then revised by the English Bishop of London, Henry Compton, for the coronation of William III and Mary II. Like Edward VIII, William IV had to be discreetly and persistently persuaded to be crowned at all during a time of severe economic depression and his coronation ceremony was pared down to the bone.

Though it is a highly decorated manuscript, the *Liber Regalis* is in fact an instruction book designed to help people organise and run a coronation. Some of the details of coronations have changed over the years, but the basic running order of the Christian ceremony remains the same. While the crowning of a new monarch may be the best-known highlight, a coronation service is profoundly a religious ceremony which takes place during Holy Communion. The most important and most sacred part of the ceremony is the anointing. This is where the Archbishop of Canterbury makes a cross with holy oil on the royal forehead and elsewhere on the body to show that the monarch has been chosen by God.

It is hard to imagine the notorious night-clubber Edward, fidgety, morose and bored, sitting through a five-hour religious ordeal. It's easier to picture Edward louchely leaning over Noël Coward's piano at some Mayfair dinner party, grimacing and shuddering with feigned fatigue at the thought of going through all that smoke-and-mirrors rigmarole in a draughty, freezing English abbey.

Wallis, meanwhile, had fled to Paris in early spring for a shopping spree on the royal aeroplane, arriving back with boxes of Mainbocher dresses and new settings of old stones by Cartier which had to be crammed into both royal Buicks. Even Philip Ziegler, Edward VIII's official biographer, reluctantly conceded 'the King had some very valuable old jewels reset for Mrs Simpson, [though] it has never been possible to identify any as having been specifically handed down from Queen Alexandra'.[16]

On the 27 March, Edward gave her the famous 'Hold Tight' Van Cleef & Arpels ruby and diamond bracelet, and in April, Wallis reciprocated with a gold memorandum case with Edward's monogram inside the cover and, in her handwriting, an engraved poem by Eleanor Farjeon:

King's Cross
What shall we do?
His purple robe
Is rent in two
Out of his crown
He's torn the gems!
He's thrown his Sceptre
Into the Thames!
The Court is shaking.
In its shoe.

King's Cross.
What shall we do?
Leave him alone
For a minute or two.

The gift-giving showed no signs of abating. A memo by Lord Davidson, an ally of Prime Minister Baldwin, reported, 'HM has already paid large sums to Mrs S and given valuable presents'.[17] It was also reported that the astronomical sum of £250,000 had been put into a trust for Wallis. A friend of Ernest Simpson reckoned a good deal of it was spirited away to the USA before Edward thought better of it and sought to reduce it.[18] But by then, it was too late.

After an official dinner at the Fort on 27 May, Wallis's name was published in the Court circular the following day prompting Queen Mary to wistfully comment after reading it, 'He [Edward] gives Mrs. Simpson the most beautiful jewels'.[19] This was followed by another 'coming out' dinner, with the Baldwins on 28 May. Guests were treated to cocktails with sausages, caviar with vodka, soup with sherry, fish with white wine, hock, champagne, and brandy. Afterwards, Wallis informed her husband she would be starting divorce proceedings. The bleary Baldwin dinner was also the last time Ernest and Wallis appeared publicly together.

This heady mix of high society, unrestricted wealth and endless horizons of infinite luxury, galloped into a glorious copper-plated English summer for Wallis. She was living beyond her wildest dreams while also acutely aware she was a hair's breadth away from a rude awakening that only such a society could deliver. It was a high-wire act, on her part, of such dazzling brilliance that it amazed and enthralled even her staunchest critics.

Everyone was sure she would fail but they were transfixed nonetheless by the performance. She owed her continuing 'existence' to the king and the king was showing no signs of his obsession wavering. If anything, it was becoming more feverish with every passing day.

The pinnacle was achieved in June when Wallis attended Royal Ascot in the king's official carriage, unashamedly on display to the world.

a coiffured timebomb that was set to detonate the English throne in just a few months. That was the high point, the apotheosis, of their joint naivety.

July was a disaster. A clumsy assassination attempt by George McMahon, targeting the king after a military review at Hyde Park, was followed by an embarrassing and shambolic formal Court presentation of debutantes in the grounds of Buckingham Palace on 21 July when a freak rainstorm exasperated everyone involved, including a visibly bored and distracted monarch.

The only thing that went according to plan was the dutiful Ernest, who checked into the Hotel de Paris at Bray in Berkshire with 'Buttercup Kennedy', fulfilling the bargain he had struck with Edward and Wallis in March to give his wife evidence of adultery so she could bring divorce proceedings against him. The lady in question was most probably Mary Raffray (née Mary Kirk), a childhood friend of Wallis.

Mary Kirk was in fact a bridesmaid at Wallis's first wedding and introduced her to Ernest Simpson in 1925. At the time of her 1936 affair with Ernest (which had been going on for months), Mary was married to Jacques Raffray, a French aviator.

July was also the occasion when the infamous *Nahlin* cruise took place. The king chartered the luxury 92m steam yacht (reputedly one of the biggest private yachts ever built in the UK) for an extensive period to explore the Dalmatian Coast and Adriatic Sea with select friends. With stops in Vienna, Yugoslavia, Athens and Istanbul, the voyage eschewed the traditional prolonged stay at Balmoral. Baldwin, naturally, was against it but Edward was adamant he needed a break and didn't need Baldwin's permission.

Dubbed 'the good ship Swastika' by journalist Malcolm Muggeridge,[20] the cruise, which purportedly cost the king a staggering £250,000 in today's money, blew the lid off their relationship, courtesy of saturation coverage by foreign press outlets, particularly American, but it was embargoed in the British media.

It couldn't fail to attract attention, especially as the white-hulled, cream-funnelled yacht was escorted by HMS *Glowworm* and *Grafton*, both Royal Navy destroyers, supplemented by Turkish destroyers when it approached Istanbul. At Šibenik, the Dalmatian port where the king and Wallis boarded the yacht, an exuberant crowd of 20,000 turned up to gawk at the famous couple.

The king and his mistress converted the onboard library on the shade deck into a suite for themselves, removing all the books to make room for stockpiles of golf balls, wine and whisky.[21]

Though idyllic, the voyage wasn't always plain sailing (Jack Crisp, the king's valet, called it 'Rotten').[22] The guests bickered and snickered among themselves at the daily shenanigans and bed hopping, growing visibly tired of the king's unrestrained enthralment as the weeks went by.

Wallis, too, was growing tired and irritable with her lover's constant fawning. She returned from the *Nahlin* cruise in September and retreated to the Hotel Meurice in Paris, where she wrote to Edward and tried to break it off, 'I am sure you and I would only create disaster together'.[23] But things were soon smoothed over when she joined the king at Balmoral as his official hostess during the truncated traditional holiday, where she was provocatively installed in the best spare bedroom with the king conveniently residing in her suite's dressing room.

The press coverage of their Mediterranean jaunt (the cuttings were provided by Aunt Bessie) had clearly spooked her and she persistently tried to get out of her 'fix' right up to the divorce hearing, set down for 27 October. But the king was equally persistent and sought to ameliorate things by co-opting the British newspaper proprietors Beaverbrook and Harmsworth into suppressing details of the Simpsons' divorce and other Wallis things pertaining to their friendship.

A further ameliorating act occurred during dinner following the end of the divorce hearing when Edward gave her the fabulous Mughal emerald, diffidently pulling the red Cartier box from the breast pocket of his midnight-blue dinner jacket at the magic moment.

But the bad omens continued to plague them and titillate their enemies. In October, just prior to the divorce hearing, during the only time Edward VIII ever hosted a shooting party at Sandringham, the flagpole at Sandringham church holding the Royal Standard snapped and had to be fixed by a carpenter working through the night.[24] It was a case of sanguinely adding another celestial mishap to the list in Edward's mind.

By this time Wallis had traded Bryanston Court for spectacular digs at Cumberland Terrace in Regent's Park. Queen Mary had also formally vacated her apartment at Buckingham Palace, moving down the Mall to Marlborough House.

There was no excuse now for the king not to take up residence at the palace and, with alacrity, he eschewed the traditional first-floor apartments for the ground-floor Belgian suite overlooking the terrace and gardens. To cushion his distaste for the imposing edifice, he installed for the head chef of Maxim's, M. Legros, a television and a squash court.

When not at her four-storey town house, Wallis dined with the king daily on dry toast, tea with lemon and a one-egg omelette for breakfast (Wallis having weaned him off his smelly craster kippers), a piece of fruit for lunch, and either grilled sole or steak and asparagus for dinner with melon for dessert. Fortunately for M. Legros, he was able to exercise his talents at dinner parties, where guests were treated to cold lobster mousse with Sauce Liberal finished in copious amounts of gin; hot curried eggs; thinly sliced rare roast beef with fresh horseradish (the king's favourite meal); Salade Russe; and Gâteau Égyptien à l'orange.

It couldn't last. The light-hearted saffron and azure frolicking of high summer and ruddy autumn was soon transformed by the dour realities of November into a nightmarish paste of smudgy browns and leaden greys.

November was always a difficult month, a dull month. In 1936, there were notable smogs in Manchester and Birmingham. Elsewhere, even in London, everything became coated with a thick, wet slime of soot despite the grudging four hours of thin, dissipating sunshine. Life became dour and severe once again, echoing Thomas Hood's famous poem of 1844:

No sun – no moon!
No morn – no noon –
No dawn – no dusk – no proper time of day.
No warmth, no cheerfulness, no healthful ease,

No comfortable feel in any member –
No shade, no shine, no butterflies, no bees,
No fruits, no flowers, no leaves, no birds! –
November!

For the country's fascists, the gloom was compounded by Franklin D. Roosevelt's landslide re-election in the United States presidential election. Roosevelt carried forty-six out of forty-eight states in the most lopsided election in American history in terms of electoral votes.

Wallis, too, was feeling the pinch of London's high society. All through November she was miserable, being privately harangued by people at every social occasion she attended to give the king up and move on, the impossibility of her becoming queen, how the whole affair was dragging the monarchy down, etc., etc.

On 30 November, the Crystal Palace was destroyed by fire. Huge numbers of people turned out to watch the spectacular blaze. Another prescient omen, it seemed, for the English monarchy.

November 1936 also represented a real and discernible quickening of Edward and Wallis's plans for escape and the Establishment's desire to fix the entire mess it had turned a blind eye to for months. The sense of an imminent showdown was palpable.

After a secret meeting with his chief advisor, Walter Monckton, at Windsor Castle (the first of many such trysts), to hammer out his next moves on 15 November, a seething Edward showed Wallis a letter written by his private secretary Alexander Hardinge two days earlier, warning him of the constitutional dangers of his continuing affair with Mrs Simpson. Hardinge's letter also hinted at a previous clandestine consultation with Prime Minister Stanley Baldwin and his Cabinet about Wallis's suitability as a possible queen and spouse of the monarch.

It was at this point that Wallis realised for the first time the full context and significance of the crisis enveloping them.

By 16 November, Edward had run out of the time and energy required to maintain the subterfuge concerning his long-held intentions and told Baldwin he was going to marry Wallis and that he was prepared to go if the government couldn't accommodate him. He also told his speechless mother at Marlborough House, and on the 19th, his incredulous brother, the Duke of York.[25] Chips Channon recorded the following conversation in his diary between the two brothers:

> 'What will she call herself?', the stammering Duke asked.
> 'Call herself? What do you think – Queen of England of course', the King replied.
> 'She is going to be Queen?'
> 'Yes, and Empress of India, the whole bag of tricks.'[26]

The febrile nature of Edward's mind ebbed and flowed. One minute he was charming and resolute, the next fidgety, chain smoking, baggy eyed and melodramatic.

After meeting with his brother, Wallis floated the option of a morganatic marriage, a proposal put to her by a member of their circle. At first, the king was non-committal but a day or two later he put it to Baldwin, who deferred to the Cabinet and consultation with the Commonwealth. It was swiftly rejected.

The strain was proving to be unbearable and the last public sighting of Wallis before her elopement to France occurred at a dinner party on 27 November, where Chips Channon noted, 'She was wearing new jewels – the King must give her new ones every day'.[27] The following evening, with Aunt Bessie in tow, she arrived at the beleaguered Fort for her personal protection at the king's insistence.

The endgame was in sight.

The brittle impasse was finally breached by the Church a few days later, reacting to the haggling between Crown and clergy over the religious format of the king's impending coronation and his ongoing religious flippancy. Robert Beaken, Cosmo Lang's biographer, explains:

> On 1 December 1936, Bishop Alfred Blunt of Bradford spoke at his diocesan conference about the forthcoming coronation. He rejected the Bishop of Birmingham's proposals for the desacramentalisation

of the coronation service. Blunt's speech was unexceptional, except in one section when he mentioned Edward VIII and said: 'some of us wish that he gave more positive signs of such awareness' [of his need of God's grace], by which he seems to have meant the king's failure to attend holy communion or any other church service [...] The bishop's speech was widely reported in the press, who now abandoned their previous restraint. For many Britons, this was the moment when they first learnt of Edward VIII's relationship with Mrs Simpson.[28]

The great game that Wallis and her lover had been playing for the last eleven months, since the reading of George V's will at Sandringham, was up.

Two days later, on Thursday, 3 December, Wallis arranged to depart the Fort for the Continent with Perry Brownlow. A ruse had been devised to shake off the plethora of press that were hanging about the Fort and Windsor: Ladbroke, the royal chauffeur, accompanied by Inspector Evans from Scotland Yard, would drive Wallis's Buick to Newhaven on the south coast where he would lodge it on the overnight ferry to Dieppe. Perry Brownlow, meanwhile, would collect Wallis in his car at the Fort and then switch cars at the ferry.

Shortly after 7 p.m., Wallis strode through the Fort's octagonal hallway, embraced both Aunt Bessie and Edward and climbed into the waiting car. Before Brownlow could take the wheel, Edward took him aside and urged him to take all care with his precious cargo – and the £100,000 worth of jewels, gems and uncut stones Wallis had on her.[29] Brownlow was mortified.

En route, the runaway couple pulled over and stopped for a few minutes in the fog-shrouded countryside to discuss whether they should instead hole up at Brownlow's house, Belton at Grantham, and try to persuade Edward not to abdicate.[30] Wallis argued that Edward would be devastated by the subterfuge and elected to carry on.

At Newhaven, Brownlow and Wallis boarded the ferry and took adjoining cabins under the names of Mr and Mrs Harris. Brownlow was awakened at some point in the early hours by howls of grief and sobbing coming from her cabin.[31] When the ferry docked, Ladbroke, Evans, Brownlow and Wallis jumped into the Buick and sped off on the 650km to Cannes.

Wallis's place at the Fort was taken by Walter Monckton, who spent the last eight nights of Edward VIII's reign there to sort out the remaining points of detail concerning his friend's abdication. The duke's unreliable 1951 ghost-written memoirs also disclosed that Edward's initial draft of his famous abdication speech was, in fact, written on the 3rd with Monckton's help, a further indication of the king's state of mind.

Meanwhile, William Bateman, Edward's private telephone operator at the palace, had been instructed to give priority to all Wallis's calls and messages while she was in France.

The king's initial plan, after Wallis had left, was to withdraw temporarily to Switzerland and let things simmer down. Piers Legh was instructed to book rooms at the Dolder Hotel in Zurich, while Ulick Alexander was dispatched to Coutts Bank to secure a letter of credit for £5,000 (despite the account being overdrawn).

Two private aircraft were chartered in the king's name and were waiting at Hendon Airport. When Baldwin was informed of this by Lord Swinton, Minister for Air, he immediately moved to close off that escape route.[32]

There was to be no wriggling free. The weekend beginning Friday, 4 December, marked Edward's point of no return. Baldwin, having spoken to the House of Commons, told the king that his situation was hopeless. To soften the blow, the 70-year-old prime minister promised to look at pushing through a special bill to guarantee Wallis's decree nisi with the abdication.

On the evening of Monday the 7th, at an impromptu dinner with his brothers York and Kent at the Fort, Edward asked Baldwin (who had unexpectedly turned up with a suitcase) for a respite of several days to get his affairs in order. The period between 8 and 9 December remains largely unaccounted for. One can only imagine what the desperate, physically drained but staunchly determined sovereign got up to behind closed doors.

The thing that Edward dreaded the most, however, was relaying the news to Wallis. The interminably scratchy, long-distance phone calls began, with Edward speaking/shouting to her and Ulick Alexander, Keeper of the Privy Purse, and his solicitor George Allen by his side to prompt him or advise him what to say.

Things moved swiftly from there. Theodore Goddard had arrived back from interviewing Wallis at Cannes, though his legal partner, Bertram Ogle, denied he had returned to London with 'his pockets stuffed with [Queen Alexandra's] jewels'.[33] On Wednesday, 9 December, Monckton met with the Duke of York at his London residence, No. 145 Piccadilly, and struck a deal with the future king that Edward would retain his royal rank and remain a royal prince after the abdication in return for two years' exile.

That afternoon, Edward broke the news to his mother at Royal Lodge and later gave his brother a draft of his abdication message. The duke showed it to Queen Mary, now back at Marlborough House, who received and read it in silence.

The following day, Edward, with all his brothers present as witnesses, signed six copies of the Instrument of Abdication at 10.30 in the morning, in the octagonal drawing room of the Fort. The copies were subsequently locked in an official red box and taken to London by Monckton.[34] Once that was accomplished, all that remained administratively was for the king and the Duke of York to agree the financial dispersal of Balmoral and Sandringham plus their contents, the royal stamp collection, the racehorses, etc., etc. This occurred later that evening at the Fort in the presence of Ulick Alexander, Sir Edward Peacock, serving as the king's personal financial advisor, Lord Wigram, advising the Duke of York, Sir Bernard Bircham, the Duke of York's personal solicitor, George Allen, the king's solicitor, and Walter Monckton.

It proved to be a traumatising experience, creating divisions and visceral wounds that would never fully heal. And if one were to pick one example of Edward VIII's behaviour as an indicator of the lengths he was prepared to go to, the goodwill he was willing to exploit and the deceit he was determined to inflict on his friends and family to fulfil his obsession, while luxuriously providing for himself and his future wife, it was the negotiations with his brother over the financial settlement of his inherited assets. And if he was capable of doing something like that, among an audience of eminent men at the top of their game, why is it so fanciful to imagine him not resisting the opportunity to grab some of the royal jewels that were in his duty of care as sovereign, that were readily accessible and within his discretion to use however he chose?

At the time of the negotiations, Sir Edward Peacock, financial advisor to George V and Edward as Prince of Wales, and former governor of the Bank of England, put Edward's wealth at £1.1 million excluding his Canadian ranch.[35] Despite this being what everyone roughly agreed was the sum of his worth, Edward is recorded as telling his brother he only had £90,000 to his name and could manage only £5,000 a year, leaving George VI 'in no doubt that he was so poor that he could not possibly survive without some sort of money from the government or the new King'.[36]

This 'suicidal lie', as Ziegler called it,[37] was made despite the people in the room knowing full well that from 1910 to 1936, Edward received substantial revenue from the Duchy of Cornwall and Lancaster which (with other investments) ensured that by the time he came to the throne he was clearly worth over £1 million. However, Edward claimed he was in debt, as the annual revenues from Cornwall and Lancaster were not due until the middle of 1937 and he had to borrow money from Barings Bank to pay household expenses and staff salaries, plus the £100,000 he had already settled on Wallis (down from the original £250,000). This was in addition to all the furs and jewels and £6,000 a year that he was paying for her upkeep.[38] There was also the spectre of income tax, which he was advised he would most likely need to pay when he returned from exile.

Perhaps to avoid embarrassing the evidently distraught new king (which, no doubt, is what Edward heavily counted on in his game plan), the room agreed to give him £25,000 annually for life as an allowance, which would include payment for Balmoral and Sandringham. The

Duke of York, as George VI, also promised he would pay his brother the agreed amount if the government did not.

When details later emerged of the deceit, duplicity and fraud that Edward had committed, the fallout was catastrophic, losing the Duke of Windsor many powerful friends and advocates, including Churchill, the future prime minister. His brother, George VI, would write to him on 10 March 1937, 'I was completely misled.'[39]

Once the last meaningful piece of the only thing that really mattered to Edward was settled, it was agreed the ex-king would address the nation the next day, Friday, 11 December, following a family dinner at Royal Lodge. The last private dinner he gave that night was for Churchill, who was teary and bleary throughout.

The next evening at 9.30 p.m., he and Monckton left the royal family for Windsor Castle, to speak at 10. They drove in silence down the Long Walk, turned into the huge quadrangle and stopped at the Sovereign's Entrance. Chaperoned to the king's former living quarters in the Augusta Tower, where things had been prepared for the broadcast by Sir John Reith, Director General of the BBC, Edward seemed perfectly at ease, even nonchalant, as the events of that evening, recorded by Reith in his diary, testify:

Left at 9.05 & got to Windsor at 9.30. I was expected & the car took me to the door of the private quarters. Here were a red-coated footman, the Majordomo & the housekeeper. Went up to the room where the broadcast was to take place. It was in a little corridor of three rooms, bedroom at end. This was the suite the King always used. The microphones were in the centre room. I had just looked around when I got an agitated message to go down to the door to receive the King who was well on his way from Royal Lodge where the family (including Queen Mary) was dining [...] No one knew who was coming with him. Actually it was Monckton [...] He (the King) had on a light suit, fur coat & was smoking a big cigar [...] He didn't seem any different from usual. 'Good Evening Reith; very nice of you to make all these arrangements and come along yourself.'

[…] Monckton told me the King had actually wanted to say good-bye to his family before the broadcast, but he had persuaded him to go back after. The King went to Pumpship (sailors' slang for urinating) in a place between bedroom & sitting room, saying he didn't know when he would use that place again, & leaving the door open. He was making changes with Monckton's help in his M.S. […] I didn't think much of what the King said. I listened in his bedroom, sitting in an odd shaped sofa before a fire. After he finished I waited for a while & then went into the room. He and Monckton looked as if they had been having an argument […] Monckton said he was glad I had come in when I did and that I got the King's mind off himself. He had had a dreadful time arguing and counterarguing […] I said I ought to get off; he said I mustn't go without seeing the King […] He came into the big corridor with me and thanked me again. He said he hoped very much that he would be able to use the B.B.C. again […] I said 'Good luck, Sir', shook hands and bowed. He smiled very nicely and rather sadly, so I bowed again and left. What an occasion. What that young man has thrown away – a greater opportunity than any King or any man ever had.[40]

After introducing the ex-king (Reith had been briefed by Sir John Simon, Home Secretary, that King George VI was very particular that his brother should be called HRH Prince Edward) and standing aside to allow Edward to take the chair, Edward accidentally and audibly rocked the table with his foot. Reith later recalled in an interview with the satirist Malcolm Muggeridge that some newspapers interpreted the sound as Reith leaving the room and slamming the door in disgust, which was not the case, he assured Muggeridge.

After the speech Edward returned to Royal Lodge to say his goodbyes. Everyone was in tears except his mother, who stood rigidly, staring at him, cold as ice while he kissed her on both hands and then both cheeks. He bowed to King George VI.

'Thank you, sir, for all your kindness to me,' Edward said. When George VI, acutely moved and stammering, offered a heartfelt protest in response, his older brother put a reassuring hand on his shoulder. 'It's right, old man, I must step off with the right foot from the first. God save the King.'[41]

Edward and Monckton then returned to the Fort, where his personal effects were being loaded in two army trucks and the royal Buick, newly returned from Cannes.

The final humiliation on home soil was the desertion by his servants, none of whom wanted to make the journey into exile with him. Norfolk-born Jack Crisp, who worked as valet and page to the former king from 1919 onwards, was cruelly one of the first not to commit to his master in exile. For twenty-seven years, Crisp had served Edward with discretion and distinction.

Such royal service and dedication ran in the family. Jack's father, Thomas, was a gardener on the Sandringham estate and a brother, Mark, was a groom. When others couldn't tolerate Wallis's behaviour, whose sole aim in life seemed to be making work for Edward's staff, Crisp kept silent and remained loyal. In 1936, he took over from Frederick Finch, who had spectacularly packed his bags after a clash with Mrs Simpson when he refused to mix cocktails the American way she had wanted, with ice. Crisp's only comment, uttered years later, on his abandonment of Edward that night was, 'He gave up his job, I gave up mine'.[42]

Edward tried to shrug it off and all the other covert slights that surfaced as he prepared to leave but it was a wrench that pained him for years. The pain was ironic, because many people in his circle echoed the views of Tommy Lascelles when it came to Edward's enduring inability to maintain long-standing friendships and loyalty:

So isolated was he in the world of his own desires that I do not think he ever felt affection – absolute, objective affection – for any living being, not excluding the members of his own family [...] if he ever looked like making a friend, he never succeeded in keeping him for any length of time; and the very devoted service given him by certain members of the staff, he appreciated so little that he could only reward them with rank ingratitude. Consequently, when he came to the parting of the ways, he stood there tragically and pitifully alone. It was an isolation of his own making: and the responsibility for it is entirely his own.[43]

Edward VIII ceased to be King of England on the afternoon of Friday, 11 December 1936. His reign had lasted less than eleven months, the shortest reign in 453 years. But that notoriety was the last thing on the former monarch's mind as he made his escape across the English Channel.

Edward VIII leaving Windsor Castle, after his abdication speech, 11 December 1936. (Getty Images)

Nicholas Rayner leads the auction of the jewels of the Duchess of Windsor in Switzerland,
2 April 1987. (Alamy)

The Sotheby's catalogue of the Auction of the Century, April 1987. (Author's collection)

Edward and Wallis after their marriage ceremony at Château de Candé in the Loire, with James Hale in the doorway making sure everything is as it should be. (Alamy)

The *Daily Mail*'s coverage of the Duchess of Windsor's death ahead of her funeral.
(Author's collection)

Yorkshire Evening Post

LEEDS   FRIDAY, OCTOBER 18, 1946   No. 17,463

'Big Five' Officer Leads Inquiries: Manhunt Extends to Continent

WINDSORS LOST £20,000: UNTRUE
REPORTS ANNOY THE DUKE

'Fence' on Golf-links as Jewels Sorted?

"Evening Post" Reporter

Death Fight in Wife's Bedroom

5 Years for Soldier

BETTER TIMES

MILLION GIFT
TO BRITAIN
From South Africa

GERMANS IN MEXICO

Caught in the Act

HAD GOERING PHIAL ALL TIME?

Broken Glass Was Found on One of the 21 Nazis

HOW JOBS ARE
TO BE FOUND

Two Speedy Placings

To Discourage Cat Burglars

BISHOP CONSECRATED

TURKISH 'NO'
Russian Plan for Straits

Sellers Near End
of Journey

'Q.E.' IN A GALE
Began in Night

INGRID BERGMAN COMING
After Broadway Play

Caption below the page: A press report of the Ednam Lodge heist. (Author's collection)

Edward VIII and his brothers marching behind the funeral cortège of George V. (Alamy)

Sotheby's lavish three-volume catalogue of their 1997 Duke and Duchess of Windsor auction in New York. (Author's collection)

9

Martyr on the *Orient Express*

High instincts before which our mortal Nature
Did tremble like a guilty thing surprised.

William Wordsworth, 'Intimations of Immortality'

A little after midnight on Saturday, 12 December 1936, a four-car convoy, comprising a chauffeured Buick limousine with drawn blinds, two police escorts and a tarpaulin-covered army truck flecked with snow, passed through the Unicorn Gate at the entrance to Portsmouth Naval Base.

Fog, drizzle and sudden bursts of sleeting rain had delayed the convoy's arrival (the Buick had to pull over several times when driving became impossible) but the blazing headlights and screeching tyres inside the base alerted the navy's lookouts and set in motion a flurry of activity at dockside.

Moments later, a hunched and pensive figure – carrying Slipper, the ex-king's sleepy Cairn terrier – together with several burly men in black greatcoats cautiously ascended the slippery gangway of the Royal Navy destroyer HMS *Fury*. Mercifully, for all concerned, *Fury* had been substituted for the Admiralty yacht HMS *Enchantress* at the last minute.[1] This was despite the *Enchantress* having better quarters, including a new accommodation deckhouse exclusively built for the Admiralty Board's use, three single 4.7in guns and an oil-fired steam turbine engine.

A small coterie of trusted officers, including the commander-in-chief, Admiral Sir William Fisher, and two other admirals, were on hand to meet the mysterious group. Fisher, in receipt of sealed orders describing the importance of his mission and passengers, led the group to the captain's spacious ward room where platters of sandwiches and smoked salmon from Fortnum & Mason had been meticulously laid out, courtesy of the linen, crockery and crystal that *Fury* had borrowed from the royal yacht.[2]

White-coated stewards promptly arrived with gleaming silver pots of fresh coffee and decanters of medicinal whisky, careful to heed the warnings given to them moments earlier to keep their eyes glued to the service and not to go a-wandering. The conversation was strained.

The principal passenger reluctantly let Slipper out of his arms for a sniff around, declined the sandwiches but accepted a small cup of black coffee. Glancing at the smoked salmon, he wondered aloud where on earth he'd be able to enjoy his favourite breakfast of heavily smoked craster kippers from Northumberland during his indefinite sojourn on the Continent. The man's chief advisor and chief fixer, the barrister Walter Monckton, piped up and replied he could always get Fortnums to send over a regular batch to tide him over until his return. This seemed to please the man and he bestowed on the group a thin, strained smile.

Fisher and his captain politely excused themselves, grateful to leave the suffocating tension in the cabin behind. Shortly after 2 a.m., the contents of the army truck safely stowed, HMS *Fury* steamed out of Portsmouth Harbour accompanied by another destroyer, HMS *Wolfhound*, which had been summoned from Portland in Dorset at extremely short notice. Both vessels were bound for Boulogne, after lying off the coast at Bembridge for a few hours.

Leaving Slipper to his own devices, the ship's principal passenger, HRH Prince Edward (soon to be created HRH the Duke of Windsor, a title dreamed up by his brother, the new king, on the spur of the moment and communicated to Edward shortly after the BBC broadcast), together with his equerries, John Aird and Sir Piers Legh, stepped out on *Fury*'s port side and stared morosely at the beach from where Lord Nelson had set off for the Battle of Trafalgar.

Monckton had already left, returning to the duke's residence, Fort Belvedere, to tidy up any personal effects the duke had forgotten in the high emotion of the abdication speech, delivered a few hours earlier, and his swift escape from servants and family. Finding a piece of paper beside the duke's bed at the Fort containing Wallis's private telephone number, Monckton assiduously disposed of it.[3] The rest of the former king's possessions were packed up in numerous tin trunks and stored at Frogmore (meticulously kept inventories were maintained by his former valet, Jack Crisp, who did so voluntarily and without rancour).[4]

The entire dismal scene, suffused with the heavy scent of bilge and oily water, was barely illuminated by the blinking navigation lights of moored vessels in the wintry harbour. There was much to ponder and little to smile about, except perhaps for one sliver of solace.

Unbeknown to both Aird and Legh, reputedly, hidden in a pocket of the duke's midnight blue Scholte jacket was a plain hessian bag containing a fabulous collection of uncut emeralds, sapphires and loose diamonds belonging to his grandmother, the late Queen Alexandra, which he had purloined from the royal vaults at Windsor.

As the destroyers manoeuvred slickly towards Spithead, the former king dismissed Aird and Legh but continued to stand on deck alone. He seemed riveted to the spot despite the choppy seas and lacerating winds that smeared the black Astrakhan collar of his fur-lined overcoat (his father's coat, worn at his father's funeral) with sea spray. Slipper, meanwhile (with nowhere apparently to go), had unobtrusively fouled the private quarters of the ship's captain, Cecil Howe, and had to be removed to another cabin by Major Ulick Alexander, Keeper of the

Privy Purse, who had been delegated by the Crown to manage the new duke's financial affairs while exiled.[5]

The *Portsmouth Evening News* later reported, 'The ex-King was sad and pensive. Indeed, he looked deeply moved. He scarcely spoke a word as he went up the gangway of the destroyer', and later stood with a 'strained face', transfixed on the gradually fading lights of Portsmouth. One eye-witness, George Hale, told the paper he was asked for directions to the naval base by Ladbroke, the Buick's chauffeur. The paper described him as 'the last civilian in England to be spoken to by the ex-king Edward VIII' as a voice in the back of the car thanked him for his help.[6]

Before dawn, the sleepless duke (who had spent the time after returning from deck drinking brandy and sending cables to friends in the wardroom until four in the morning),[7] his entourage of aides, two detectives and the Surgeon Commander of the royal yacht,[8] plus twenty-two pieces of luggage personalised with his royal cypher (the bulkier items from the Fort were to travel separately south to Cannes) were met at Boulogne by the *Orient Express*, which had been specially diverted to make the connection. First-Class passengers had been alerted to the diversion, but the cheaper seats resorted to poking their heads out of the windows to get a better look at all the commotion. The train's army of stewards and cooks knew nothing, so they had nothing to say.

All the arrangements had worked perfectly thus far, except for the rather sad farewell when the duke disembarked *Fury*. A telegram from Downing Street received during the crossing emphasised there was to be no saluting by officers, citing the express wish of Buckingham Palace. Not that the prince would have noticed. He never looked back, carrying Slipper into the waiting limousine for the short trip to Boulogne railway station and pulling down the blind once they were settled.

The ducal party, occupying eleven compartments, were travelling overnight to Baron Eugene de Rothschild's fairy-tale hunting lodge at Schloss Enzesfeld. At the station, the *Orient Express*'s comptroller, Roger Tibot, was instructed to serve all the duke's meals in his special sleeping car, 3538, a specially modified first-class suite with private washing salon, intricate mahogany, rosewood and ebony marquetry wall panels and a shower.

The duke was adamant that, apart from meal services, he was not to be disturbed. Tibot remonstrated with Aird and Legh that he'd made provisions for the duke to use the restaurant car after all the other passengers had left and that the only way to serve the ex-king in 353E was to put the food on trays and set them on suitcases to compensate for the absence of a table.[9]

The equerries were likewise perplexed by the duke's reluctance to leave his compartment, but their employer was not to be dissuaded. He was not to be disturbed, except for meals and the attentions of his valet (a duty performed by the luckless Aird because Crisp, his usual valet, refused to accompany him into exile), until he was met by his escort in Vienna.

As the train sped through the frozen, misty French countryside, the duke changed his clothes and with Slipper picked at his personally prepared breakfast: scrambled eggs with fine herbs, clear soup, delicate cream cheese, poached chicken breast cooked without sauces, boiled white fish, assorted cereals, fruit compotes and pastries, coffee and brandy. Apart from visits from his equerries, he was to remain secluded for most of Saturday and Sunday.

Meanwhile, at the accession meeting of the Privy Council of the United Kingdom in London, King George VI was announcing to the elderly, pop-eyed men seated around the table that he had decided to make his brother the Duke of Windsor with the style of HRH, a decision he had privately come to only a day earlier.

On board the *Orient Express*, Aird, Legh and Alexander were finally at a loose end and took the opportunity of the duke's confinement to catch up on some sleep. After clearing another of Slipper's transgressions, they proceeded to snore their heads off between brandies and the clink of cocktails being delivered to the duke's compartment (Edward had excised lunch from his daily routine since his early twenties).

The duke's security, in the meantime, was maintained by the two detectives, Chief Inspector David Storrier and Detective Sergeant

Hatfield, who had accompanied him across the Channel, together with successive detective crews from the forces of France, Switzerland and Austria. Part of Storrier's remit was to report on Edward's moods and movements by letter to Sir Philip Game, Commissioner of the Metropolitan Police, on a fortnightly basis.[10]

On arrival in France, Storrier wrote his first report on *Orient Express* stationery. He was concerned that Edward was being 'over-policed' by seven burly men from the *Sûreté* (the French equivalent of Special Branch) and thirty fidgety, bored *gendarmes*.[11] After representations, the *Sûreté* numbers were reluctantly reduced to two, he wrote.

By the time the train arrived at Vienna's Westbahnhof station on Sunday, 13 December, the duke's official entourage had been swelled by over sixty reporters and photographers. Quite how and where they all fitted in is a mystery.

After spending Saturday night drinking brandy alone with Slipper into the small hours, the duke rose at 3 p.m. on Sunday and was served oysters, soup with Italian pasta, turbot with green sauce, chicken à la chasseur, fillet of beef with château potatoes, a chaudfroid of game animals, lettuce, chocolate pudding, a buffet of desserts and two bottles of his favourite Pol Roger, the 1928 vintage. At 5 p.m., he alighted from the train at Salzburg for a few minutes, wearing his black winter coat and a dark red muffler with a dark bowler hat pulled well down over his eyes. Police and detectives surrounded him. A crowd gathered at the station and sang 'God Save the King' and cheered.

The *Manchester Guardian* later reported that when the train finally arrived in Vienna at 10.05 p.m., Austrian police formed a cordon round the duke's special sleeper, allowing none of the passengers or reporters anywhere near it. Inside the cordon were Dr Skubl, Police President of Vienna, and Sir Walford Selby, the British Minister in Vienna. No representatives of the Austrian government were present.

For a couple of minutes, nothing happened, until the duke suddenly appeared and stepped on to the platform. Detective Storrier, who carried Slipper, followed him. The ex-king looked well. 'Any messages for me?' was Edward's first question on leaving the train.[12]

He was handed a bundle of telegrams and letters, which he crammed into his coat pocket.

Then, after heading for the Imperial Waiting Saloon en route to his car, he suddenly said, 'Let the photographers come along. They have had a tough journey and deserve some pictures. Let us turn back.'[13] The party returned to the platform where the cameramen, many of whom had been on the train for the entire twenty-five-hour journey, secured pictures by means of flashlights. After a spell in this crossfire of light, Edward said in German, 'Well, I guess, gentlemen, this is enough.'[14]

Two minutes later, a large black Mercedes whisked him away through the snow and ice, the police detaining the cars of the impatient reporters for a further five minutes to give him a start. Edward was accompanied by Legh and Storrier, Hatfield and Slipper.

What happened next is a matter of conjecture. The newspapers reported that Edward's party drove straight to Enzesfeld, arriving at 11.15 p.m., and that he immediately telephoned Mrs Simpson. But the attaché, Dudley Forwood, who was part of the Embassy group supporting Sir Walford Selby at the station, recalled many years later that the duke was required by protocol to pay his respects to the Austrian President Miklas and did so after leaving the Westbahnhof.[15] It would have been very late, and the weary duke would probably have done anything to avoid it, but Forwood is insistent it happened.

In the scheme of things, it is not a significant variance from the accepted details, but it does illustrate the challenge of piecing together a story that has been shattered into a million pieces by the passage of time, familiarity, receding memory and conflicting contemporary accounts. Whatever transpired immediately after the duke left Vienna station remains an annoying mystery, but his new life as the Duke of Windsor (it was not until after the new king's coronation on 12 May 1937 that the style and title were given legal form) had certainly begun, and although the past traumatic forty-eight hours was by no means the start, it was the end of Edward's blatant theft of heirlooms and gems from the vaults of the Royal Collection, which had been conducted over many years.

He had the opportunity, he had the means, and he certainly had the motive. In fact, he had a series of enduring motives, which drove him perpetually onwards and dictated the course of his emotional life and indeed the purpose of that life, as he saw it.

Sir Alan Lascelles, Edward's assistant private secretary at the time of his ascension to the throne, before resigning in disgust at his dissolute and profligate ways, was convinced he was driven by these motives, drenched in an overriding selfishness:

> His only yardstick in measuring the advisability or non-advisability of any particular action was 'Can I get away with it?' – an attitude typical of boyhood. As a matter of fact, he usually *did* 'get away with it'; his one conspicuous failure to do so, however, cost him his throne.[16]

It was simply that Edward truly believed that he and the duchess were made for each other and that nothing else truly mattered except their happiness.[17]

The decades of deceit and deceptions, betrayals and sleazy cover-ups willingly carried out by compliant jewellers, gem merchants, auction houses, police forces and Windsor cronies was a small price to pay for that conviction to play out. It was the single motivating force behind all their subsequent madcap conceited schemes for getting away with it.

Even the press seemed to acknowledge their genius, especially the drive and determination of the dominant personality in the irresistible self-serving equation of their lives. When 1936 ended, *Time* magazine named Wallis Simpson 'Woman of the Year', the first time the magazine had ever given its 'Man of the Year' award to a woman. In a year of three English kings sitting on the throne, the field of other notable candidates she beat was impressive: an American President (Franklin D. Roosevelt), Mussolini, Eugene O'Neill, Chiang Kai-shek, Stanley Baldwin, Lou Gehrig, Jesse Owens and Margaret Mitchell. According to *Time:*

In the single year 1936 she became the most-talked-about, written-about, headlined and interest-compelling person in the world. In these respects, no woman in history has ever equalled Mrs. Simpson, for no press or radio existed to spread the world news they made.[18]

Both had achieved what they wanted, sort of, but of course it was never, ever enough. And when the chance came later to get even more of what they always wanted, they naturally took it.

10

The Adventure of Ednam Lodge

We must look for consistency. Where there is a want of it we must suspect deception.

Arthur Conan Doyle, 'The Problem of Thor Bridge', *The Casebook of Sherlock Holmes* (1927)

The Duke of Windsor, by October 1946, was a shadow of the man who had dazzled his subjects in the previous decade as Prince of Wales and King Emperor. It was all very sad and unfortunate, especially as the man's physical and emotional decline in the years since 1936 was so obvious.

One side of his face was visibly sagging and the purple bags under his eyes were as deep and tender as soft golf bunkers. He looked drained and the strain of the war years was etched deeply across his forehead like depleted volcanic fissures. Even unsympathetic observers like Tommy Lascelles, who spoke with him a year earlier in October 1945, during his lightning visit to London (without the duchess) to see the king and his mother, tried to put a positive spin on his condition:

The first thing that struck me about him was his voice, which seems to have got shriller, and is now more pronouncedly American than that of many Americans [...] He is noticeably, almost painfully thin, and his face is much lined though not unhappily.[1]

He was only 52.

Fans of the duke still remembered the time he flew from Hendon to Hamble Aerodrome in his De Havilland Puss Moth to inspect the new Canadian Pacific liner *Empress of Britain* at Southampton in May 1931. Immediately afterwards, he jauntily crossed Southampton Water in a speedboat to Hythe, where one of the new Imperial Airways flying boats was waiting for him. Climbing into the pilot's seat, he took off, roaring over the *Empress of Britain* as she steamed into the Solent, dipping the plane's wings in salute, before handing over the controls to the Imperial Airways pilot. When all this was done, he then nonchalantly returned to Hamble in a speedboat and flew in his own machine to Hendon, where he touched down at Walton Heath Golf Club in Surrey to play in a club competition. Just another day in the life of the most glamorous Prince of Wales in history.

How things had changed. The ennui that was an important facet of his nature, even charm, some would say, was of a different sort now than at the height of his dashing kingly presence. He seemed somewhat pummelled, as if all the zip and verve and charisma of his previous life had been squeezed out of him by the realities of his new position (or non-position) and status as perhaps the most famous has-been and cuckold in the world. His wife's increasing disdain, rapidly diminishing respect and icy contempt for the once mighty king, that had begun well before the start of the marriage, and which had manifested itself in reckless and wanton sexual promiscuity in the years since, was a major contributing factor.[2]

Life hadn't turned out the way the two of them had imagined. All their friends knew that Wallis, as a consequence of the huge intervening let-down in wealth, status and emotional compatibility, couldn't stand the little man – couldn't even stand to be alone with him – and took every opportunity to belittle and wound him as a substitute for her own pain. Lady Diana Cooper, a close observer of Wallis and Edward's relationship over time, summed up the common view of her circle, 'The truth is she's bored stiff by him, and her picking on him and her coldness towards him, far from policy, are irritation and boredom.'[3]

The war had changed everything and everybody, of course, but the Duke and Duchess of Windsor had endured an especially humiliating time of it. Nobody wanted them and nobody knew what to do with them. They were an expensive embarrassment and a blot on the British war effort.

Dragged back to Britain by Lord Mountbatten in September 1939 aboard HMS *Kelly*, the duke was reluctantly made a major general attached to the token British Military Mission in France. When Nazi Germany invaded that country in May 1940, the Windsors, along with a good chunk of the population, fled south to the relative safety of Vichy France. This was after the duke had provocatively asked German Wehrmacht forces to place guards at his Paris and Riviera homes.[4]

In June, they were in Spain. In July, the pair moved to Portugal, where the duke golfed, sunbathed and pursued a bizarre obsession for sardines while Nazi agents tried repeatedly and unsuccessfully to persuade him to return to Spain.

It was all too much for Churchill and his incredulous War Cabinet, who were exasperated by the pair's incessant demands and capacity for getting involved in diplomatic scrapes, conniving and escapades that bordered on treason and possible court martial (the duke was a commissioned serving officer). They were unceremoniously packed off to the Bahamas (described by the duchess as the 'moron paradise')[5] in August 1940, when the duke was appointed Governor. The appointment was scathingly received by everyone, including the Windsors. It was said the duke 'used to be First Lord of the Admiralty, but now he's third mate on an American tramp'.[6]

The Windsors spent the war bored and stuck in the petty bureaucratic backwater of this third-rate British colony, dogged by controversy after controversy: the continuing suspicion of collaboration with the Nazi regime, racism, anti-Semitism, money laundering, currency fraud, even complicity in a murder.[7] It seemed that wherever they went, they were rarely out of the limelight, whether benign or scurrilous. It was all part of the Windsor package.

No one in government seemed to trust them. There were always reservations. The Windsors frequently shot themselves in the foot when giving interviews, citing misquotation. It was never, ever their fault. Roosevelt bugged them whenever they holidayed in the United States, and they were under surveillance almost continuously throughout their Bahamian tenure.

They tried everything to escape. The duke's brother, King George VI, recorded in his diary one such attempt made directly to Churchill:

MAY 5, 1942: David has written to W [Churchill] asking to leave the Bahamas in August where he has been for two years. Where can he go, and what can he do? He cannot come here, anyhow, W & I are certain of this, the Dominions don't want him, there is nothing he can do in America, and he wants a temperate climate to live in. W suggests Southern Rhodesia, which is vacant.[8]

At the war's end, relieved and exhausted, a haggard duke resigned his post in March 1945 and the Windsors fled back to France as soon as they could. Britain was not an option, and that was made plain to them through various unofficial channels.

The previous summer, on 20 July 1944, the king and Churchill had a pleasant lunch in the air-raid shelter at Buckingham Palace, where the distasteful subject was discussed. The following Tuesday, the pair of them glumly agreed that, in the national interest, the duke and duchess could not be allowed to return to Britain after the war.[9]

At least France wasn't as grim as the UK, but it was still bad Food and fuel were in short supply and electricity could be cut off suddenly, sometimes for five hours at a stretch, with no advance warning. The restaurants were either closed or dependent on the black market, charging exorbitant amounts of black-market dollars for inferior food Only embassies could afford to give dinner parties.

The Windsors had access to British Army rations, so they were a good deal better off than most of their impoverished friends. Armed with a resourceful French chef and contacts everywhere, they still managed to put on a good show in the circumstances. The duchess told her Aunt Bessie of a dinner party on 2 January 1946, where they hosted seventeen friends at their Boulevard Suchet apartment, 'We had a buffet of hot dogs from the US, ham mousse from tinned ham, salade russe from tinned vegetables, sandwiches of cheese and cress, and black market eggs stuffed – our only extravagance',[10] – washed down with thirty bottles of champagne and three of whisky …

On another occasion, 'Halfway through dinner, a footman came in, carrying a bowl piled high with baked beans. Another followed with some form of meatloaf. There we were, in this very swank room, dressed to the nines, eating beans and hamburger.'[11]

By 1946, Wallis was already fed up and restless, endlessly decorating and redecorating their exquisite leased house, the Château de la Croë, on the Cap d'Antibes peninsula of the Côte d'Azur. The stockpiles of antique furniture, paintings, silver, porcelain and crystal, and the priceless heirlooms looted from royal residences in 1936 and stored at Frogmore, could finally begin their journey across the Channel to be reunited with the former king and his former mistress. The anticipation of finally surrounding themselves with the trophies of their former life wasn't, however, enough. It was never enough.

The duke was in a pitiful state, almost wholly dependent on the energy, verve and resourcefulness of his glamorous, flinty wife. He freely admitted to dinner partners that he had no purpose and was utterly bored with what he was doing. He told the wife of an American diplomat:

You know what my day was today? I got up late, and then I went with the Duchess and watched her buy a hat, and then on the way home I had the car drop me in the Bois to watch some of your soldiers playing football, and then I had planned to take a walk, but it was so cold that I could hardly bear it […] When I got home the Duchess was having her French lesson, so I had no one to talk to, so I got a lot of tin boxes down which my mother had sent me last week and looked through them. They were essays and so on that I had written when I was in France studying French before the Great War [...] You know I'm not much of a reading man.[12]

To alleviate *her* ennui, Wallis was rumoured to have begun an affair with Ireland's premier peer, Edward FitzGerald, 7th Duke of Leinster (dubbed 'the Shy Duke' by Wallis), who lived in a villa nearby with his third wife, the former musical comedy star Denise 'Jo' Orme.[13] Wallis, it was said, literally threw herself at 'Fitz' Leinster and would not take no for an answer.

The duke, meanwhile, sniffed an opportunity for redemption, perhaps even reinstatement. He could hardly believe his luck and jumped at the sheer implausibility of it, such was his desperation to be *doing* something. It would mean spending time in his former kingdom (the first since the truncated 1939 visit), something that Wallis dreaded. But the prize on offer (which included providing her pathetic husband with an occupation of sorts) was thrilling. She counted herself in, despite the shivering thought of leaving her sunny, lush life in the South of France and her twenty-two servants for another round of deprivation and humiliation.[14]

It was no mean sacrifice on her part. The difference between serious Britain and the easy-come, easy-go South of France in October 1946 couldn't be more pronounced. The Cap d'Antibes peninsula of the Côte d'Azur had attracted multimillionaires and celebrities from all over Europe since the belle époque, earning its moniker as the millionaires' playground. It seemed the logical choice when the duke and duchess were hunting for a home of their own after the abdication, eventually settling on the vacant Château de la Croë.

An eccentric American publisher, Sir Pomeroy Burton, had commissioned the construction of the château in 1926 as an elegant, colonial-style villa with seventeen bedrooms and eight bathrooms. White with green shutters and a red-tiled roof, it looked like a Christmas decoration, and directly faced the sea from its unobstructed rocky vantage point on 12 acres of cool woodland and immaculately manicured lawns.

The château, described as cool, serene and aloof, perfectly mirrored Wallis's personality. It was also massively proportioned and needed renovating to the duchess's taste. While this was done, the couple opted to stay nearby, renting suites at the Hotel Cap d'Antibes, which had a natural pool and an artificial *piscine* where fashionable Americans cavorted and bathed during the Season.

When the refurbishment was completed, the Windsors frequently hosted lavish receptions with liveried footmen and lackeys. Edward wore full Highland dress at dinner and pipers came out to play the bagpipes after the plates were cleared, which struck many guests as rather out of place in such a beach setting. The food was superb and fresh, the champagne and wine exclusive, the linen crisp, white and heavy.

On Christmas mornings, the Windsors and their visitors headed to the nearby small Anglican church, which the royal couple helped maintain for as long as they leased the château. In the afternoon, the Windsors would assemble their retinue of servants in the château's great hall and stand together in front of the Christmas tree to receive each one of their household staff and their respective families. They would shake hands and exchange pleasantries with their retainers, handing over gifts. Wallis and Edward were the king and queen of their world and their servants were their loyal subjects.

The Côte d'Azur, with its climate, casinos and exotic mix of tanned, well-fed people, was the place to have fun, experience luxury and eat and drink too much. It was an experience in excess; a fantasyland. It was a syrupy cocktail of delusion and degeneracy that was unsuccessfully satirised by Cyril Connolly in his only novel *The Rock Pool*. From the Carlton in Cannes to the Negresco in Nice and the Hôtel de Paris in Monte Carlo, from exotic châteaux and sparkling villas, life was a game of roulette, where fortunes, friendships and luck turned on the slap of a card or a furtive smile glimpsed on the run from the Belle Epoque casino by rich drifters, fickle heiresses, party animals, whores and gigolos, and the endless gravy train of war-damaged aristocrats.

Britain, by contrast, was bleak, damp and cold, without proper food and proper warmth; an austere, grim, permanently grey place exuding deprivation and devastation on a scale never seen before or since. The war was never as bad as the peace that now existed.

In Britain, the national debt had risen from £760 million to £3.5 billion by the end of the war and reserves of gold had fallen from £864 million to £3 million. The country had lost 30 per cent of its total wealth and had spent close to £7 billion on the war effort, spending £2 billion a year abroad in 1946 while earning only £350 million in return. Loans from America were vital, a matter of survival.

One in three houses had been destroyed by bombing while factories and shops had also been destroyed in large numbers. Twenty per cent of schools had been levelled or damaged. Britain had suffered 264,433 military and 60,595 civilian deaths during the war. Many others were physically and mentally scarred and unable to resume normal life. The post-war divorce rate was high, with over 60,000 applications processed in 1947. In total, 177 merchant ships and two-thirds of the navy had been sunk, meaning food supplies were a continuing problem.[15]

Rationing remained in place and continued to be in place until 1954. When it was first introduced in January 1940, sixty-six coupons a year were issued, but this soon dropped to forty-eight coupons a year, and by 1945, thirty-six coupons a year were given to each adult. A dress could cost eleven coupons, compared to a pair of stockings, which may only cost two. Another item, men's shoes, might cost seven coupons, with women's shoes costing five coupons. In 1945, an overcoat (wool and fully lined) was a grand total of eighteen coupons, a man's suit twenty-six to twenty-nine coupons (according to the lining), with children aged 14–16 getting twenty more coupons.

Meat was of course rationed, as was soap. Newspapers were limited to 25 per cent of pre-war consumption. Wrapping paper for most goods was prohibited. Items such as tinned goods, dried fruit, cereals and biscuits were rationed using a points system. The number of points allocated for each item accorded to the availability of that item and consumer demand. There were priority allowances of milk and eggs given to those most in need, which included children and expectant mothers. Bread, which was never rationed during wartime, was put on the ration in July 1946.

It wasn't all doom and gloom, although the bright spots were not on the sunshine scale of the Côte d'Azur. The cost of the average house was £620 in 1945, while the average salary was £214. The price of the average car was £310 and the price of a litre of fuel would have been 2p. The cost of a grocery shop would have been 45p.

So, what could possibly make the Windsors leave their sunny, bling-infested nirvana for a seriously gloomy place and the prospect of a seriously gloomy experience?

The answer is contained in the duke's correspondence with Kenneth de Courcy, a maverick, sometimes delusional, minor aristocrat. The letters, discovered in America and unearthed by Christopher Wilson in 2009, show the duke trying hard to contain his excitement while plotting his return from exile in France and regaining power in a compromised regency as the delicate health of King George VI deteriorated.

A heavy smoker, like his brother, father and grandfather, and prone to excessive stress and suffering because of his chronic stuttering and the visceral burden of being a sovereign in wartime, George's life was blighted by all kinds of physical ailments, including chronic stomach problems as well as knock knees, for which he was forced to wear painful corrective splints as a child. The subsequent development of lung cancer, among other setbacks (including arteriosclerosis and Buerger's disease), which affected his life after the war, posed the very real possibility in the minds of family and government that he might not be physically capable of continuing as monarch.

Some courtiers feared that George VI would become too ill to rule and the young Princess Elizabeth, 23, would effectively reign under the decisive political and social influence of Earl Mountbatten and Prince Philip of Greece. It was an unthinkable possibility – even more unthinkable for some than the unpalatable prospect of the return of a reviled ex-sovereign and his scheming wife. It was all a question of degree, as most soft *coup d'états* are.

For the Windsors, it was the mouth-watering prospect of revenge and tapping reinvigorated veins of wealth and privilege. For some sections of the Court (or was this just in de Courcy's head?), the anathema of Edward's return in a limited capacity was euthanised as a case of 'my enemy's enemy becoming my ally'. However, de Courcy was also aware of the possibility of treason and Edward's propensity for going after the full bag of tricks yet again. He suggested the duke resist regaining the throne and instead lay 'entirely fresh foundation-stones in place of those which are now endangered'.[16]

Edward was reinvigorated by the idea of a regency and answering de Courcy's call to thwart Mountbatten's burgeoning power grab for the Windsor dynasty. After relocating to Britain, the duke would simply wait in the shadows to be called to safeguard the throne. It was so much better than the alternative, as Wallis confided to Harold Nicholson, 'He was born to be a sales-man. He would be an admirable representative of Rolls-Royce. But an ex-King cannot start selling motor-cars.'[17]

In a letter to de Courcy dated 19 March 1946 and signed 'Edward', the duke refers to:

… the subject we discussed in Paris […] It certainly is a situation of great delicacy but, at the same time, one in which it would seem I hold fifty percent of the bargaining power in order that the Duchess and I can plan for the future in the most constructive and convenient way.[18]

The duchess was in on the scheming from the start. In a handwritten note to de Courcy on 18 July 1946, she wrote, 'We are always busy turning things around and around in our heads – there's no doubt that something must be done […] Anyway I can't sit by and see the Duke of Windsor wasted.'[19]

The original plan, as espoused by de Courcy, was for the duke to:

… buy an agricultural property somewhere near London and the Duke devote a good deal of his time to experimental farming on the most advanced modern lines. This would make a great appeal to the country

[...] Your property here ought to be sufficiently near London to make it possible for people to drive down for dinner, etc, and the [guest] lists should be most carefully considered [...] I venture to say that if this advice were followed, the results would be remarkable.[20]

The Windsors demurred to the next best thing: borrowing a supporter's country seat while they waited for the appropriate moment to arrive.

In the early hours of Saturday, 12 October 1946, the slumbering green fields and misty narrow laneways of Sunningdale in Berkshire were shattered by the wrenching progress of three army lorries under the command of an officer from the Royal Army Service Corps, transporting the duke and duchess's luggage to Ednam Lodge, the home of the Earl and Countess of Dudley. The Windsor visit was meant to be low-key (naturally, no attempt was made to solicit his sick brother's help in securing a suitable royal residence); the pretext given was a series of private visits with the duke's family and checking the inventory of the hoard of possessions that had been stored at Frogmore since the abdication for safe transfer to their residences in Paris and the Côte d'Azur.

To accommodate the privacy and security of the couple while on English soil, the Dudleys intended to decamp to temporary lodgings at Claridge's but were on hand to greet their guests at their 'suburban villa'.[21] The Windsors were met at Dover on 11 October by supporters and driven to Ednam Lodge, with a brief detour to Fort Belvedere, which they found in a sad, dilapidated state. Unbeknown to his family, the duke had been quietly disposing of Belvedere furniture not deemed valuable enough to be stored at Frogmore through the aegis of George Allen, Wallis's solicitor, who had drawn up her will when she was last on English soil.[22]

Eventually arriving at close to midnight with maids and servants in tow, including Sydney Johnson, the Bahamian valet the duke had employed in the Bahamas who would spend the next thirty years in his service, the Windsors sat up for a while sipping brandy and smoking. The next morning, the duke and duchess were due to meet the press in the gardens, after which they planned for a quiet weekend settling in at the house, travelling to London for some family visits the following week and several trips to Frogmore. Fort Belvedere was out of bounds under direct orders from an ailing king.

At some stage, while the duke and earl drank and smoked during the small hours of the 12th, Laura, the Countess of Dudley, claimed that Wallis gave her a peek at the jewellery she had brought with her, housed in its specially constructed case. The countess was aghast. The normal travelling case that was used by the aristocracy in such circumstances (usually a plusher version of Mrs Ronnie's black tin box) was in Wallis's situation a trunk – one of three identical trunks she travelled with to confuse would-be thieves.

The trunk was so big (about the size of a large carry-on suitcase) that the countess prevailed on Wallis to store it in the burglar-alarmed strongroom where the family silver was kept in the butler's pantry. Wallis declined, laughing that she always kept her babies under whichever bed her maid was using at the time.

It wasn't just the bulky nature of the trunk that amazed the countess but also its contents. In her autobiography, *Laughter from a Cloud*, she claimed she 'examined the contents' of the duchess's jewel box and it had contained 'a great many uncut emeralds which I believe belonged to Queen Alexandra'.[23] Scotland Yard's case file challenges this claim. According to the police report released by The National Archives in 2003, 'They [Lord and Lady Dudley] naturally assumed that the Duchess would have brought some jewellery with her, but neither had any idea that she had brought such a large quantity'.[24]

The confusion on such a mundane, routine matter as the contents of Wallis's jewellery trunk is just one of the enduring mysteries of the Windsors' stay at Ednam Lodge in October 1946. A precise inventory of the jewellery the duchess brought with her has never been found and probably never will be. This absence continues to cloud the veracity of later claims made by the royal pair in the days following their installation in rural England.

But for now, the Windsors settled in to their first-floor rooms overlooking the front of the house and the Dudleys moved out.

On Wednesday, 16 October, the duke and duchess travelled to London to dine with the Dudleys. Following the set below-stairs lodge schedule, at 5.30 p.m. the evening bell rang, calling the sixteen members of staff and the detective guarding the house to their evening meal, which was taken in the staff dining room, quite a distance from the duchess's bedroom.

Meanwhile, for some unfathomable (and ultimately extremely suspicious) security reason, the duchess had ordered her maid to move the trunk containing the various jewellery boxes into the duchess's bedroom after she had left for London, where it was to be rested in front of the fireplace. The duchess's maid at the time, a Miss Martin, later told police she was going on holiday the following Friday and she and the duchess had thought it best to bring the trunk to the duchess's room on the Wednesday and not leave it until the day she (the maid) went away.[25] It later transpired that this Miss Martin was the only one, apart from the duchess, who knew which of the identical trunks contained her jewellery.

The inscrutable Miss Martin made her way to the staff dinner a few minutes later, returning to the duchess's room around 7 p.m., where she discovered the resting trunk had been crudely pried open; some pieces of jewellery lay scattered about the room like confetti and some individual jewellery boxes were missing.

The mystery of Ednam Lodge had begun.

11

The Mystery of Ednam Lodge

'Is there any point to which you would wish to draw my attention?'
'To the curious incident of the dog in the night-time.'
'The dog did nothing in the night-time.'
'That was the curious incident,' remarked Sherlock Holmes.

Arthur Conan Doyle, 'Silver Blaze',
The Memoirs of Sherlock Holmes (1893)

News of the Windsor burglary was gleefully published across the world with its customary loose attention to detail. The front page of the *New York Times* for 18 October reported:

In one of Britain's most audacious robberies, thieves escaped with jewels belonging to the Duchess of Windsor after having broken into the holiday home of the Duke and Duchess last night. The jewels were worth $100,000. [...] Scotland Yard detectives declared today that the robbery was the work of an expert. They had been called in by the local police at the request of the Duke.[1]

Time magazine followed up a few days later:

In the misty Berkshire dusk, while the Windsors were in London (he at
the Palace to see the King, she, excluded, to have tea with an unnamed
friend), a nimble burglar had slipped past two Scotland Yard detectives, clambered up a drainpipe at rambling, red brick Ednam Lodge
and gained entrance to the Windsors' white-walled bedroom. He went
to a Gladstone bag, removed a brown leather jewel case. From a small
leather box on the Duke's bedside table, he plucked a valuable watch.
Two hundred yards away, he stopped, picked through the jewel case,
discarded some inexpensive hatpins. Then he drove away. According
to the Duchess, he had stolen every jewel she owned except those she
had on. The loss: (Windsors' estimate) $80,000. At week's end, those
few clear facts had been culled out of the mad confusion of the world
press. In London, the *Daily Mail* fell overboard, estimated the value of
the loot at $2 million. U.S. papers wildly reported that two socialite
women were under suspicion, and that the Duchess had stored part
of her million-dollar collection in a safe-deposit vault. The Duchess
regretfully denied that one: 'It was stupid. I've been kicking myself all
over the place.' The Duchess was asked to describe the basis on which
she selected jewels to match her costumes. She said: 'A fool would
know that with tweeds or other daytime clothes one wears gold and
with evening clothes one wears platinum.' Among the missing was her
famous diamond stork-shaped clip; a pair of diamond and sapphire
earrings; a 58.2 carat aquamarine ring.

Although the chic Duchess was calm, the proud, pathetic little
Duke was blazing mad. His never-good chance of a Government job
(he wanted the Governor Generalship of Australia) had been crushed
between the rollers of Fleet Street's presses. An $80,000 jewel collec-
tion stood for the kind of life no longer popular with austerity ridden
Britons or Australian socialists. Said Windsor: 'I don't think I will play
very good golf this afternoon.'[2]

In the immediate aftermath of Miss Martin's discovery, the police were
called and the duke and duchess quickly returned from London with the
Dudleys. Several police officers also converged on Ednam Lodge and its

surroundings, including Assistant Commissioner R.M. Howe, Chief Inspector Capstick from Scotland Yard and fingerprint experts.

The burglary was the worst possible thing that could have happened during the Windsors' planned low-key, discreet visit. The resulting PR fallout was an unmitigated disaster in a country still suffering under the clenched fist of austerity with rising disgust at the flaunting of personal wealth that may have been acceptable in the previous decade but was certainly not in the present straitened circumstances. The Windsors, seemingly incapable of realising the change in mood and responding in fashion, contrived to contribute to the false and incomplete information that floated out. Or maybe the duchess realised, in a savvy flash of inspiration, the disaster had a silver lining after all: if only one had the courage to *grasp* the chance of glory it tantalisingly offered? But that wasn't the immediate reaction.

The duchess's fury on returning to Ednam Lodge was palpable. She insisted on the police grilling the Dudleys' household, much to the annoyance of Lady Dudley, and then the duke insisted on the police arresting a demented vagrant who had been seen in the vicinity of the house and Sunningdale golf course. After a spell behind bars, the poor man was released when it became clear such a hopeless case could not have been responsible for such a physically demanding theft.

There was one ray of sunshine in the whole unsavoury business. One of the items that escaped the robbery was the duchess's Cartier brooch made of rubies and sapphires forming the couple's intertwined initials, 'W' and 'E', which the duke had given her during the abdication crisis and which she wore the day of the robbery. The couple had been using 'WE' in a variety of ways in their correspondence since early in their relationship and it became an important symbol of their union. It was either extremely lucky or, as some with a jaundiced view of the Windsor predicament maintained, it had been previously arranged to reside on her lapel and not in the jewellery trunk at Ednam Lodge. Either way, it couldn't be added to the stolen list because it was so obviously on the duchess's person throughout the immediate aftermath as witnessed by the police. Not even the Windsors could wave that fact away.

But that didn't prevent another extraordinary development, typical of the mixture of absurdity and farce which suffused the entire situation. Wallis's mood sank even further into the abyss when it was discovered that another piece of jewellery (a brooch) that was not in her jewellery trunk, and therefore not part of the stolen haul, was also missing. The blame fell on the hapless, befuddled figure of the duke, who had been the last person to have handled it.

The poor man was compelled to turn over the house, even to the extent of getting down on all fours to peer under beds, chairs and other pieces of furniture when it suddenly dawned on him that for some completely inexplicable reason he had left it under a vase for safekeeping! Apparently pale and exhausted and on the verge of tears, the trembling ex-king presented it to Wallis, receiving an icy, disbelieving stare in return for his efforts.[3]

The story of the recovered brooch becomes even more extraordinary when it appears it was a brand-new brooch delivered by Cartier on the morning of the robbery. Described as a jewelled bird of paradise with a large 65-carat cabochon sapphire forming the bird's breast and at least 350 small diamonds and no fewer than a dozen other precious gems, it was created using gems purportedly in the Windsors' collection. Later, the duke enigmatically said he knew that Cartier shouldn't have delivered the brooch when they did.[4] Much later, the Windsors claimed it (valued at the time at £20,000) was also part of the stolen cache of jewellery.[5]

More incomprehensibility was to follow. Several unmatched earrings were found by an eagle-eyed caddie, scattered around the golf course, and Ednam Lodge staff found abandoned Fabergé boxes belonging to the duke, which were kept on a tray at the bottom of the trunk, bizarrely still on the tray and resting on a windowsill. Most intriguing of all were rumours that a string of pearls worth £5,000 that had belonged to Queen Alexandra was one of the items found by the caddie. This is strange because the most significant pearl necklace in the duchess's collection was the one she wore to the duke's funeral, which had been passed to the duke by his mother, Queen Mary. Which also begs the question why such an immensely valuable piece, if it existed, was discarded or abandoned?

Discrepancies and anomalies like the pearl necklace (as noted by Scotland Yard in the case file and subsequent amateur sleuths around the world during the past seventy years) began piling up almost immediately from the start of the investigation. They are:

1   At the time of the burglary (between 6–7 p.m. on 16 October) none of the servants saw or heard anything and none of the dogs belonging to either the duke and duchess or the Dudleys barked. The dogs either knew the culprits or they had been removed from causing any disturbances. The Scotland Yard case file confirms that the Dudleys' head housemaid was out walking at least one (and perhaps two) of the dogs during the time the burglary was committed. Why wasn't the housemaid at the staff meal?

2   The thief or thieves knew exactly what they were doing and where to go. It was all over in a matter of minutes. Ednam Lodge was entered via an upstairs open window in the bedroom of Lady Dudley's daughter, sometime after the bell sounded calling all staff and servants (including the detective guarding the house) to the evening meal. Once inside the house, the thief/thieves walked through a short corridor and straight into the duchess's bedroom, where the locked (or was it, in fact?) jewellery trunk conveniently and appealingly rested in front of the fire. The burglars most probably escaped via the same window where the duke's Fabergé boxes were later found. Nothing else was taken that night and there was no sign of forced searches elsewhere in the house, including Lady Dudley's bedroom, where some of her jewellery lay in plain sight on the dressing table.

3   Accounts also diverge over the means of entry. While Scotland Yard concluded the burglars climbed up a drainpipe, crossed a flat roof and entered via the open window, most contemporary accounts

suggested the burglars shimmied up a white rope attached to the window. Maybe the reason for the rope was the added burden of coping with jewellery boxes?

4   Another discrepancy involves the number of items that were dis-covered on the Sunningdale golf course and their location. No one – Scotland Yard detectives, so-called eyewitnesses, let alone the media – could agree on either at the time of the robbery.

But perhaps the biggest discrepancy or controversy, in true Windsor fashion, concerns what exactly was stolen and their real versus their insured values.

Most historians generally agree that around ten significant pieces were stolen and never recovered. News reports at the time sensationally estimated the stolen jewellery was worth the nice round obscene figure of £500,000. The befuddled and acutely embarrassed duke, reacting to offensive rumours that he had instigated the entire robbery himself, told journalists the loss was worth only a paltry £20,000. This is a strange assertion considering the new Cartier Bird of Paradise brooch that had been delivered on the morning of the robbery and, though later found, had subsequently 'disappeared' with the rest of the stolen jewels was worth £20,000 on its own. The value of the recovered jewellery alone (the eighteen mismatched earrings found on Sunningdale golf course nearby) was estimated at £5,000.[6]

The valuation of the Bird of Paradise brooch and the duke's evasive behaviour and misleading comments regarding how much the other jewels cost did little to dispel the belief that the Windsors were some-how complicit in what was obviously an 'inside job' of some kind. The police report had an each way bet on both theories, indicating that while it 'seems incredible that this offence could have been committed with-out collusion, past experience proves that most climbing thieves operate with the knowledge that all the staff are absent from the upper rooms at meal times. This was clearly planned by an experienced cat burglar.'[7]

The stolen jewels were officially insured for £400,000, according to the Windsors' assessors, Summers, Henderson & Co. of Leadenhall Street. Here is their list of the stolen items which was published under press duress, along with some photographs:

one diamond bird clip
one diamond aquamarine brooch
one platinum & diamond bracelet w/6 large aquamarines
one aquamarine ring w/solitaire aquamarine (58.2 carats)
one gold ring set w/one golden sapphire (41.4 carats)
one solitaire square cut emerald ring (7.81 carats)
one pair diamond & sapphire earrings
one pair of diamond ball earrings
one pair of earrings in shape of a shell (one set w/blue sapphire, the
    other w/yellow sapphire)
one double gold chain necklace w/one large blue sapphire and one
    yellow sapphire
et cetera.[8]

No one knows what the words 'et cetera' implied, although some have interpreted this to mean the mythical, uncut Queen Alexandra emeralds as cited by Lady Dudley.

As previously stated, Nicholas Rayner, Sotheby's 1987 auctioneer of the duchess's jewellery collection, disputed the existence of these mythical gems altogether, 'I don't believe the Alexandra emeralds ever existed. We've found no evidence of them at all. I believe the story was simply malicious gossip started by people who were offended by the marriage. They wanted to believe the Duchess stole jewels belonging to the royal crown.'[9]

Rayner, like any good auctioneer worth his salt, was determined to keep things simple. The only provenance that mattered to Sotheby's was the certainty the jewellery was the Duchess of Windsor's. Where the Windsors sourced them from was their own private business. Probably the safest bet is that 'et cetera' was meant to include the missing odd earrings from the duchess's jewellery trunk.

A striking omission from the published list, although surely not covered by the words 'et cetera', was the imposing diamond Cartier tiara the duke had given Wallis as a wedding present, which contained four large centre diamonds and three curved upright fingers of smaller diamonds mounted on platinum. The duchess specifically mentioned this item in interviews with reporters and it is strange that such a stand-out item wasn't included in the Summers, Henderson & Co. inventory along with the Cartier Prince of Wales feather brooch.[10]

At some point between the date of the robbery on 16 October and the Windsors' eventual departure from the country with their dogs and servants and 155 pieces of Goyard and Louis Vuitton luggage (eighty suitcases in their suite, seventy-five cabin trunks in the hold)[11] bound for the United States aboard the *Queen Elizabeth* on 6 November, the opportunity for reaping a lucrative return out of the chaos of the ghastly situation was tenaciously grasped. Perhaps it was precipitated by the gradual recovery from illness of King George VI at the end of October, which made the whole purpose of the Windsors' visit itself somewhat moot.

Throughout the late 1940s King George was in and out of hospital with increasing regularity and, despite the urgings of de Courcy, the Windsors never really took the whole regency proposition seriously again. By 1949, the king had undergone an operation on a nerve at the base of his spine to mitigate the arteriosclerosis caused by the stress of the war and his heavy smoking. In a letter dated 13 May 1949, de Courcy wrote to the duchess:

The King is gravely ill and out of circulation and he will not be in circulation again [...] the King faces the fearful tragedy of losing first one leg then the other [...] The King will be able to do extremely little and moreover that those around him will gain greater and greater power. I may tell you most confidentially that a Regency has already been discussed and it seems likely enough that presently a Regent will be appointed.[12]

This time, the Windsors did not bite, having already been previously bitten by de Courcy's colourful imagination and exaggerated prospects for the duke and duchess. By the time the king died in February 1952, they had settled into their rather aimless, louche lives on the high society social scene, reduced to watching Queen Elizabeth II's coronation on the television screen at the Paris home of Mrs Margaret Biddle, the American millionaire.

The Ednam Lodge episode was rather a watershed moment for them, scuppering whatever chances they had of ever returning to England permanently. They seemed to take the setback with a pinch of salt and marched purposely onwards into trivialities and their infinite scrounge for free money.

Their change of tack regarding the 1946 burglary was perhaps intended to salvage something out of the wreckage of these misplaced hopes. Whatever the reason, it wasn't long before the mischievous couple went on the offensive about the stolen jewels and deliberately created and contributed to the false, incomplete and misleading information that seeped out (e.g. the Cartier brooches and tiara). Safely aboard Suite 58A on the main deck of the luxury liner, the duke was able to console himself with a special batch of 30-year-old whisky sourced from supplies still maintained by his Jermyn Street wine merchants and a hefty cheque, courtesy of his jittery insurers eager to honour the claim and draw a line under the entire sorry affair in their books.

The secrecy surrounding the pay-out amount is natural enough, but the speed of the settlement is simply astounding. The settlement was not only extremely generous, uniquely paying for all the lost pieces to be replaced and reinsuring the new collection for £800,000, it was conducted with such alacrity and deference that even the police were struck by the goodwill of the insurers at a time when there was not a lot of goodwill being splashed around the country. Scandal and bad publicity were never far from the Windsors, and seemed to follow closely in their wake, which perhaps was another contributing factor in Messrs Summers, Henderson & Co. paying out so quickly.

Subsequent events seemed to reinforce their haste to put the distasteful mess behind them and the possibility of further embarrassment. This included the absurd rumour that Buckingham Palace was responsible for the robbery in an attempt to rescue some of the jewels previously looted from the Royal Collection by the ex-king.

A few days after the theft, Lady Dudley was shopping in Mayfair when she was approached by a plain-clothes policeman, who asked to inspect her heirloom diamond clip that was in the form of Prince of Wales feathers, much like the sapphire and diamond Cartier clip the duchess had worn at her wedding and was now missing. Obviously, she was being tailed and obviously, she was under suspicion. She was left feeling rather annoyed and soiled.

Almost immediately after the burglary, people claimed to have either seen the duchess wearing gems that were purportedly stolen or seen the stolen gems in different settings. This included an incident in late 1946 when Frances Goldwyn, the wife of movie tycoon Samuel Goldwyn, thought she recognised some of the stolen jewels in a Bond Street jeweller before they were quickly withdrawn.[13]

One authority who was convinced of the Windsors' duplicity and fraud was Leslie Field, author of *The Queen's Jewels: The Personal Collection of Elizabeth II*, written with the co-operation of the royal household. She emphatically told the biographer Charles Higham:

I believe the Duchess of Windsor defrauded the insurers by overstating the numbers and identifications of the jewels which had been disposed of. At least thirty items she named as being stolen turned up in the Sotheby's catalogue at Geneva in April 1987 and were sold for high prices. She clearly could never wear those jewels again after she and her husband had collected the insurance. They had from the beginning been in a strongbox in Paris and remained there.[14]

Or maybe not. A year after the robbery, the duke and duchess provided Cartier with a large quantity of loose stones, including amethysts, emeralds, diamonds, sapphires and rubies, which were incorporated into new

Windsor pieces and settings. Then, in the 1960s, the duke and duchess deposited at Cartier a further five 'cloudy deep green'[15] emeralds and a large quantity of diamonds that were used to create one of her fabulous necklaces.

This steady stream of immensely valuable gems seems to indicate the couple had recourse to a large bank of jewels after the robbery. Of course, after the insurance settlement there was plenty of cash to buy new jewels and revamp old jewellery settings by remodelling them in the latest fashion, such as her 20-carat emerald engagement ring reset by Cartier in 1958. This would have been a clever ploy to blur a perceived fraud based, as it was, on the perfectly natural and plausible desire of an eminent and fashionable lady to keep up to date with the latest trends. By breaking down the stolen jewels into loose stones for resetting and using the insurance money to fund the new work, the Windsors were covering their tracks in the most ingeniously contrived way.

If this was the case, then it is reasonable to assume that the Prince of Wales feather Cartier brooch listed in Sotheby's 1987 auction is a replica of the original. And Cartier, far from covering up the action, recognises that it was and still is a commonplace practice. The issue of Windsor replicas even made its way into a gushing Cartier publication, the author Hans Nadelhoffer disingenuously noting, 'The replacement pieces were of artistic rather than obvious material value'.[16]

The questionable practice was not so much the replication of favourite items but the passing them off as originals.

12

The Secret of Ednam Lodge

Holmes took up the stone and held it against the light. 'It's a bonny thing,' said he. 'Just see how it glints and sparkles. Of course it is a nucleus and focus of crime. Every good stone is. They are the devil's pet baits. In the larger and older jewels every facet may stand for a bloody deed.'

Arthur Conan Doyle, 'The Adventure of the Blue Carbuncle',
The Adventures of Sherlock Holmes (1892)

So, whodunnit?

The Ednam Lodge case was closed in 1961 and the stolen Windsor jewels have never officially been recovered. Although the haul was estimated to be worth £13 million in today's money and was the biggest reported theft of 1946, it pales in comparison with other heists before and after.

For the record, probably the biggest, most audacious heist in modern history (jewellery or otherwise) is commonly thought to be Natwarlal's con. 'Natwarlal' was the alias of Mithilesh Kumar Srivastava, who, posing as a government official, purportedly 'sold' the Taj Mahal to various wealthy foreign industrialists. Not once, but three times!

In India, felons who pull off particularly smart cons are often called *natwarlal*. This particular *natwarlal* started off selling autographs of celebrities and moved on to bigger things like the Taj Mahal, the Parliament House of India (included in the purchase were the Members of Parliament themselves), the Red Fort and the Rashtrapati Bhavan.[1] He was a master of disguise and had over fifty different aliases. At one stage, he faced fourteen convictions with gaol sentences running to 113 years and was last officially spotted at the New Delhi railway station on 4 June 1996 while he was being transported from prison in Kanpur to the AIIMS hospital for treatment. He vanished from the wheelchair at the age of 84. Though active in 1946, it is unlikely he was seduced by a syndicate to rob the Windsors in dreary, cold, austerity-riven Britain. He had bigger heists, in sunnier climes, on his mind.

Despite the absence of a glamorous *natwarlal*, the conundrum of the stolen Windsor jewels still fascinates. Its allure, despite the release of Scotland Yard's case file by The National Archives at Kew, is possibly due to many of the known facts and acknowledged clues surrounding the burglary remaining a bit of a puzzle, if not downright perplexing.

Take the apparent disarray in the duchess's bedroom, the Fabergé boxes on the windowsill and the various unmatched earrings strewn about the rough at Sunningdale golf course. This might be evidence of panic on behalf of the robbers, spooked by the provenance of the jewels they had snatched, or it might be a deliberate ruse to throw suspicion off a sophisticated and seasoned operator on to the possibility of an amateur out of their depth. Or it just might be sheer incompetence on behalf of a thief, or even bad luck, which is not uncommon in spectacular heists.

Car trouble got in the way of what would have been the biggest art heist in history in April 1991 when armed gunmen took twenty Van Goghs from the Vincent Van Gogh National Museum in Amsterdam. One of the thieves hid in the museum until after closing and then let his accomplice in after nightfall. The gunmen forced the guards (one of whom was later named as an accomplice) to disarm the security systems and then tied them up. Not in any hurry, the duo took a leisurely approach, spending over forty-five minutes perusing the works before choosing their favourites and tucking their selections into garment bags.

In a surprising twist, the Van Goghs were found in a car at a nearby railway station less than an hour later. Another car was meant to rendezvous with the robbers, but it had got a flat tyre and when it failed to arrive, the spooked bandits abandoned the Dutch master's sunflowers, irises and potato eaters in the first car and disappeared. The haul was estimated at nearly $500 million in value. Four men, including a guard, were later arrested for the crime.

Even more ridiculous, in 2012, a pair of would-be vandals broke into a Stockholm house with plans to abscond with a trio of paintings including 'Clair-Obscur', a sentimental canvas by painter Carl Larsson, creator of the so-called Swedish style of painting. But the bandits hadn't accounted for the size of their vehicle. When the 4ft by 3ft work refused to fit inside their compact Ford car, the thieves were forced to ditch the painting, nearly running it over as they fled. Two smaller paintings were discovered in a nearby dumpster.

One aspect the Ednam Lodge robbery was never short of was suspects, however lunatic, improbable or downright incapable they may have been. Suzy Menkes, in *The Windsor Style*, even wrote that the mystery was bizarrely solved in 1960 when a man named Richard 'Tiptoe' Dunphie confessed to participating in the theft along with three accomplices.[2]

Ignoring the lunatic fringe that always attaches itself to notorious cases, the Scotland Yard case file maintains that a former bricklayer, Leslie Arthur Charles Holmes, was the primary suspect for many years. Holmes was also a prominent housebreaker, living in Sunningdale and working as a handyman on the Dudley estate, making repairs to a statue in the garden when the robbery was committed. He was questioned but not detained. A year later, he was sentenced at Surrey Quarter Sessions to three years in prison for twenty-six cases of housebreaking and larceny. There was never enough evidence to try him for the Windsor robbery, however. When he lost his appeal on the severity of the original sentencing, the Court of Appeal (Criminal Division) increased it to five years.

Holmes never confessed to the Ednam Lodge robbery. Despite his denials, Detective Inspector John Capstick of Scotland Yard (seconded to the investigation from Special Branch's 'Ghost Squad') was so sure Holmes was the thief that he frequently visited him in gaol and sent him a Christmas card every year to gain both his trust and information about the location of the jewels. Police even dug up Holmes's garden to find evidence. In 1951, Capstick told the FBI, 'There is little doubt that he has buried the jewellery and I am convinced that he is afraid to dispose of it.'[3]

Apart from Holmes, police naturally believed the robbery was, to a large degree, an inside job but couldn't prove it. Prior to his obsession with Holmes, and with no immediate strong leads and few clues, DI Capstick initially believed a London gang was responsible for the robbery. This was after discounting household servants, the Dudleys, the Windsors themselves and even the royal family, who it was rumoured had orchestrated the robbery to recover jewels that had belonged in the Royal Collection.

It wasn't long before the investigation was drowning in a surfeit of exotic foreign and homegrown suspects (there was a very sophisticated jewellery theft ring operating around London at the time). The 1930s, 1940s and 1950s represented the golden age of solo jewellery heists, when the glamorous Mediterranean-style cat burglar, in the fictional mould of John Robie (played by Cary Grant in Hitchcock's *To Catch a Thief*), represented the sexy superstar of world thievery.

Given that Ednam Lodge was, by all appearances, breached by a thief or thieves who shimmied up a drainpipe and exited roughly the same way through an upstairs window, the attribution of the crime to a cat burglar or cat burglars seemed plausible. Defined as a particularly stealthy kind of burglar who gains undetected entry using agility, newspapers first coined the phrase 'cat burglar' in 1907 to describe someone with a particular 'skill in climbing'.[4] It was in the 1930s that the profession achieved a steady rise in notoriety.

The key to the cat burglars' fame was the fact they were sensationalised as practising a more daring form of burglary than had ever been undertaken before. Not only daring, but also supremely cool and calculating, their demeanour oozing with sangfroid. No wall was too high, no rooftop too treacherous to prevent them from reaching their quarry. In their published memoirs, biographies, even in the transcripts of their police interrogations and court cases, they attributed the adrenaline rush, the buzz, the sheer exhilaration of pulling off a job and getting away with the fabulous hoard of loot as the driving force behind their actions.

Writing about it in *Nine Lives: Confessions of a Master Jewel Thief*, the canny thief Bill Mason, who plundered more than $70 million worth of jewels in three decades at the tail end of the twentieth century, maintained there was nothing in the world quite like hanging by your fingertips from a parapet, 200ft above the ground, knowing that a treasure trove of precious stones is only a few metres away:

> You get addicted to the thrill. You know someone is living up there in Penthouse B with a couple of million in jewels, because you have done your homework and read the gossip columns. And they have all this security, from the cameras in the lobby to the guards who patrol the corridors, but you have done all the planning, very, very carefully, and you have got around it all. So you are hanging there by your fingertips, like climbing a mountain, and in a few minutes all the pieces of the jigsaw fit together and you are in. And the jewels! Because you know that this lady is having her hair fixed before tonight's ball, it is all there, right there, laid out on the bed for you. And she has left the safe open. Boy. Let me tell you: it feels really, really good.[5]

John Robie in *To Catch a Thief* had a more prosaic way of putting the other side of the equation, the drab thrill of the detective nabbing a suspect in the act, to Frances Stevens, his love interest played by Grace Kelly:

> Frances Stevens: I've never caught a jewel thief before. It's stimulating. It's like ... It's like...
> John Robie: Like sitting in a hot tub?[6]

Cat burglars were sexy. Their escapades were tinged with fear, suspense and menace. They sliced through the defences of the rich and untouchable and breached their inner sanctums with all the finesse of a silky surgeon. The newspapers loved them. Mark Benney, the self-proclaimed perpetrator of more than 100 cat burglaries, described his crimes in a series of newspaper articles in 1937. In the process, he disclosed a particularly creepy fetish for stealing 'the gossamer silk underwear' of women as they lay sleeping.[7]

The public fascination was mirrored in popular Victorian and Edwardian fiction. The 'gentleman thief' Arthur J. Raffles, the fictional criminal mastermind whose burglaries were rarely ever traced, adroitly described the compelling motive behind this particular branch of crime, 'Why should I work when I could steal? Why settle down to some humdrum uncongenial billet, when excitement, romance, danger, and a decent living were all going begging together?'[8]

Convicted burglar George Smithson (or 'Raffles in Real Life', as he dubbed himself in his autobiography of 1930) was one of a growing number of criminals who tried to leverage the Raffles tactic of only targeting the mansions of wealthy aristocrats to garner public sympathy for their crimes. Smithson described how, having breached the country mansion of Lady Helen Salt through 'the servants' parlour window on the second floor [I] crawled inside, panting, breathlessly waiting to see if any lights appeared or if anybody knew I was there'.[9] Though frightened, he recalled his determination that, 'given a stroke of luck, there were coronets, tiaras and a multitude of heirlooms and family jewels, as can be found only in the mansions of the old and established families of our land [to steal]'.[10]

Another burglar lionised by the popular press of the day was Robert Delaney, who was arrested for the first time in 1925 for breaking and entering the Duke of Rutland's mansion near Green Park in London. People like the larger-than-life Delaney, who lived life on the razor's edge, seduced their victims when invited and generally flaunted the stuffy conventions of rigid British society (he was also later charged with bigamy), sold newspapers. 'Cat burglar who holds women fascinated!'

declared the *Daily Mirror* headline on 20 December 1934, the ensuing breathless story labelling the profligate Delaney the 'king of cat burglars'.

The most glamorous and audacious twentieth-century cat burglar operating in Europe at the time was a woman. The plush corridors of the Hôtel Impérial on Nice's illustrious Promenade des Anglais in the bluey predawn hours of 8 March 1908 were silent as only a luxury hotel's corridors can be. But down one thickly carpeted dark hallway, a slim woman in a menacing black outfit moved noiselessly, caressed by the slumbering shadows. On her person she carried a set of English, custom-made silver lockpicks. Newspaper accounts breathlessly detailed what happened next:

> ... thinking that she was no longer watched, [she] started out on one of her adventures. She naturally took the precaution to change her costume, and, whereas during the day she went about in most stylish toilette, she now had nothing on but a tight-fitting jacket and skirt of knitted wool, sandals with felt soles, to make as little noise as possible, and a black veil over her head [...] detectives were surprised at the transformation, and watched her stealing noiselessly down the dimly-lighted corridor until she was in front of the room occupied by a wealthy couple.[11]

What this woman did not realise was that after years of near misses, blind alleys and fruitless pursuits (she had first come to the attention of the French police in 1892 but continued to operate around the Mediterranean for another sixteen years until her arrest), French detectives were finally about to catch the extraordinary Comtesse de Monteil in the act:

> Two detectives finally followed her to the Riviera, where she stopped in one of the finest hotels. The pseudocountess was quick, however, to suspect that she was being watched, and changed her hotel, after sending her baggage to the railway station, as if she were going to take a train. But the police detectives were not so easily hoodwinked, and followed her to her new hotel, where they took rooms near her own.[12]

The 'pseudocomtesse', as the newspapers dubbed her, was a jewel thief, cat burglar and con artist, as well as the alleged leader of a ring of thieves that stretched across the Mediterranean's most opulent tourist destinations. The capture of the Comtesse de Monteil was an immediate media sensation, making international headlines. Reports emphasised her beauty and cunning, calling her 'The Spider' and 'Queen of Thieves'.[13] Exhaustive coverage detailed her lavish lace evening gowns and state-of-the-art luggage, which transformed into a full-size armoire:

> … when her room was examined it was found stocked with all sorts of housebreaker's instruments, small electric pocket lamps, and keys of all descriptions, together with a list of the hotels to be visited, and the location and numbers of the rooms where wealthy guests would be staying. She had besides some 20,000f. worth of jewels and 4,000f. in cash in her possession.[14]

It's no surprise that the arrest, and most of her crimes, took place in Nice, one of the most famous cities of the Côte d'Azur, which includes the principality of Monaco and the seedy French Riviera, 'a sunny place for shady people', as novelist W. Somerset Maugham called it.[15] It was an area full of wealthy 'marks' attracted by the area's popularity with movie stars, business moguls, royals (like the Windsors) and wealthy, bored people who indulged in flouting the laws and conventions of their stuffy home countries and cloying families.

Though based in Paris, the Comtesse de Monteil (a name she gave herself) apparently restricted her criminal activity to locations associated with elegant luxury travel: Geneva, Alexandria, Monte Carlo and the towns of the French Riviera. Her chosen beat was not without its dangers. French nobility was a closed society and the pseudocomtesse risked giving herself away on a daily basis through a minute slip in etiquette or by mispronouncing a particular name ever so slightly. However, she had chosen the location of her nefarious dealings well as the aristocracy rarely visited the Riviera during this period and she could execute her deceptions undetected.

In fact, hoteliers and wealthy foreign tourists welcomed the Comtesse de Monteil, delighted to host a supposed member of the elite who deigned to rub elbows with them, 'Reports have it that at Biarritz, Arcachon, and other places where she stayed, she was very well considered by the genuine nobility, who took no trouble to inquire into her title'.[16]

Her method of operation was simple enough. She would observe her fellow hotel guests and travellers, calculating their habits, idiosyncrasies and difficulty as targets – a notebook detailing her assessments was discovered in a search of her luxuriously furnished Paris apartment following her arrest:

Mr and Mrs A? cabin No.? – Leaves key in lock at night. Press hard.
Mr B – Bag on the right-hand contains his pocket-book. Very rich. Eats little; very strong. Chloroform.[17]

A considerable quantity of chloroform in handy little flat bottles was subsequently found at the apartment.

After her arrest, Europe's newspapers portrayed her as an attractive, charming and considerate woman:

... far from being of the accepted criminal type, she is a very pretty woman, and although well over forty looks only twenty-eight. She plied her trade with marvellous skill and success [...] Her charm of manner and her beauty, joined with her excellent style, won her many friends of both sexes and in very many cases she was an intimate of the families she robbed, and offered to help to try to track the robber [...] Her arrest has come as a great surprise to those who knew her in Paris as she had a wonderful reputation for respectability, and was well received everywhere.[18]

Even the catty *Le Petit Parisien* newspaper gushed in print that her maid liked and respected her and that she was a generous tipper.[19]

The pseudocomtesse was convicted and sentenced to ten years in prison. After her release in 1918, she melted back into the shadows.

Nobody knows what became of her. It was as if she had never existed and her fate is unknown.

Was the pseudocomtesse lured out of retirement to mastermind one last heist at Ednam Lodge, where the Duchess of Windsor's fabulous collection was not only available but spectacularly vulnerable owing to the Windsors' loose security arrangements? In 1946, she would have been nudging 80, so it is highly unlikely she would have physically participated in the assault, but she may have put together a team capable of carrying out the heist, as she frequently did during her heyday.

Or were there other soloists, more conveniently available, and agile?

Peter Scott, also nicknamed the 'King of the Cat Burglars' or the 'Human Fly', was often referred to as a 'master criminal' but Scott cheerfully described himself as a 'master idiot'.[20] He would have been 15 at the time of the Windsor robbery but that wouldn't have ruled him out of the frame because, as Peter Craig Gulston, he had been operating as a prolific burglar since the age of 12. Scott had a reputation as an athletic cat burglar, able to climb and penetrate the best-guarded Home Counties mansions. He specialised in stealing from the very rich or, as he put it, 'the real meaty jugular vein of society'.[21]

In the 1950s and 1960s, he forged a partnership with George 'Taters' Chatham, then known as the most celebrated 'cat burglar' in London. The duo engaged in heists that bagged them art and jewellery worth over £30 million from Bond Street jewellery stores to Mayfair art collectors, the Shah of Iran and movie stars like Vivien Leigh, Zsa Zsa Gabor and Sophia Loren. The 1965 film *He Who Rides a Tiger*, directed by Charles Crichton, was lightly based on his career. Tom Bell played the Scott character and Judi Dench a besotted girlfriend. At the time, Scott was in Dartmoor Prison and made little money from the film.

Scott was said to have bought a new suit before each job so he would blend in. 'I felt like a missionary seeing his flock for the first time,' he said when reliving the burglary of Dropmore House in Buckinghamshire, where the press baron Viscount Kemsley lived. 'I decided these people were my life's work.'[22] During another burglary, he claimed, 'A titled lady appeared at the top of the stairs. "Everything's all right, madam," I shouted up, and she went off to bed thinking I was the butler.' He also said that on other burglaries, if he was disturbed by anyone there he would shout reassuringly, 'It's only me!'[23]

In his 1995 memoirs, *Gentleman Thief*, Scott admitted to 'an obscene passion for larceny' and described himself as 'a man who has made all the mistakes that vanity, envy and greed create'.[24] He always justified his exploits by saying, 'The people I burgled got rich by greed and skulduggery. They indulged in the mechanics of ostentation – they deserved me and I deserved them.'[25] He always denied having anything to do with the Windsor burglary.

Another candidate was Barry Redvers Holliday, a man about town with bucket loads of cash derived from mysterious sources, who first came to police attention in 1924 as Barry Fieldsen. Holliday attended hunt balls, was a regular racegoer and owned several properties including a Chelsea townhouse and a house at Sunningdale. He wore Savile Row suits and drove a Bentley and a Mercedes. The secret to his success lay in his deft ability as a cat burglar and it was estimated he amassed a fortune which in today's terms would total £7 million.[26] Some of the robberies attributed to him included the theft of £52,000 worth of jewels from the Mayfair home of Lord and Lady Docker, £40,000 of precious stones from the Sunningdale residence of Miss Marjorie Cunliffe-Owen and £20,000 from the London home of Lord Bearsted.

DI Capstick didn't consider him a suspect for the Windsor burglary and it was only when Detective Inspector Robert Lee took over the case that Holliday entered the frame. Holliday made a stupid mistake, astounding in its banality, which altered the course of his life forever: he slipped a meat pie from the counter of the Dumb Bell Hotel at Taplow, where he was a regular customer, into his pocket. The barman saw him do it (perhaps Holliday thought he'd got away with so much for so long he was immune to harm) and Holliday knew he knew about it, but 'The Squire', as Holliday was called by locals, swaggered out nevertheless.

The barman didn't raise the alarm, marking it down as eccentric toff behaviour, but did mention it jokingly to a local police constable.

Somehow, the story got back to DI Lee, who, presumably having scraped the bottom of the barrel when it came to Windsor suspects, took an interest and became even more interested when a search at the Criminal Records Office matched Holliday with Fieldsen.

With nothing better to do, Lee set up a surveillance detail on exclusive Friary Island, which confirmed Holliday was indeed Fieldsen. But with a sixth sense that all successful burglars seemed to possess, Holliday sensed he was being followed and decamped to Earl's Court Square.

Lee wouldn't let it go and kept tabs on Holliday's movements in the following months and years. And then in December 1949, he caught a break. Holliday was seen entering a bank near Sloane Square with a parcel under his arm and was observed leaving the same bank without it. A search warrant was sought and granted, and a safety-deposit box in the name of Holliday's wife was found to contain £10,000 worth of gems, some of which were identified as stolen. He was arrested, his house was searched, and a large amount of silver and jewellery was found. Charged with receiving stolen goods, Holliday was bailed at West London Magistrates' Court on 14 December 1949. Though Lee kept up the surveillance, Holliday always seemed one step ahead.

Then, three days before Christmas, Holliday booked into a room at the Wheatsheaf Hotel in Virginia Water (coincidentally, a stone's throw away from Fort Belvedere) and blew his brains out.

After his death, more safety-deposit boxes he'd rented were discovered, and jewels to the value of £100,000 were recovered, with seventeen items identified from burglaries that occurred in the Sunningdale area from 1932 to 1949.[27] None of the recovered jewellery belonged to the Duchess of Windsor.

The burglary of Ednam Lodge remains unsolved, its secrets intact. But that is the least of its significance. The episode's greatest impact would be felt some forty years later and 1,000km away in Switzerland. But even here, apart from a few complicit players, the vast majority of the impacted would be blissfully unaware of this last and greatest Windsor con.

13

Auction of the Century

A lie that is half-truth is the darkest of all lies.

Alfred Lord Tennyson, *Harold: A Drama*

Over forty years after the burglary at Ednam Lodge, the penultimate act of greed, deceit and drama that the Windsor jewels always seemed to coax from its coterie of players was destined to be spun out over two nights in the Swiss city of Geneva. To facilitate it, an impressive cast of brilliant characters waited in the wings of what was billed as the greatest jewellery auction of the twentieth century, a cast that rivalled the best theatrical Agatha Christie ensemble ever assembled for television.

First to emerge from the shadows is Nicholas Rayner, the suave auctioneer, who leapt off the page from the venerable firm of Sotheby's dog-eared Windsor script like a David Niven cameo. It was perfect casting.

Nicholas Rayner grew up in Ashcombe, near Teignmouth, the son of Brigadier Sir Ralph Rayner, the MP for Totnes from 1935 to 1955, and a Deputy Lieutenant and High Sheriff of Devon. After Eton, he was commissioned into the army and, as a young officer serving with the 11th Hussars in Northern Ireland, his personal Auster plane lost a wing colliding with power lines but somehow managed to land unscathed.

A passionate sportsman, in England he rode point-to-points and hunted with the South Devon. His brother Andrew was a prominent banker in the City of London.

On the Continent, he created a record for the skeleton bob on the famous Cresta Run in the Swiss resort of St Moritz and to celebrate the centenary of the Cresta Club, he organised a classic car race from London to St Moritz across the Alps in winter. On arrival at St Moritz, he raced his classic 1936 Aston Martin convertible on the frozen lake.

By the age of 28, he had left the military to set up restaurants in Malta and later Italy, where he met his first wife, Marina, with whom he had a daughter, Desideria. It was in Italy that he learned how to set gemstones from an expert. After stints with Cartier, Chaumet and Andrew Grima in Paris and London, he persuaded Sotheby's Simon de Pury (appointed the firm's Geneva chairman in 1986) that he was the man to run their small Swiss jewellery auction business. He began by initiating Sotheby's very successful and lucrative jewellery sales in St Moritz, shrewdly held in the second week of February to coincide with the height of the ski season.

All these escapades proved to be perfect preparation for the trials ahead in securing the commission to sell the Windsor jewels for Sotheby's against stiff competition. Among the competition was the second major character in the unfolding drama, the wily Mohamed Al-Fayed (owner of Harrods and the Hôtel Ritz Paris), the newly acquired holder of a fifty-year lease on the Windsors' last house at 4 route du Champ d'Entraînement. The lease was mysteriously granted by the Mayor of Paris, Jacques Chirac, for 1 million francs a year on the condition that Al-Fayed spend 30 million francs restoring the Villa Windsor to its former splendour.

To secure the commission, it seemed all Rayner had to do was woo the formidable Maître Suzanne Blum, the Windsor estate's executor and the third notable character in our story. In the end, he didn't even have to do that as the commission was literally handed to him and Sotheby's by virtue of some high-powered Parisian pillow talk.

From her vast and gloomy apartment, flanked by embassies, in the prestigious rue de Varenne (the Parisian equivalent of Downing Street

— the house of the French prime minister was a few doors away), the elegant and incisive Maître Blum was described by a 1994 *Independent* obituary as a 'striking-looking woman, with the dignity of Queen Mary, her forceful personality veiled by an old-world French courtesy which soon disappeared when journalists telephoned'.[1]

Maître Blum first became involved with the Windsors when her husband, Paul Weill, became the duke's Paris attorney. After the duke's death in 1972, the duchess (already suffering from arteriosclerosis) was largely left to her own devices but leaned on the services of the distinguished lawyer, Sir Godfrey Morley of Allen & Overy; her private secretary, John Utter (a retired American diplomat); and her personal secretary, a multilingual Swiss girl, Johanna Schutz. However, in 1973 the services of Allen & Overy were abruptly terminated and it was made clear by Maître Blum (by now the duchess's Paris lawyer) that she would be handling all her legal affairs. To this effect, the duchess signed over her personal power of attorney to the French lawyer.

Most disturbingly, Sydney Johnson, the duke's trusted valet, was dismissed soon after the duke's interment at Frogmore, allegedly because he had asked to go home early one evening to be with his family. John Utter was also officially 'retired' in 1975 and the duchess gave most of her private papers to Maître Blum, along with permission (asserted by Maître Blum) to publish them, if and when she thought fit. The duchess also made a new will (under the guidance of Maître Blum) in 1975 in which she apparently appointed the Pasteur Institute in France as her principal beneficiary.

It has long been a source of conjecture why the Pasteur Institute became the principal beneficiary of her largesse but, as Maître Blum's assistant Michael Bloch has since pointed out, perhaps it was a way of expressing her gratitude to the French nation for years of token rent on the Bois de Boulogne house as well as her continued tax-free status (in 1973, she was informed by Maurice Schumann, representing the French government, that she would also not be charged death duties and the Villa Windsor would be hers in perpetuity). Another motivation might have been that the institute was at the forefront of AIDS research at the time, though Hugo Vickers contends she wouldn't have even known what AIDS was.[2]

In the absence of any legitimate documentary evidence such as photographs, signed documents or letters, it would seem the decision to appoint the Pasteur Institute as sole beneficiary of the duchess's estate, although a good one, was not made by the duchess. In April 1978, Maître Blum forcibly exercised her discretionary powers and dismissed Johanna Schutz on the grounds that she was unstable and frequently absent.

The duchess, of course, is the fourth principal character in the story of the 1987 auction. Tragically, most of the important sequential changes to her network of support and care coincided with the duchess's physical and mental deterioration.

She was terrified of being murdered or kidnapped and kept a toy revolver next to her bed (she thought it was real). She never slept through the night but kept getting up and peering out of the window, myopically checking to see if the French soldier she had hired was standing on duty. When she went to restaurants like Maxim's, she insisted there was a guard outside the restaurant.

She broke her hip and ribs on various occasions and was hospitalised for extensive periods. The doctors found it difficult to put an anaesthetic tube down her throat because of the extensive plastic surgery on her neck. In November 1975, she again fell gravely ill, haemorrhaging from an undiagnosed stomach ulcer, which was only partly cured after treatment in the American Hospital.

She returned home in the summer of 1976 a virtual wreck; a taut sack of bones that protruded from her skin like struts from a threadbare sofa. At the hospital she was petulant, muddled and difficult. She rejected the food and introduced her own Michelin-style menu supplied by her personal chef. Appalled by the linen, she brought her own pillows and sheets, and stuffed her private room with magnificent displays of flowers. The doctors succeeded in cutting down her consumption of alcohol, but she ate scarcely anything and lost more weight.

By 1978 she was a total invalid, unable to speak or move, confined to her personal wing on the first floor of the Villa and spoon-fed by nurses.

She lost the use of her hands and feet and had to be carried from her bed to a clinical couch. She was almost completely blind.

By 1981, doctors were describing her as a vegetable. In 1982, Maître Blum told the BBC's *Timewatch* programme, 'Everyone knows that for seven years now she has been bedridden, being only able to be taken to an armchair in front of the windows to look at the trees and to hear the birds sing'.[3]

It was indeed a terrible decline and a far cry from the luxurious routine she enjoyed every day of her life while the duke was alive:

> Every day of her life the Duchess had Édouard, from Alexandre's, come to the house in the Bois de Boulogne and comb her hair. Once a week she went to Elizabeth Arden to have it washed. The Duchess never took a nap. Occasionally she would rest on her chaise longue, but she really relaxed only while having her hair, face, and nails done. Every afternoon a makeup artist came to the house to do her face. The tones he used varied with the color of what she was wearing, and he applied false eyelashes so discreetly that people didn't realize she wore them. She had a manicurist come in three times a week, and she rarely altered the color of her polish, which was bright red.[4]

The Villa, once a hive of activity and luxury, had become a shell of its former self, a gloomy totem of decay and atrophy:

> Over the wall through the grey, misty atmosphere one could see a kind of living tomb. All the windows on the ground floor were shuttered from the outside world, but I thought the drawing room window was open. Upstairs where what remains of the Duchess [sat] surrounded by nurses, there were two lights – one on the side, which is her bedroom, and one in the far window of what I think is the upstairs sitting room.[5]

Johanna Schutz, in an interview with the duchess's biographer, Anna Pasternak for the *Daily Telegraph* in February 2020, laid the blame for this sad state of affairs squarely with Maître Blum: 'Blum really threatened the Duchess. She told her the French government would make her leave the house unless she bequeathed everything to the Pasteur Institute. She was totally menacing.' Schutz also claimed that nurses hired by the lawyer were 'drugging the Duchess'.[6]

It is a picture that is somewhat confirmed by a visit in 1980 by Lady Caroline Blackwood, who was commissioned by the *Sunday Times* to write about the duchess's lifestyle since the death of the duke in 1972 (Lord Snowdon was to have taken the pictures). In scenes reminiscent of Billy Wilder's *Sunset Boulevard*, Lady Caroline managed to get past the high-wire fence and massive steel gate – which was riddled with security locks and bolts and surmounted by golden steel spikes – and as far as the front door of the rundown Villa Windsor, only to be barred by Georges, the duchess's butler, and his glowering wife, Ophélie. She soon realised there was no one else in the creepy and depressing house except, perhaps, a bedridden figure upstairs. It is telling that publication of Lady Caroline's narrative was delayed until after Maître Blum's death at the age of 96 in 1994.[7]

Someone who did manage to breach the security fences, gates and servants was Aline, the Countess of Romanones, an old friend. When she arrived, she noted an eerie, disturbing silence due to the absence of the loud, excited barking of the Windsor pug dogs (they had been given away because the duchess could no longer tolerate the sound).

Entering the boudoir, she found the duchess seated in her wheelchair wearing a handsome brocade dressing gown, her hair elegantly drawn back behind her ears, wearing her favourite sapphires. She told her she looked like a Chinese empress.

Returning several months later, she found things had taken a turn for the worse. The duchess's hair was white and lifeless, and her face was splotchy and creased. Staring out of the window, she said, 'Look at the way the sun is lighting the trees … tell David to come in. He wouldn't want to miss this!'[8]

In a further series of fantastic revelations, Johanna Schutz also claimed she wanted to rescue the duchess in 1975 with plans to whisk her off to New York where the Windsors kept an apartment. 'We were all set to go, then the Duchess suffered a perforated ulcer because Blum had worried her so much. That's when all her troubles started. After that, she was too ill to travel or impose her wishes.'[9]

That's when the sale of Windsor objects began. 'The Duchess would say, "Why don't we go down and have dinner in the library?" I had to say, "You are too frail. It's not heated." Any excuse so she didn't see the truth.'[10]

Ms Schutz also approached Queen Elizabeth II's private secretary, Sir Martin Charteris. Charteris persuaded the queen's lawyer to travel to Paris with a doctor but 'Blum wouldn't let them through the door'.[11] The duchess had become a prisoner in her own home.

According to Elvire Gozin (who was the duchess's nurse from 1976 to 1986), less than a year before the most lucrative auction of personal jewellery ever held, the duchess 'died in a slum', sleeping in ratty sheets, her favourite expensive make-up brands having been replaced years ago by cheap alternatives.[12]

One person, however, was permitted to penetrate the duchess's inner sanctum during the last few years of her life. The Reverend Jim Leo of the American Cathedral in Paris made a weekly visit to the Villa, where he prayed before the partly paralysed and comatose figure on a bed in her boudoir. The duchess's hands were always bound to stop her from pulling the black nasal feeding tube out of her nose. Abdominal feeding tubes were available and considered more humane but were deemed too expensive by Maître Blum. Leo's weekly pilgrimage to the Villa continued right until the duchess's death, seven weeks short of her 90th birthday.

Whatever and whomever you choose to believe, one thing is certain: Maître Blum was a polarising figure in the latter part of the Duchess of Windsor's life. But, whatever people thought about her, the Columbia-educated Blum was a formidable lawyer in her own right.

Born Suzanne Blumel in the village of Niort, she began practising law in 1922 at the age of 24 and progressed quickly through the ranks of her calcified, male-dominated profession to represent such diverse clients as Warner Brothers (against the composer Igor Stravinsky in a copyright case, converting his damages from $1 million to one franc), Twentieth Century Fox, MGM, Charlie Chaplin, Walt Disney and Rita Hayworth (in her divorce from Aly Khan). As if this wasn't enough, she also managed to find the time and energy to pursue a writing career, producing three crime novels under the pseudonym L.S. Karen. When Paul Weill died in 1965, she married the distinguished soldier and Arabic scholar George Spillmann.

Supporting Johanna Schutz's claims, it was well known in the auction business that Maître Blum, on behalf of the duchess, had been quietly disposing of Villa Windsor furniture since the late 1970s to pay for the duchess's mounting medical and care expenses. This was despite the duchess signing an agreement with the French government on 30 March 1973 giving the state nearly 140 important pieces of furniture and art. The pieces stipulated in the agreement were transferred to the French state following her death and included all of the Louis XVI furniture (worth about £7.5 million today), several of her gold boxes (now in the Louvre), a Stubbs painting (which went to Versailles) and important pieces of eighteenth-century porcelain which were donated to the National Ceramics Museum.

The non-agreement pieces that Maître Blum released from the Villa Windsor were placed on the open auction market, while others were offered to Windsor friends such as Nathan and Joanne Cummings, who purchased the table from the dining room along with various silver pieces and the famous Meissen Flying Tiger dinner service. The remaining pieces, upon the duchess's death, became tangled up in the disposition of her estate to the Pasteur Institute, her principal beneficiary.

But the institute did not want to take on the onerous and additional burden of curating historical valuables and personal possessions, so it was decided the best course of action was to auction everything off. This was perfectly understandable as the duchess, for example, had kept everything in the duke's rooms exactly the way it was when the duke died, even retaining the cigarettes she hated. The cobwebbed pipes were still in their racks and the cigars lay neatly in their dusty, expensive boxes.

The desk was untouched. In the cupboards hung all the duke's suits, immaculately preserved in mothballs.

At this point, in the summer of 1986, in stepped Mohamed Al-Fayed, who successfully struck a deal with Maître Blum to purchase the contents of the Villa. Al-Fayed declared he was in love with the Windsors' love story and planned to create a museum dedicated as a permanent memorial to the royal couple, which must have appealed enormously to Maître Blum – especially when Al-Fayed lost no time in spending even more money refurbishing the objects of his love affair.

The Chippendale table at which the duke signed his letter of abdication was sent back to English furniture experts, who reglued its joints and rejuvenated its tooled leather top. The duke's polo trophies and his ceremonial sword were sent to silversmiths to be reburnished and the tattered sovereign's Garter banner was rewoven by French craftsmen. Under the supervision of an Anglo-American team of decorators, the leaky roof was also repaired, the interior was given a coat of paint and other tapestries and woodwork were restored.

Everything remaining in the Villa Windsor at the time of the duchess's death was included in the Al-Fayed sale except the duke's uniforms (including his Garter robes and all his orders and decorations, which were returned to the Crown on the advice of Lord Mountbatten) and the jewellery collection. And there was no doubt in Al-Fayed's mind that, after parting with $4.5 million to secure the Villa Windsor furniture, personal effects and bric-a-brac, he was in pole position to add the jewels to the proposed Windsor museum.

So things didn't look all that promising for Nicholas Rayner and Sotheby's when word leaked out that the indefatigable Mohamed Al-Fayed and Maître Blum had reached an agreement in principle for the sale of the collection at a sum which, ironically, represented a small fraction of the sum ultimately achieved by Sotheby's at auction.

But then, as was sometimes the case with the tenacious and manoeuvring Al-Fayed, he stole defeat from the jaws of victory when he resorted to various ploys to influence or induce Maître Blum to reduce the agreed price. Maybe he was having cash-flow problems or maybe he was intent on securing the duchess's jewels for an even greater knockdown price. Whatever the reason, Al-Fayed's jockeying reputedly exasperated Maître Blum and in a fit of French pique, she awarded the sale to the charming and attentive Nicholas Rayner of Sotheby's.

Naturally, Al-Fayed was furious and then almost catatonic when he was advised that legally there was nothing he could do about it. Maître Blum had made her decision and no amount of threats, legal or otherwise, would reverse it. Al-Fayed never forgot or forgave the insult. Sensing an Establishment conspiracy, his manic response was to hoover up as many Windsor artefacts that were available on the open and private market as his money could buy through connected intermediaries. A lot of dubious people made a lot of money from Al-Fayed's emotional immaturity.

Another source of irritation leading up to the Sotheby's decision was Lord Louis Mountbatten, the duke's second cousin and friend, who had a habit of turning up at the house and walking around the rooms as if he owned the place. Pointing at objects, Mountbatten would say, 'Those are going to Charles',[13] or touching the duke's Fabergé gold boxes, he'd announce, 'The duke intended those for me',[14] and then proposed removing them. It got so blatant that Maître Blum insisted that someone was always present during these visits to dissuade Mountbatten from following through with his intentions.

Even when the duke was alive, Mountbatten was indefatigable in his quest to secure certain items. 'Who are you going to leave that to?' he asked, pointing at the Copenhagen dinner service once owned by Queen Alexandra and George IV's Lowestoft porcelain in their Chippendale cabinets.[15]

'How dare he!' the duke exclaimed indignantly (according to Lady Alexandra Metcalfe, the wife of his best man). 'He even tells me what *he* wants left to him!'[16]

At one point in 1973, the duchess claimed Mountbatten insisted upon her making a new will to the effect that everything would go to the royal family (the duke's estate was estimated at £3 million by those privy to his sealed will). He even volunteered to act as her executor and to find another English lawyer associated with the royal family who would draw it up. The duchess was apprehensive and suspicious.

When that didn't work, Mountbatten tried to make the duchess sign a document in which she placed all her property in a foundation that Mountbatten would administer with Charles, Prince of Wales, as its chairman. The wily Lord Louis was obviously acting for the family, in a none-too-discreet way, to retrieve the many historical artefacts the royal family believed ex-King Edward VIII had looted from royal homes and collections prior to his abdication and removal to France.

Bizarrely, Maître Blum alleged that individuals authorised by Lord Mountbatten *had* succeeded in removing some of these items by obtaining the keys to the duke's boxes and confidential filing cabinets in his study, burgling the contents and walking them downstairs to the concierge's lodge, where they were loaded on to a van and driven away under cover of night.[17] Even crazier, Maître Blum's charges were supported by statements from John Utter, Sydney Johnson and Johanna Schutz – this is despite Sir Robin Mackworth-Young, the librarian at Windsor Castle during the alleged theft, having documentary evidence that categorically refuted the charges.

These shenanigans were finally called out when the duchess wrote to Mountbatten on 9 December 1974:

> It is always a pleasure to see you, but I must tell you that when you leave me I am always terribly depressed by your reminding me of David's death and my own, and I should be grateful if you would not mention this any more.[18]

After this final rebuff he retreated, telling the family they would have to wait until her infatuation with Maître Blum had run its course.

Amid the continual jockeying and counter-jockeying of interested parties surrounding the fate of the duchess's jewellery collection, the decision to suddenly award their disposal to Sotheby's in the late autumn of 1986 was astounding. It was the most tremendous coup. In fact, the firm could hardly believe its luck and required proof before they could officially congratulate their charming but mercurial Swiss-based jewellery expert.

Rayner's 'coup' was officially vouched for by none other than the head of Sotheby's Paris office, whose relationship with the head of the Pasteur Institute paved the way for Sotheby's capture of the year's most prestigious auction. And yet, despite the affectionate understanding reached by the principals of Sotheby's and the Pasteur Institute, the solution to the Al-Fayed problem still had to meet the approval of the vendor (in this case, the executor of the duchess's estate) before it became a done deal. But as Maître Blum was well acquainted with both principals, this wasn't a problem.

Maître Blum duly summoned the proposed auctioneer Nicholas Rayner (who had been quietly soliciting the commission at the urging of Sotheby's director Sir Angus Ogilvy, husband of Princess Alexandra, who was privy to gossipy information about the flagging Al-Fayed negotiations) for a tick-the-box, in-person pitch, at her rue de Varenne office:

> Arriving in Maître's rooms, he was duly nervous. Rayner was shown into Blum's presence and found her sitting on a sofa at the end of a room. 'Avancez!' she commanded. She invited him to sit on the sofa beside her and he launched into his pitch. Part of this was to show her some catalogues. He opened one on her knees so that she could inspect how they laid out their images. He realised that he was getting nowhere. She said to him: 'I am terribly sorry, but I am completely blind.' Rayner was so embarrassed that he burst into tears. He put his arm around Blum and she began to cry too. The jewellery sale went to Sotheby's.[19]

Once confirmation of this most tremendous outcome had been obtained, the news soon galvanised Sotheby's entire worldwide organisation. Everyone realised the marketing potential of what was soon being touted as the biggest and most glamorous jewellery auction event of the century.

By the time the tedious and protracted disposal of the jewels had been sorted out, both Maître Blum and the Pasteur Institute also wanted the whole thing wrapped up within a year of the duchess's death on 24 April 1986. This meant Rayner and the Sotheby's organisation had just under six months to catalogue the lots and work through all the required logistical, marketing, publicity and legal aspects necessary for a successful event.

But that was a minor headache compared to the treasure that was under Sotheby's management. During the long years of what fashion journalist Suzy Menkes described as the duchess's 'half-life' following the duke's death,[20] her jewels were kept in the substantial safe of her Paris notaire, Maître Lecuyer, and in 1976 they were moved to the Morgan Guaranty Bank in the Place Vendôme.[21]

After her death, it was a different story. For safekeeping prior to the auction, the jewels were secreted under cover of night to the safest location in Paris. It was here that Nicholas Rayner and two colleagues made their way via the rue du Colonel-Driant in central Paris to inspect them in their temporary home: the gold vaults of the French central bank, the Banque de France, located in the subterranean maze of corridors beneath the bank's headquarters near the Musée du Louvre. Rayner freely admitted he was simply unprepared for the experience that was to follow when he inspected the jewels for the first time over the 1986 Christmas period.

The Banque de France's gold vaults were completed between May 1924 and November 1927 using over 10,000 tons of steel and 20,000 tons of cement. They were specifically located in a set of chambers known as 'La Souterraine', situated in the eighth level basement, 28m below ground level, in an 11,000-square-metre space. Only five bank officers had permanent access to it.

The men from Sotheby's first had to take a rickety elevator down to the fourth basement level where there was an antechamber with a 7-ton thick armoured door that led to a small corridor with rail tracks in the floor. When the access passage was closed, another 17-ton, 2m-wide steel block moved on these rails via a 35-ton rotating turret, blocking the entrance to the passage. There was then a second elevator ride down to the eighth basement level with another security door before reaching the actual gold vault area. This was where the duchess's jewels were stored, courtesy of Maître Blum's well-heeled connections.

In a nondescript steel cabinet with a wire grille door, one of 100 inside 'La Souterraine', near a pile of US Assay Office gold bars which were stacked towards the ceiling in a pyramid, sat the duchess's jewellery collection – or what was left of it. Rayner and his colleagues were gobsmacked by the boxes and boxes of embossed red Morocco leather jewellery cases that required several large metal trolleys to move them around the fourth basement level antechamber.

Rayner's colleague and later worldwide chairman of Sotheby's jewellery department, David Bennett, was in the Banque de France cataloguing the Duchess of Windsor's pieces. 'The first of these huge red Morocco leather boxes came out, with the Duchess's monogram on,' he recalled, remembering that the first piece to emerge was the famous ruby bracelet:

> Up until that point, nobody knew apart from the men who engraved them that the jewels had been inscribed with this very personal language between the Duke and Duchess. And almost every single piece bears some kind of literal message, a love note, pet name or phrase in a childish language with meaning then known only to them.[22]

Bennett was also involved in writing the sales catalogue, and consequently, spent time in Cartier and their Place Vendôme neighbours Van Cleef & Arpels archives:

> Jacques Arpels was still alive when I was writing the catalogue, and I was able to spend some time with him in Paris. He could remember the Duke and the Duchess coming in and designing, picking the stones, arriving with jewels. He mentioned that the Duke was extremely involved, loved gemstones, loved jewellery. You do get the idea that it was a collaboration between the two of them.[23]

The duke's penchant and enjoyment of haggling for rare stones and working closely with jewellers on special designs (once he had worn them down on price) was legendary. 'The Duke would spend hours at our shop on the Place Vendôme overseeing every detail himself,' Ferdinand Ripoll drolly confirmed at Van Cleef & Arpels.[24]

Cocooned inside this subterranean cavern of untold wealth, for Rayner's team the entire experience felt like something out of the *Count of Monte Cristo*, only here, Edmond Dantès' oaken coffer, bound with cut steel and crammed with jewels and gold, was multiplied 100 times over in red leather. The effect was the same. Rayner had to pinch himself, rubbing 'his eyes in order to assure himself that this was not a dream'.[25]

Of course, both Sotheby's and Maître Blum knew that auctioning the duchess's jewellery collection represented a major deviation from the Duke of Windsor's repeatedly expressed wish that the jewels should be broken up after the duchess's death so no other woman could wear them. This was due, in part, to the many private messages of affection inscribed on each piece.

There was, however, a practical reason why this was not carried out: the Windsors had not made any legal provision to break up the jewellery. There was an additional, more devastating reason, which the Windsors, Maître Blum, Nicholas Rayner and Sotheby's were all privy to and which, in Sotheby's case, they chose to ignore. For there was a gigantic secret at the heart of the 1987 auction in addition to the most obvious secret, which most people involved with the duchess's jewels already suspected. That there were secrets is no surprise; as one dedicated Windsor watcher expressed at the time, 'Speculation about the Duchess's jewels began the moment she died.'[26]

Aside from the question whether the sale contained all the duchess's jewellery (it did not), the other question is, what jewellery might have been 'lost'?

There are stories that Maître Blum withdrew jewels from the duchess's collection in 1977 and gave the Windsor heirlooms as gifts to various people, such as the Duchess of Kent, Princess Alexandra and later, Princess Michael of Kent.[27] She also sold certain pieces to notable associates such as Jacques Arpels of Van Cleef & Arpels (who was curious as to why only fifteen out of the forty pieces his firm created especially for the duchess were listed in the Geneva sale)[28] and Estée Lauder, who bought a jonquil diamond shaped like a heart for $150,000 in 1977.[29] But generally, most Windsor watchers agree the jewels that disappeared in the duchess's lifetime were thankfully not the most famous, readily recognisable ones.

Maître Blum attempted to kill off the most obvious secret when she released in May 1986 the news that the duchess had named the Pasteur Institute as the main beneficiary of her fortune before her death. After declining to estimate the estate's value or provide the names of the other beneficiaries (they were the Claude Pompidou Foundation for the Handicapped, the American Hospital and the Association of Villages for SOS Children, the Royal National Lifeboat Institution, Guide Dogs for the Blind Association, the Honourable Artillery Company and the Soldiers, Sailors, Airmen & Families Association), she then sensationally stated that several members of the royal family had inherited a number of small items.[30] When asked to elaborate, she declined.[31]

When questioned about the jewellery collection and the controversy regarding the delicate provenance of some of the items ('whether her estate included jewels supposed to be crown property'),[32] Maître Blum steered the press to unnamed Buckingham Palace sources who would verify 'any jewels belonging to the crown were returned after the Duke's death in 1972',[33] knowing full well the Palace would never comment on such private matters. The ruse worked and syndicated news outlets duly reported the required confirmation by these anonymous royal 'sources' in their filed stories.

Maître Blum was obviously making a deliberate, pre-emptive attempt at provenance cleansing before deciding how the Windsor haul was to be sold off. She was particularly careful about unnecessarily provoking the royal family by inadvertently drawing attention to its rather testy relationship with the duchess, even going to the extent of vetoing any pictures in the subsequent auction catalogue that featured the duchess wearing her jewellery, either in the presence of Queen Elizabeth II or at English locations such as Buckingham Palace and Windsor.[34]

If unchecked, Blum knew these controversies would have a damaging effect on the value and saleability of the duchess's remaining assets. She probably convinced herself (that's supposing she needed convincing) that she was protecting her client's wishes from potential harm by taking all reasonable steps to negate any threats that might jeopardise their fulfilment.

The other delicate question of provenance conveniently obliterated after her death concerned the deal the duchess struck with Cartier and Van Cleef & Arpels in the 1950s. Both firms were persuaded to lend her jewels for public events, as long as the name of the jewellery house was leaked to the press and they were promptly returned. Needless to say, the practice was manipulated by the duchess and poisoned her relationship with the two houses, as the journalist Christopher Wilson observed:

[The Windsors] only kept to the first part of the bargain – they borrowed, but didn't return. Unfortunately, it is no longer possible to identify which items in the collection were paid for and which were not. A wholesale clear-out of all correspondence at the time of the Duchess's death in 1986 ensured that we shall never know the full extent of this dishonesty. However, one former servant told me grimly: 'Rarely was anything handed back'.[35]

Presumably these were the 'borrowed' pieces farmed out or sold by Maître Blum to friends and associates during the duchess's twilight years, which also may account for Jacques Arpels' comments on the Van Cleef & Arpels pieces that were missing from the collection.

But these weren't the greatest secrets at play during the auction. There was another secret that Maître Blum's assistant, Michael Bloch, curiously says he continually drew Sotheby's attention to, which was intentionally covered up so it wouldn't negatively impact potential auction proceeds.[36]

In a business where provenance is everything, the auction of the duchess's jewels as depicted in the official catalogue was a ruse of the highest calibre. Such a deception required a degree of 'front' by both the auction house and auctioneer who would be introducing the lots described in the sale catalogue. Maintaining such a bluff would challenge even the most skilful members of a nation's intelligence service, and Nicholas Rayner certainly had that 'front' – the nerveless, cold-blooded poise and precision, never wavering in doubt or hesitation. All successful auctioneers must have that ability to some degree to pull off an event that has millions and millions of dollars at stake. It is perhaps almost a basic requirement.

'Basically, you have to be a combination of entertainer and performance artist,' says Aurel Bacs, probably the most famous auctioneer of fine goods in the world today and the man who sold Paul Newman's Rolex Daytona watch for a record auction price of $15.5 million in 2017:

> The best auctioneers are effortless, they know when to push and when to stop. They also know what they are selling, and by that I mean they understand what they are selling. They have an intimate knowledge of the product and the clientele that will make a serious effort to acquire what's on offer. In my case, I know what is in my client's watch collections and what they should be looking for to enhance them.[37]

But in tandem with this confidence in one's ability to execute a sale successfully, there's also the mental and physical toll, the attrition, the stress that standing in front of hundreds of people and countless others around the world has on one's body. 'I can see how my body does funny things to me in the lead up to an auction,' explains Mr Bacs:

> I sleep much less, my appetite goes and people say I look pale. My circulation seems also to be affected and my hands are frequently cold. And then there's the paranoia: what if no one turns up? What if nothing sells? What if I can't speak? But then, the evening of the auction, I have my first proper meal for weeks as the adrenalin starts to kick in. Later, as I mount the rostrum, I get the feeling because of all the preparation I've done, that the room is cordially welcoming me. Then I'm away. Of course, after it's finished and I 'come down'

from that pitch of performance I invariably also physically come down with some bug and I have to spend a week in bed just to properly get over things.[38]

For Nicholas Rayner, it was the same. His friends and family say his health never fully recovered from the effects of the 1987 auction. It led to a stroke in 1994 and his retirement from the auction business. His last days were spent tragically at the mercy of a carer who was convicted of the systematic extortion of his estate while he lay bedridden and incapacitated.

The other potential problem with the auction were Sotheby's questionable saleroom practices that were rife in the 1980s, as described by the historian Peter Watson in his study, *Sotheby's: Inside Story*. Watson's investigations also spawned a 1997 Channel 4 *Dispatches* television programme. The allegations were also taken up by CBS's *60 Minutes*. As a result of these exposés, Sotheby's commissioned their own report into illegal trading and made assurances that only legal items with published provenances would be traded in the future.

They were, of course, not alone in practising deception in their salerooms. Christie's were also implicated and both firms were investigated by New York's Department of Consumer Affairs, the Department of Trade and Industry in London and the Environment Committee of the City of Westminster for 'routine deceptions of the auction process' in the 1980s.[39]

Sotheby's insisted at the time, 'The reputation and integrity of Sotheby's are the two things that matter the most.'[40] Professor Watson's book, however, showed it was riddled with unethical and illegal practices throughout the organisation. In the case of the 1987 Geneva auction, of the three forms of auction manipulation that were most rife in the 1980s, the most relevant to this blockbuster auction concerns the curious phenomenon of commission bids.

An auction is supposed to be a transparent system of buying and selling: a vendor puts an object into a sale, specifying the minimum price or reserve they will accept for it. On the day of the auction, the highest bidder for the object, providing the offer exceeds the minimum price, gets the object. If a potential bidder cannot attend the auction or does not wish to be seen at the auction, they can send an agent to bid on their behalf or they can leave a commission bid with the auction house. A commission bid puts the auction house in a very privileged position because it not only knows what the owner wants for the object it also knows how far a buyer is willing to go, price wise, for that object This conflict of interest can be extremely lucrative to auction houses:

> When an auction house is in possession of both sets of information – what the seller wants and what a buyer is prepared to pay – the temptation may exist to sell the object for a higher sum than strictly speaking it should go for.[41]

Of course, auction houses the world over say this does not happen. It is a question of trust and integrity, relying as it does on two parts of an organisation not divulging to one another such lucrative information. When an organisation's share price, staff remuneration and brand value depend on how much it makes and how much it exceeds the previous year's performance, the pressure to succeed is obviously enormous. But this is not the principal ethical weakness of the practice (the paper-thin veneer of self-regulation).

The main weakness is that during the sale itself the auctioneer must know the reserve on each lot and whether there are any commission bids for it. This puts the auctioneer in a supreme position of power: they know (whether they act on it or not is solely at their discretion) what can be achieved once the price clears the reserve. If that is the case, what is there to stop an auctioneer from making fictitious bids to push up the price once it has cleared the reserve? The answer is nothing.

It's an accepted practice. John Marion, Sotheby's chief auctioneer in America and later company chairman, wrote in an internal memo dated 23 August 1985, 'It is not uncommon for the auctioneer to make the first few bids on his own in order to move the sale along'.[42]

In 1987 Sotheby's utilised what they called the 'Comm Box', in effect, a plain, non-digital box where all commission bids were placed in advance of sales, the contents of which theoretically could not be seen by those fixing the reserves. The box of commission bids for the Windsor jewels is long gone so we'll never know what it contained or be able to match the winning bids against the contents. But generally, a reasonable guide as to how much a commission bid may have affected the outcome of a sale is usually indicated by how much the eventual price clears the published pre-sale estimate. The greater the gap, the greater the potential for skulduggery. It is an imperfect measurement, but still worth noting.

In Geneva, on that dark, chilly evening in April, armed with a supreme confidence in his abilities, Nicholas Rayner was ready for the biggest day of his life. Clutching a sheaf of marked-up notes and dressed in a superb Brioni tuxedo with a raffishly set crimson silk hanky peeking from his top pocket like a bloodied shark's tooth, he threaded his way purposely through the noisy, perspiring crowd and bounded up the steps of the auctioneer's rostrum.

Braced by several cigarettes, copious amounts of black coffee and 'settlers', Rayner had a few moments before the start of proceedings at 9 p.m., central European time, to study the crowd and absorb the pulsating energy in the marquee, which was filled to overflowing. The three Givenchy models were in place, engaged to hold up the lots on stage as they were announced (pre-filmed images of each jewel were also shown on television monitors scattered throughout the saleroom), as were the cream of Sotheby's worldwide executives, including the Earl of Gowrie (previously Britain's Minister of Arts). Above the auctioneer's rostrum another giant screen displayed all the jewels at fifty times life-size and two electronic currency converter boards hung like suspended bodyguards from the ceiling.

It was incredibly hot and stuffy, despite the early spring chill, the product of rows and rows of overdressed people dripping in jewels, illuminated by huge arc lights connected to banks of TV and closed-circuit cameras from around the world. The audience fanned themselves with their catalogues in excitement; pet dogs in studded collars panted at the feet of elaborately coiffed matrons with sleek fur coats draped over their shoulders; pumped-up waiters were making a fortune in tips; thickset men yanked at their stiff collars and lusted after a cigar in the cool night air; and plain clothes detectives in rented dinner jackets and ball gowns tried to appear as bored and as smug as the clientele jabbering around them.

Among all the hullabaloo, Rayner was probably reminded of those famous opening lines from Ian Fleming's *Casino Royale*:

The scent and smoke and sweat of a casino are nauseating at three in the morning. Then the soul-erosion produced by high gambling – a compost of greed and fear and nervous tension – becomes unbearable and the senses awake and revolt from it.

Rayner would have inwardly relished the similarity. Like James Bond, he was about to embark on the greatest game of bluff in his life, and the stakes couldn't be higher. But unlike the fictional Bond, the stakes here were for real.

However, now was not the time to get all maudlin about it. The die had willingly been cast a long time ago, not only by Rayner, but notoriously by the two major protagonists themselves. It was up to him, at this moment, after decades of deceit, fraud and calumny, to tie the knot in this royal caper once and for all.

Steadying himself, he flicked open the first page of his notes, cleared his throat and picked up the glossy little blonde gavel. The 'buzz' was deafening, a cacophony of almost every language on the planet. He was in the eye of the universe.

Perfumed bosoms heaved in anticipation. Clouds of pheromones erupted in relief. All the important international gem dealers were in the tent: Graff, Gol, Moussaief and Horowitz, plus the jewellers Cartier, Van Cleef & Arpels, Harry Winston, Garrard, Fred Leighton. Even Verdura was there, represented by its new owner, Ward Landrigan.

A colleague gave him the signal, it was bang on 9 p.m. Nicholas Rayner opened his mouth and heard himself saying, 'Ladies and gentlemen, the jewels of the Duchess of Windsor, Lot 1, and I shall open the bidding at seven thousand francs.'

The first round on 2 April lasted four hours. Some of the spectacular sales included Lot 15, the duke's diamond dress suite, bought by Mr Wafic Saïd for £247,000, over fifty times the advertised estimate, and Lot 27, the sparkling Prince of Wales diamond plumes at £350,000. Laurence Graff, the London jeweller, paid £823,000 for Lot 81, the Great Mughal emerald engagement ring set by Jeanne Toussaint of Cartier, for his wife for their 25th wedding anniversary. It was given to Mrs Simpson by King Edward after her decree nisi was granted in 1936 and he originally bought it for £10,000.

The best was saved for last: Lot 95, the McLean diamond, provided the contest of the night, a brilliant duel between Mr Takagi from Japan in the Geneva tent and a telephone bidder from North America. At 4.1 million Swiss francs, the telephone bidder deliberated for three nail-biting minutes, testing Rayner's nerve, only for Mr Takagi to eventually win with a breathtaking £1.8 million. Curiously, the London *Daily Mail* bought several items, including Lot 33, the gold and gem-set powder compact by Hermès, as prizes for various competitions.

Generally, the pieces with the greatest sentimental value sold for the most, like Lot 31, the historically important and emotionally charged Cartier charm bracelet of crosses, going for £214,000. Lot 32, a Cartier 18-carat gold and gem-set cigarette case engraved with maps and routes for holidays in 1934, 1935 and 1936 (including the infamous *Nahlin* voyage) went for £165,000, 100 times the pre-sale estimate, and a little circular framed photograph of Queen Mary, which she gave to George V on the day of their silver jubilee, sold for over 1,000 times its estimate. Two bejewelled panthers, a brooch and a bracelet made by Cartier in the late 1950s were purchased by Andrew Lloyd Webber as a gift for his wife at the time, opera star Sarah Brightman, to celebrate the couple's success in the hit musical *Phantom of the Opera*.

Lots on the second day mopped up most of the duke's remaining trinkets: various desk seals, *objets de vertu*, silver and gold cigarette cases, including a beautiful 18-carat gold Cartier case given by Edward to his favourite brother George on his marriage to Marina of Greece in 1934, snuff boxes, gold cufflinks, sporting trophies, gilt and silver Georgian candlesticks, Royal Navy presentation swords, regimental knives and a range of well-worn sporrans. Mohamed Al-Fayed bought ten desk seals for 2 million Swiss francs.

The whole show was an unprecedented success. The three ingredients of a successful jewellery auction (provenance, quality and design) had created a perfect storm of bidding. From the lightning sale of Lot 1, the ruby and sapphire beaded clip that opened proceedings at 7,000 Swiss francs and sold for 65,000 Swiss francs, everyone connected with the auction made a killing. The clip's buyer was Alexander Acevedo, who was determined to buy the first lot at practically any cost because he had heard that somebody intended to buy the whole collection, lot by lot.[43] It set the tone for the remaining auction and estimates were on average exceeded by as much as thirty times.

The pre-sale estimates of $7 million weren't merely smashed they were obliterated by the unfettered, unrestrained blitzkrieg of big money flexing its awesome power, bombing the record books. The duchess's favourite piece (according to Rayner), the Burmese ruby and diamond necklace given to her by King Edward VIII on her 41st birthday on 19 June 1936, fetched $2.6 million.

It didn't matter who or what you were, how you made your money or where it was kept, all that mattered was you had it. Yes, celebrities were well represented in capturing certain prizes, but it was the big money men (including Al-Fayed, who ironically purchased several pieces for more than the total amount he had offered for the entire collection several months earlier), the Wall Street men, the oil men, the real estate titans, the emerging tech gurus, who were gorging themselves at the trough.

Aside from Sotheby's golden boy Nicholas Rayner, the other star of the show was a nondescript, middle-aged Middle Eastern man with glasses who sat in the marquee's fifth row. Gliding into action when the auction moved from the last of the duchess's jewels to the personal possessions of King Edward VIII of England, he soon became the centre of attention. With each nod of Sam Moussaieff's head, the price jumped by $6,666 (10,000 Swiss francs) on whatever seemed to catch the Iranian-born dealer's fancy.

When Rayner (visibly red-faced with exhaustion and almost hoarse after two days of spruiking) pounded the gavel on the auction's final item, a George III silver-gilt horse-racing cup that went to Moussaieff for $200,000, the audience stood and applauded the soft-spoken dealer who ran a jewellery shop in London's Hilton Hotel. During the final afternoon and early evening, Moussaieff's quiet nodding had won him more than twenty-six lots, ranging from old silver and alabaster frames with pictures of the duke and his parents to a cigarette case, to royal and personal seals, Buckingham Palace candelabra, ceremonial swords, drinking tankards and those sealskin sporrans the duke wore over his kilts.

It was little known at the time, but Moussaieff was one of the auction's big spenders (the eponymous singer Shirley Bassey was in attendance), parting with more than $4 million of the two-day auction's astonishing $50.2 million total. 'I haven't decided what I am going to do with all these purchases,' Moussaieff told the *Washington Post*, which cornered him after he'd left the tent for the sanctuary of the Beau Rivage Hotel's bar. 'But I will definitely take them all back to England, because that is where they came from and that is where they belong.'[44]

There was a strong suspicion among the sniffy punters bested by Moussaieff that he might have been buying many of the items for Middle Eastern sheiks or exiled Iranian millionaires, but the shy, retiring gem dealer insisted that was not the case. 'I have always been an admirer of history, and I have long collected historical things,' he said diplomatically. 'I admired the Duke of Windsor and am delighted to have been able to acquire so many of his belongings and treasures.'[45]

Even objects that weren't quite in the show-stopper class excelled. One four-piece lot, including a plain platinum wedding band, went up to $120,000 in a dizzying forty seconds, almost 200 times the estimated price. A modest gold medallion commemorating the death of 'our principal wedding guest', the couple's Cairn terrier, Slipper, who died of a snakebite shortly before the ceremony at Château de Candé, sold for $73,320.

Other trinkets, such as a gold pipe cleaner given to the duke for Christmas in 1945 and listed in the sales catalogue as 'slightly imperfect', still brought in $20,000. Bidding, however, was slower on items unconnected to the 'grand love story'.[46] Four wedding rings, including ones from the duchess's two previous husbands, both Americans, sold for a mere $16,665.

The *New York Times* caught the high-octane reek of money, arrogance, avarice and greed when it reported midway through the sale:

The night seemed entirely a seller's market as bidders like Marvin Mitchelson, the Los Angeles divorce lawyer who has made his fortune on the failed loves of the rich, persisted in the hunt. Mr. Mitchelson stayed in to buy a diamond bib necklace for $373,996 and announced that he dedicated the achievement to his mother [...] Elizabeth Taylor phoned in from poolside at her Los Angeles home to buy a diamond clip in the shape of the plumes and crown of the Prince of Wales. It cost her $623,327, and she said it was worth it because of the friendship with the Windsors that she had shared with Richard Burton [...] the sale was attended by a thousand invited bidders, with a thousand more competitors participating in New York via satellite television and open checkbook. 'All done New York?' the auctioneer, Nicholas Rayner, took care to ask as each bidding contest peaked. Then he pronounced 'Adjuge!' signifying that the piece had been sold. The most active and successful bidder in New York was Alexander Acevedo, a Madison Avenue dealer in American art who bought 10 pieces for a total of about $2.7 million. He bought the ruby and sapphire clip that was the first offering in the sale, as well as a natural pearl necklace, at $733,326 the most expensive ever sold. Afterward Mr. Acevedo said he had already resold the necklace in the salesroom during the auction 'at a profit'. After months of buildup for the sale, the auctioneers intended to deny the television cameras the right to show the faces of the bidders in action, as if something intimate were occurring. But pandering to prurient interest soon seemed a reasonable policy once such shimmering behemoths as a 206-carat sapphire pendant were brought forth. The pendant went for $373,996 as everyone craned and stared – while the cameras recorded them – at the glittering residue of the oft-told love affair of Wallis Warfield Simpson and her King.[47]

Not surprisingly, Sotheby's was publicly ecstatic with the results. 'This surpasses even our wildest estimates,' said John D. Block, their New York-based senior vice president in charge of jewels and precious objects.[48] Privately, the company's pay day was described as 'extraordinary'[49] and Rayner and his team rightly celebrated on the company's tab after calculating their enormous commissions.

Perhaps they were also celebrating their good luck and the fact that the auction was nearly a spectacular failure. Apparently, the scores of television lights installed in the tents to capture the event had been frying the electrical cables running back to the Hotel Beau-Rivage. If it hadn't been for the back-up electrical generator that Sotheby's executive Michael Ainslie insisted was hired for $40,000, the $50.2 million outcome would have gone up in smoke![50]

And perhaps, more tellingly, they were also trying to obliterate the devastating, tightly held corporate knowledge their customers were blissfully unaware of: that some of the pieces in the collection were, in fact, replicas/copies of the original pieces that were stolen from the Windsors under mysterious circumstances in 1946.

As Maître Blum's assistant, Michael Bloch was inextricably involved in the packaging of the auction, rendering Sotheby's significant historical advice and other assistance over several months, including dashing off an article for their magazine. He was their guest at Geneva and invited to all their lavish junketings. He still has the pile of auction catalogues they gave him as recompense for his efforts.

Mr Bloch was also privy to the truckloads of confidential Windsor papers entrusted to Maître Blum and has written extensively on the Windsors. He is quite certain that:

There was, so to speak, a lie at the heart of the sale. Much of the Duchess's jewellery had in fact been stolen in a robbery in 1946 during the Windsors' first postwar visit to England as man & wife. Many of the pieces offered for sale in Geneva were not therefore the original pieces which the Duke of Windsor gave her to mark various milestones in their romance, but copies later produced by the original jewellers, paid for with the insurance money. Though I pointed this out to Sotheby's on a number of occasions, it was nowhere mentioned in their catalogue, which gave the impression that they were offering the original pieces for sale.[51]

This was the gigantic secret at the heart of the auction that was not disclosed in the 1987 sale catalogue and subsequent Windsor jewellery publications. It perhaps also explains why the duke 'romantically' wanted the sets broken up after their deaths, to further disguise both the extent of the theft in 1946 and the original provenance of the collection.

But, at the time of the 1987 Geneva sale, this didn't matter. What mattered was that the auction exceeded its estimate of $7 million, ensuring everyone made money (including Maître Blum) and the maximum amount possible went to the Pasteur Institute, in accordance with the duchess's will. Blum was quoted later as saying with uncharacteristic understatement, 'The mission that the Duchess asked to fulfil has been more than accomplished.'[52]

Not quite. Ironically, at the close of the twentieth century, there was one final, embarrassing denouement of their lushly created life together that played out in a city where they often found unconditional approval and sanctuary from the incredulous, prying eyes of a desiccated, wary Europe.

14

A New York State of Mind

Poor playthings of the man that's gone,
Surely we would not have them thrown,
Like wreckage on a barren strand,
The prey of every greedy hand.

Fast ride the Dead! Perhaps 'tis well!
He shall not know, what none could tell,
That gambling salesman bargain'd o'er
The books he read, the clothes he wore,

The desk he stood at day by day
In patient toil or earnest play,
The pictures that he loved to see,
Faint echoes of his Fantasy.

> Frederick York Powell, on the sale of his friend Lewis Carroll's
> personal effects 'At a Certain Auction'

It was a Manhattan February like no other. Absent were the howling
flurries of translucent snow that often swirled around the enclave's sky-
scrapers like the unleashed banshees at the conclusion of *Raiders of the*

Lost Ark. Absent were the cross-country skiers, criss-crossing the usually snowy meadows of Central Park and its bridle paths. Even the Arthur Ross Pinetum, from 72nd to 102nd Streets, which was planted to hide the views of buildings and look beautiful in winter, was denuded of snow. The habitual 6in of ice that covered the Rockefeller Center skating rink and both Wollman and Lasker rinks appeared razor thin and there were no sleighs or snowmen on Pilgrim or Cedar Hill. It was weird.

In its place was the mildest February on record (since passed by 2012, 2017 and 2018), that was 7°F above the average. And there was no snowfall, the only February on record ever to have this distinction. It followed an equally mild January, which was 8.5°F above average. And today, Thursday, 19 February 1998, continued the unusual trend with temperatures that were 11°F above the February average.

But apart from the weather, things were mostly the same in Manhattan that winter of 1998. The billboards around Times Square were promoting movies like *The Wedding Singer* and *Titanic*, and television shows like *Frasier*, *The Nanny* and *Stargate SG-1*. Newspapers were either leading with the Clinton–Lewinsky sex scandal or salivating about the wedding of Mötley Crüe drummer Tommy Lee and *Baywatch* actress Pamela Anderson.

'Nice and Slow' by Usher was on top of the singles charts, finally taking over from 'My Heart Will Go On' by Celine Dion. CDs had taken over from vinyl and cassettes as the dominant format for music. People were splurging on CD players and portable CD players. The post-Christmas sales were still in full force, trying to flog off excess vinyl stock that nobody wanted.

This was not the case with Sotheby's blockbuster auction of the Duke and Duchess of Windsors' accumulated possessions, rescheduled for February 1998 in Manhattan. It seemed everyone wanted a piece of the Windsors and their hoard of bric-a-brac (whether 'borrowed' from the Royal Collection, inherited or just plain looted was beyond knowing or even caring by those who attended).

Unlike the Geneva auction of the duchess's jewellery collection a decade prior, the New York offering was both exhausting and humiliating. Exhausting because it lasted nine fatiguing days, and humiliating because the buyers were predominately the kind of people the Windsors disdained their entire lives. This was obviously not the same well-heeled, filthy-rich, celebrity crowd habituated by the Windsors during their lifetime, who took over the city of Geneva in 1987 and proceeded to bleed it dry of booze, hospitality and, yes, cheese.

And, of course, there was no Nicholas Rayner, just a conveyer belt of in-house auctioneers, and no brooding Maître Suzanne Blum figure hanging over the entire event like some unrelenting, omnipotent vulture. There was just the cloying, disinterested figure of Al-Fayed, grieving from a distance, and an inexhaustible crowd of curious royal spectators.

The 1998 auction crowd were typically mundane American bourgeoisie, armed with a savings stash of a few thousand dollars and braced by a packed lunch of sandwiches and a thermos of home-brewed coffee, who were mostly thrilled to be spending a fun day in New York as one might be thrilled to be spending time at an amusement park or a night on Broadway. One thing, however, was common to both bookended Sotheby's auctions: like Geneva 1987, nobody cared where the New York money came from as long as it came. The Windsors might have looked down their noses at the clientele, but they would not have refused their money.

Unlike the elegant, haute society affair the Geneva sale aspired to create, New York, despite Sotheby's totemic, three-volume sales catalogue, was a glorified garage sale that lacked the refinement and poise of Christie's auction of Jackie Kennedy Onassis' estate the year before, and which every American instantly recognised for what it was – a rummage around the fusty closet of a deceased celebrity, albeit a royal one.

The 44,000 items for sale were originally scheduled to go under the hammer in September 1997, but this was postponed to February 1998 because of the premature deaths of Diana, Princess of Wales, and her boyfriend Dodi Fayed.

There was a last-minute hitch when Maîtres Jean Lisbonne and Paul Bailly, both of whom had worked with the formidable Maître Blum and described themselves as 'Exécuteurs Testamentaires de la Duchesse de Windsor', made a joint eleventh-hour protest against the sale. They claimed that when Al-Fayed had taken over the lease of the Villa Windsor and bought the Windsor furniture for 15 million French francs, he had promised to retain the house as a historical monument in memory of the Windsors. But nothing came of the protest.

The overhanging allure, mystique, drama, tragedy, pathos, or whatever you want to call it, of the collection's Diana connection didn't appear to influence the audience's bidding tendencies. It wasn't in the front of the minds of purchasers when they were interviewed in the spotlight of victory or in the margins of defeat, though it had been stoked occasionally and subliminally by the auction house and the collection's owner. 'I had hoped to be at Sotheby's tonight to welcome you to the beginning of this historic sale,' Mohamed Al-Fayed said in a statement. 'But, as I am sure you can understand, it is too difficult for me.'[1] Proceeds were earmarked to benefit the Dodi Fayed International Charitable Foundation and charities favoured by Diana.

The pall that now permeated the Windsor bric-a-brac for Al-Fayed was a far cry from the euphoria on display at the champagne garden party he had hosted on 10 December 1989 to celebrate the three years and $14.4 million he'd spent on recreating the Windsor mansion as it was before the duke died in 1972.

Guests swooned at the reverent attention to detail: the duchess's perfumes lining a bathroom shelf; the duke's pipes waiting by his desk; their clothes, a reminder of how tiny they both were, hanging in wardrobes. 'This is how it used to be,' said Sydney Johnson, the former footman who, together with the Windsors' chauffeur of twenty years, Gregoire Martin, and his wife, Maria, were kept on by Al-Fayed when he took over the lease of the mansion in 1986.[2] Except, Johnson noted, there were no dogs around.

But their images were represented everywhere: on cushions, in porcelain and in photographs. Only the duke and duchess appeared framed on tables, desks and mantelpieces more often than their beloved pugs.

Al-Fayed had rescued the Villa when he acquired the lease in 1986 from Paris Mayor Jacques Chirac. The structure of the house needed reinforcing, the roof had to be retiled and the central heating and electrical systems were replaced. At the chilly 1989 party, while the bubbly flowed and the canapés circulated, guests were encouraged to open drawers, rummage through closets and touch things to absorb the Windsor effect.

Golf clubs, walking sticks and wardrobes full of the duke's clothes could be fingered and tried on along with the duchess's weighing scales, fur coats and shoes. Personal valuables were placed where they were supposed to be, including framed intimate letters and photographs and silver and crystalware on the dining room table as if the Windsors were expecting guests.

Countless porcelain pug dogs were dotted around the house, commemorating the family pets who were always given pride of place. Even King Charles III, who as Prince Charles visited the mansion twice while the restoration was going on, was encouraged to savour the Windsor experience and then go one better. 'I told him if there were any items that he would like for his family collection, to please take them,' Al-Fayed confided to the *Washington Post*. 'He took a couple of things, but I won't say what!'[3]

'I feel on top of the world,' said 69-year-old Sydney Johnson at the time, dressed once more in gold and red livery, as he did in the old days. 'I cried all through the party Mr Al-Fayed gave three years ago to celebrate his lease on the house,' he continued. 'The restoration is so authentic I expect to see the Duchess stepping down the staircase asking, "How do I look?".'[4]

To compensate for the Windsor furniture and *objets d'art* from No. 4 route du Champ d'Entraînement that were clandestinely and deceitfully sold off during the last fourteen years of the duchess's life (when she became increasingly disorientated and incapacitated), the restoration team tracked down items from the Windsors' other home, 20 miles south-west of Paris, at Ville de Gif-sur-Yvette.

Le Moulin de la Tuilerie, a converted eighteenth-century mill house, was purchased as a weekend escape from their trophy house in the Bois where they felt like 'animals in a gilded zoo'.[5] It was the only house they ever owned. Here, the duke waved his arms around and tried to communicate with his French, Spanish and Alsatian gardeners, who disregarded his instructions when he left, and the testy American-born duchess drove her servants mad with her fluctuating moods and nagged her expensive Michelin-starred chefs to use more tinned and frozen American produce:

> I wonder often if American housewives appreciate their good fortune in having so many excellent frozen foods … In France, these foods are few and expensive. Inevitably this must change when electric refrigeration becomes more general. In our household I have waged a long fight on behalf of frozen foods.[6]

No wonder 'the Dook' took refuge in ultra-thin slices of the rarest of rare roast beef whenever he could. It was a far cry from their early days at the Château de Candé and the expert household tutelage of Fern Bedaux. By Monday afternoon, the relief of getting back to the Bois and its rigid, spacious routine for all and sundry was palpable.

In its heyday, the 26-acre estate featured eighteen bedrooms, sixteen bathrooms and had 1,328 square metres of internal living areas spread across six buildings. In total, it could sleep thirty-six people. It was made for entertaining. In 2010, the British charity the Landmark Trust marketed it for holiday lets stripped of the duchess's eccentric decor ('Chi-Chi and overdone', as photographer Cecil Beaton put it) [7] with the main house advertised at £2,800 to rent per week. In 2020, the owner decided to sell the estate, which included three self-catering properties – Le Moulin, La Maison des Amis and La Célibataire – for £5.6 million.

While the showy gardens of the Mill (the name the duke referred to it by) were the sole responsibility of the duke, the interior, of course, was the duchess's preserve. Like the Villa Windsor, the highly developed and stylised taste at the Mill (some less generous souls might describe it as a tacky Palm Beach) was influenced by her friend, Elsie de Wolfe. Not everyone was in tune with it. Fashion writer Suzy Menkes called it 'pioneer homestead meets the American Dream'.[8] Diana Vreeland was kinder – the duchess's style was 'soignée, not degagée [polished but not relaxed]'.[9]

The duchess put the Mill on the market a year after the duke's death. Most of the furniture and bric-a-brac was put into storage and, over time (as the duchess lost control of her faculties), discreetly sold off by Maître Blum at various auction *privées*.

Fundamentally, furnishing the Mill was an exercise in shopping, as most of the Windsors pre-abdication household possessions were already absorbed by the Bois de Boulogne Villa. It was something the duchess had always excelled at. She often described her life as 'Wallis in Wonderland'[10] and shopping was her overwhelming super-power. Laura, Duchess of Marlborough, expressed what everyone knew, that 'her life's work was shopping',[11] and everyone in her circle knew she would rather shop than eat, a fact her rail-thin figure through the years attested to. It was fitting, then, that in the lead-up to the 1998 Sotheby's New York auction, one of Manhattan's premier department stores, Bergdorf Goodman, decorated their windows with the duke and duchess's clothing and held a special event on 5th Avenue to commemorate the sale. 'They did for shopping what Einstein did for physics,' Bruce Wolmer of *Art and Antiques Magazine* told CNN Interactive. 'They took it to a whole new dimension.'[12]

It set the tone for the marathon, post-Christmas shopping spree to follow, occurring conveniently at the height of the bonus season on Wall Street. The American mania for anything royal, especially British royalty with an American connection, was prodded, coerced, teased and stroked until it had sensationally prevailed through that drab February and the largest, longest-running sale ever held at the 254-year-old auction house. The American papers were full of it, the quirkier and whackier the better. And there was plenty to write about over the course of nine gruelling days and eighteen selling sessions (such as the duchess's 135 pairs of gloves that took up one whole display cabinet).

Bidders eventually parted with a total of $23.3 million on 44,000 items that had been expected to fetch only $7 million. Though some items, such as the table on which Edward VIII signed the instrument of abdication, went for eight times the pre-sale value ($415,000), the overall ratio was just over three times the expected outcome. This failed to match Sotheby's 1996 sale of Jacqueline Kennedy Onassis' estate, which brought in $34.5 million and seven times the pre-sale estimate. As the journalist Malcolm Forbes once cannily observed, 'I think that anyone could live very comfortably for the rest of their life on the difference between Sotheby's estimates and what they actually sell for.'[13]

To celebrate securing the Windsor sale (and perhaps endeavour to trump the legendary status and allure of the sensational Geneva jewellery auction), Sotheby's New York decided to do something rather special – something that wasn't possible or even conceivable in Geneva.

To break up the vast mannequin displays of Windsor clothes and demonstrate the Villa Windsor's shrine-like setting and aura (where too much was never enough), the auction house hired the New York firm that created the exhibition for the wildly successful Jacqueline Kennedy Onassis estate sale to inject some show-business razzmatazz into the dreary showrooms. 'What we wanted to do was really to create a ghost house, a phantom of a lost age,' Francis O'Shea of Ralph Appelbaum Associates told Cynthia Tornquist of CNN Interactive.[14]

Great attention was paid to getting things just right, to the extent that a long-time socialite friend of the Windsors, Lucy Douglas 'C.Z.' Guest (described by the New York Times as 'one of the monarchs of New York society'[15] – the Windsors were the godparents of her children), was brought in to set the dining room table. 'I think people who come here who didn't know the Windsors will get the feeling of the taste they had and the beauty of all the wonderful things they collected,' she told CNN,[16] echoing the duchess herself, 'The possession of beautiful things is thrilling to me'.[17]

Sotheby's attempt at recreation was no mean feat and a valiant attempt given the exactness of the Windsor effect. Of course, some things, such as the intrinsic ambiance of the Villa's settings, could not be recreated. What was included in the attempt was the vintage madder-red Khorasan carpet that grounded the decor. The north Persian textile was repurposed, like the other furniture from the Windsors' former residence at Boulevard Suchet. Practically the only other important thing missing from Sotheby's recreation was the room's English ostrich candelabra that incorporated an actual egg.

To this fabricated regal setting (behind the auctioneer's rostrum hung the Munnings portrait of the duke on horseback, accompanied by two images of the duke and duchess, ironically printed back to front, with his Garter banner attached to the ceiling), the great unwashed of American society flocked, gaining admittance to the 'ghost house' by virtue of their wallets, just as they would have done to the actual Windsor residence.

Although, it wasn't necessarily the size of the wallet that counted in 1998, but the desire of ordinary Americans to open theirs. Take the story of Rick Patrick, a 42-year-old painter from Michigan. Mr Patrick submitted the winning bid of $4,250 for a 'medicine spoon' that had once been owned by the duke and which a Sotheby's expert had valued at no more than $600. The *Baltimore Sun* reported Mr Patrick:

> ... sat back, reached beneath his folding chair in Sotheby's auction room, and pulled out a small paper bag. Inside was his lunch. 'It's important to economize,' he explained. Patrick's home-packed meal – a sandwich and a Coke – was the only thing that came cheaply this week at Sotheby's.[18]

The prices for all the objects on sale, from mundane ashtrays to rare paintings, were supercharged by emotion for some buyers, just as the Geneva jewellery from 1987 had been.

'The Duke and Duchess had a beautiful love story, but it certainly boosts the market beyond all comprehension,' said Gayle Nemeth, who owned a pet-related antique store, Doggy Dames, at the time of the auction in Manhattan.[19] 'There were pieces here that sold for $28,000 that you couldn't get $2,800 for at the priciest antique show. I'm exhausted. I've got to go home and rest from price shock.'

Auction observer Trudy Ebanks Dyer, a nurse who grew up in the UK, was equally indignant, though in a very British way, 'And they are such commonplace things! It's hard to imagine spending that kind of money to take them home.'[20]

Such was the feeding frenzy that, against their better judgement, many antique collectors and dealers stuck around for all nine days in the hope that prices would drop as bidders became fatigued. If they were hoping that through sheer exhaustion and inaccessibility, prices and bidders would magically drop towards the end, they were resoundingly disappointed. Newspapers reported the mix of onlookers seemed to grow *curiosa* and *curiosa* as the closing hammer drew near, with antique dealers and Manhattan's fashionably fabulous set of socialites and designers rubbing shoulders with an eclectic diorama of expatriate Brits, nurses from various East Side hospitals, and even the occasional cabbie.

The *Baltimore Sun* reported that an Italian menswear designer paid $27,600 for the duke's wedding suit, and a Tennessee man successfully bid $123,500 for a rectangular gold Omega wristwatch that had been expected to sell for perhaps $1,500 to $2,000. A silver-mounted walking cane given to the duke on his eighteenth birthday sold for $20,700. Even the Baltimore-born duchess's hometown Maryland Historical Society purchased a dozen outfits that had belonged to her.

Several buyers came to the auction seeking to reclaim items that they or family members had once sold to the royal couple. Alexis Kirk, a New York jewellery designer, spent nearly $20,000 on costume jewellery he had designed for the duchess in the 1960s and told the *Sun*:

> It's business and pleasure ... I'll use the pieces as the basis of a special collection. And they mean something special to me, too. The Duke and Duchess couldn't have been nicer or more helpful when I knew them. They treated me like royalty.[21]

Kirk had positioned himself in the front of the auction room, near representatives from fashion houses Dior, Tommy Hilfiger and Yves St Laurent, who, he reported, spent heavily even as they snickered at the tastes of a duchess who was (as one remarked to him) 'a little too Baltimore'.[22] Particular items for snickering were a Christian Dior couture 'Stewart Old' tartan kilt from 1963–64 and matching diamanté-studded, wing-shaped spectacles in tartan; a reversible organdie stole appliquéd with butterflies and the duchess' cyphers from the 1950s; and a group of flashy handbags and purses from the 1960s.

The opening night of the auction, attended by over 1,000 punters, was lit up when a tiny piece of the Windsors' wedding cake sold for $29,900 in spirited bidding. The *LA Times* quoted the San Francisco buyer, 31-year-old entrepreneur Benjamin Yim, 'It represents the epitome of a great romance – truly romantic and elegant like Fred Astaire and Ginger Rogers'. Yim told the newspaper he was going to preserve the sentimental morsel packed in a white silk-covered cardboard box inscribed in ink by the duke and duchess. 'We intend to keep it. We're sure not going to eat it,' he joked.[23] The 61-year-old piece of cake was valued at between $500 and $1,000 in the auction catalogue.

Other items in the first night's sale included Prince Edward's christening portrait, photographs, books and the king's red-leather dispatch box (it brought $65,750 after an estimate of $15,000), amassing a nice start at $1.92 million. The most expensive item, a pair of Regency-style tables with ornately carved eagle decorations, was bought by clothing designer Tommy Hilfiger for $134,500. The same price was paid for a Cecil Beaton watercolour portrait of the duchess wearing the ruby and diamond necklace the king had given her on her fortieth birthday, one of several drawings Beaton made on the afternoon of 20 November 1936, less than three weeks before King Edward VIII signed the instrument of abdication.

The only downside for Sotheby's was a ceremonial sword given to Edward in July 1911 to mark his installation as a duke, which failed to find a sufficient bidder. The double-edged sword was valued at up to $55,000 but it was withdrawn when bidding only reached $42,500.

The *Deseret News* reported on two quirky sales during the second day, Friday, of the scheduled nine-day auction. By then the auction had taken in $2,805,128 and the highest price on Friday was the $52,250 paid by an anonymous bidder for a gold medal, one of five, struck to commemorate the maiden voyage of the RMS *Queen Mary* in 1936. It had been presented by the board of the Cunard Line to the duke while he was still King Edward VIII. It had been estimated by Sotheby's at between $7,000 and $10,000.

The second was the sale of a silver-plated plaque presented to the Prince of Wales in 1936, which was bought for $460 by Matthew Coleman, a 17-year-old high school student from Woodmere, New York:

> I'm ecstatic. I came into Manhattan with my two friends today especially to attend the auction and bid ... I was so nervous I was shaking. It feels nice to hold a piece of history in my hands ... to pass down to my children. I paid with cash and a check endorsed from my grandma.[24]

The *Hartford Courant* chose to focus on the unlikely story of Jane Dayus-Hinch from Lichfield in Staffordshire, who as a 14-year-old schoolgirl was assigned to write a book report on the duchess. In 1998, as a fortieth birthday gift, her family sent her across the Atlantic to New York City so she could spend the day trying to buy a memento of her favourite royal.

She chose Wednesday, the seventh day of the marathon sale, because of its focus on the duchess's once highly touted wardrobe. As of late afternoon, she was still empty-handed, but hopeful that something – anything – at the higher-priced evening session could fall into her hands. 'My maximum cash-in-hand is 800 to 1,000 pounds,' Dayus-Hinch told the *Courant*.[25] It was a lot of money for her, but not for New York, where just the auction catalogue set you back $90 and the conservative estimate of $7 million for the entire collection had been surpassed days ago. The running total stood at $18.2 million as of 5 p.m. on Wednesday, 26 February.

The daytime sessions on that day focused on the duchess's clothing and accessories. Devotees shelled out just over $1 million at the 10 a.m. and 2 p.m. sessions, buying dresses, gowns, furs, hats, shawls, hankies, linen and even mink garters. Auctioneers passed the $1,000 mark in seconds with several of the items.

The biggest seller, at $26,450, was the midnight-blue velvet 'Lahore' evening gown created by Christian Dior in the 1940s, which was snapped up by a representative of the Paris fashion house. A printed silk commemorative scarf bearing what the *Courant* called 'A King's Farewell', the abdication address of King Edward VIII, sold for $25,300. An ivory silk chiffon scarf embroidered with tiny steel beads, bearing the duchess's cypher, a monogram, sold for $21,850. Both scarves were purchased by anonymous telephone bidders.

The *Courant* sadly noted that Dayus-Hinch didn't stand much of a chance with her £1,000, especially with the likes of Pat Kerr of Memphis, Tennessee, in the audience. Kerr had collected royal memorabilia for thirty years and bought four of the gowns that belonged to Diana, Princess of Wales at the 1997 Christie's auction. She was a committed aficionado. For her, the 44,000-item Windsor auction was a gold mine.

By Wednesday afternoon, she had purchased fifty lots – and she was still below her self-imposed budget of $250,000. 'I have an enormous collection and this will all be a part of it,' Kerr told the *Courant*. 'Someday, I might have my own museum.' She had bought in quick succession an ivory, satin and lace-edged cloth embroidered with the duchess's cypher for $2,185; another embroidered cloth for $4,025; and two quilted pink satin lingerie cases bearing the duchess's cypher for $3,162.

Some punters wished to be spared the glare of publicity offered by circling media hacks, for obvious reasons. A 'youngish-looking man sporting a goatee, shoulder-length hair and modish glasses' was spied by the *Courant* paying $3,200 for the duchess's mink garters. The newspaper tried to get him to talk, but he wouldn't, and 'left fast'.[26] A Sotheby's spokeswoman later said the man had made the purchase as an anniversary gift for his wife.

Julie Fitzgerald of Camp Hill, Pennsylvania, came to New York for two days of close contact with the Windsor collection, never dreaming she would actually buy something. The *Courant* reported there was a look of 'slightly dazed satisfaction on her face' when she found herself the owner of four pairs of the duchess's gloves for $1,150 and she planned to exhibit them along with her copy of Sotheby's three-volume, 4.5kg catalogue in a shadowbox table.[27]

Jane Dayus-Hinch from Lichfield left with nothing but the experience.

Although the back of the auction room throughout the nine days was divided among three classes of punter – antique dealers, curiosity seekers and amateur historians – no member of the motley auction audience cut a more distinctive figure according to the *Baltimore Sun* than Mr Patrick, the Michigan painter, who said he was attending his first auction. Wearing a plaid jacket in a crowd dressed mainly in chic Manhattan black, he passed on the couple's paintings but won the bidding for the silver medicine spoon and the Windsors' 495 poker chips.

As the prices rose, Mr Patrick's sister-in-law was there to egg him on, reminding him in an emphatic whisper of his purchase's charitable upside, 'Tax deduction! Tax deduction!'[28] Mr Patrick told the *Sun* he would use the spoon to encourage his eleven nephews and nieces to take their medicine. The poker chips, which he'd nabbed earlier in the week, had already been used by late Thursday night in a quarter-ante poker game. 'I've got to leave in ten minutes,' he said, as he bit into his bag lunch, 'but I wish this auction would never end'.[29]

But this was the end, and although Windsor possessions and jewellery would appear in ad-hoc auctions following the 1998 event (including, most notably, Sotheby's twenty-lot auction of *Exceptional Jewels And Precious Objects Formerly In The Collection Of The Duchess Of Windsor* on 30 November 2010 in London, which lasted a little over an hour and raised $12.5 million, including a top price of just over $7 million for the 1952 Cartier panther bracelet set with diamonds and onyx that was bought by Collection Cartier – in 1987, Mohamed Al-Fayed had purchased it for over $1.4 million, along with at least nineteen more Windsor pieces), the New York marathon represented the couple's last big hurrah on the world auction stage.

Even though the jewels were secretly released in dribs and drabs during the 1970s and 1980s, it is still to be determined which pieces of the dispersed collection are replicas and which are originals. To answer that conclusively, we need the co-operation and goodwill of a plethora of litigious vendors, anonymous buyers and secretive haute jewellery makers. And the chances of that occurring in the interests of the truth is practically zilch, for all the obvious reasons of client confidentiality, client embarrassment and dire legal consequences.

But then again, stranger things have happened in the labyrinthine story of the Duchess of Windsor's jewellery collection and the messy, murky business of its creation and disposal.

Postscript

The Only Thing That Ever Truly Mattered

This woman has taken possession of me in spite of myself, in spite of my fear and my knowledge of her; and she possesses me as if she had plucked out, one after the other, my every last aspiration.

Guy de Maupassant, *Alien Hearts*

After another tedious luncheon at a French forward defence post near the Maginot Line, Major General HRH Prince Edward, the Duke of Windsor, informed his driver they would be taking a slight detour through central Paris en route to his billet at the British Military Mission in Vincennes. 'It's alright, Corporal,' the duke no doubt said in response to his driver's nervous reaction to this wanton disregard of imperial standing orders, 'I'll deal with any flak that comes of it.'

Paris at this time (Monday, 4 March 1940) was in an unreal situation, six months into a period of relative calm known as the Phoney War (*La Drôle de guerre*). Since the spring of 1939, city workers had dug 20km of trenches in city squares and parks intended for bomb shelters. Municipal plans were in place to distribute gas masks to civilians and post signs on street corners to guide Parisians to the nearest shelter when the inevitable blitzkrieg arrived. The previous August, the French government had begun evacuating 30,000 children from the city to the regions and streetlights were turned off as a precaution against anticipated German air raids.

In August 1939, workmen had also begun taking down the stained-glass windows of the Sainte-Chapelle and curators at the Louvre, aided by packers from the nearby La Samaritaine and Bazar de l'Hôtel de Ville department stores, began cataloguing and packing major works of art into crates labelled with numbers to disguise their contents. The 'Winged Victory of Samothrace' statue was carefully wheeled down the Louvre's long stairway on a wooden ramp and put on a truck for transportation to the Château de Valençay in the Indre. Trucks used to move scenery for the Comédie-Française theatre company were requisitioned to move the larger paintings, including Gericault's 'Raft of the Medusa', in a slow convoy to châteaux of the Loire Valley. Other architectural landmarks of the city were protected by sandbags.

Ration cards for fuel and food had just been introduced but cafés and theatres were open for business, albeit with escalating regulations and shortages. Meat could only be served on certain days, and certain products, such as cream, coffee and fresh produce, were becoming extremely rare and expensive. It prompted the great restaurants to become innovative and scrupulous in their attention to unnecessary waste.

But one can only dine on noodles with water, turnips and beets for so long. Black market dining was thriving. Almost overnight it had become the chic new Parisian symbol of wealth and privilege. For 500 francs, one could demolish a reasonable pork chop and cabbage, served with a litre of Beaujolais and real coffee, while sitting anonymously in a room on the first floor of a house at rue Dauphine, listening to the BBC with Picasso, Chanel or Jean Gabin.

The bars of the Champs-Élysées and other parts of Paris became common meeting places between black marketeers and their clients. It was the only way for Parisians not in the upper echelons of government or the armed forces to obtain cigarettes, meat, coffee, wine and other necessaries. The hunt for food was to be an enduring pursuit for the citizens of Paris for the next five years.

Due to a shortage of fuel, the number of automobiles dropped from 350,000 before the war to just under 4,500 by the time the city fell to the Germans in May 1940. Older means of transportation, such as the horse-drawn *fiacre*, were coming back into service. Trucks and automobiles that did run often used *gazogene*, a poor-quality fuel carried in a tank on the roof, or coal gas, or methane extracted from the Paris sewers.

The Metro ran, but service was frequently interrupted and over-crowded. Three thousand five hundred buses had run on the Paris streets in 1939, but only 500 were still running by September 1940. Bicycle-taxis were becoming popular, and their drivers charged a high tariff. Bicycles became the means of transport for many Parisians and their price soared – a used bicycle would soon cost a month's salary.

Though two-thirds of Parisians (particularly those in the wealthier suburbs like Vincennes, 7km to the east) had fled to the countryside and the south, many illustrious inhabitants continued to go about their daily lives or use the city as the hub of their commercial activities. Picasso continued to sell paintings at the Hôtel Drouot auction house and the Galerie Louise Leiris, formerly Daniel-Henry Kahnweiler's. Braque, Kandinsky and Henri Matisse continued to sell their work in the back rooms of Paris galleries. The actor Fernandel, film director and play-wright Sacha Guitry, and singers Édith Piaf, Tino Rossi, Charles Trenet, and Yves Montand stayed and performed, while 67-year-old Colette continued to work quietly on her *mémoires* in her apartment at No. 9 rue du Beaujolais, next to the gardens of the Palais-Royal, and the philoso-pher and novelist Jean-Paul Sartre continued to write and publish, along with his companion Simone de Beauvoir and friend Marguerite Duras.

The Duke and Duchess of Windsor had returned to the city after being evacuated to England in September 1939 aboard HMS *Kelly* at the behest of the duke's brother, King George VI. They'd had a rotten time in England. They had nowhere to stay and spent the first night with Sir William James, commander-in-chief at Portsmouth. They were then forced to stay at the Metcalfes (Fruity, Baba and their children) when requests for accommodation and a car were denied by the Palace, though the duke did manage to sneak a secret visit to Fort Belvedere.

Humiliated, the Windsors met with no other member of the royal family except the king, who Edward saw on 14 September. By the end of the month, they were back in France, the duchess at the Trianon Palace Hotel in Versailles and the duke assigned to the British Military Mission attached to the French General Headquarters in Vincennes.

While the duke was in Vincennes, the duchess became the honorary president of the French relief organisation Colis de Trianon, which distributed kits of clothing and necessities to the Front. She learned to knit and donated money to a soup kitchen in Montmartre. In addition, she volunteered for the Section Sanitaire of the French Red Cross.

On the surface, they were engaged in meaningful work but it was, as usual, hard work keeping up the pretence. The duke's reports on French military readiness were ignored in Whitehall and his days were largely preoccupied with keeping his prickly ego in check in the face of all kinds of supposed slights and humiliations. It was the same, intolerable existence all over again, exacerbated this time by their separation and the absence of the usual comforts of a proper home.

Wallis needed cheering up and the duke's destination this gloomy Monday afternoon was to provide for that, plus a fitting present for her forty-fourth birthday on 19 June. The rue de la Paix, a half-kilometre-long street leading from the Opéra Garnier to the Place Vendôme, was lined with flashy automobiles that, because of recent petrol rationing, had nowhere to go. The duke's mud-splattered military car pulled up outside the marbled, elaborately gilded façade of No. 13, and he sauntered out smoking a pipe with a marshal's baton clenched firmly under his armpit.

After a few words to his driver, the duke glided by the ebony window frames and royal crests flanking the entrance to Cartier and pushed open a door marked with a card bearing the words '*fermé pour entretien privé*' beneath a spotless white awning.

The duke was expected, and he was ushered into a cavernous showroom, walled with blonde wood diffused by a crystal teardrop chandelier. The floor was chequered marble, and every surface was punctuated by lavish displays of fresh roses provided daily by florists operating around the Opéra Garnier. Against the walls were mirrored cabinets containing all manner of silverware and, of course, jewellery: diamond studded necklaces, multi-coloured settings of gems, sapphires, rubies and emeralds of all shapes and sizes, a cacophony of colour and dazzling reflections. Above the display cases were sketches of iridescent birds and fantastic animals, with leopards, panthers and other big cats predominating. A lithographic reproduction of Corot's 'Bacchante with a Panther' (the original was on its way to the Louvre) stood on an easel.

The duke removed his hat. He loved this room. It was largely unchanged from the time he first began coming here in the 1920s as Prince of Wales and it was wonderful to be back here again with its soothing memories, even though it was freezing. Coal was becoming scarcer and scarcer in Paris and electricity was being shut off at eight-thirty in the morning. You could generally tell the time in Paris because at five in the evening, the streets were filled with the clacking of wooden shoes from workmen heading home because the electricity had been turned off in offices and shops. Like everyone in the store, the duke kept his gloves on.

After a moment a small, slender, birdlike woman in a rose-pink turban with a triple band of luxurious Persian pearls draped around her neck appeared, dissolving the duke's reverie. This was 53-year-old Jeanne Toussaint, Cartier's Director of Fine Jewellery, a woman with startling blue eyes and skin as smooth and white as a duck's egg. A vivid Schiaparelli jacket of multi-coloured shards and embroidered Russian boots dating from the *ancien régime* completed her outfit.

An assistant with a tray containing two flawless Baccarat glasses and an opened bottle of Krug appeared, unobtrusively serving the duke and Mademoiselle Toussaint while they chatted and exchanged pleasantries. 'At least the champagne doesn't need chilling,' remarked the duke.

Jeanne nodded, 'Yes, and imagine the workmen up on the sixth floor using their hands all day long for the finest of work.'

'It's the same everywhere,' the duke replied. The duchess had remarked to him only this morning about a fitting she went to at

Schiaparelli at Place Vendôme, where the seamstress kept dropping her pins her hands were so cold.

Intent on changing the subject, Jeanne steered the duke casually to an ornate Louis XV desk where she wanted to show him an important new diamond that Cartier had recently obtained. Opening a drawer, she extracted a crimson velvet wrap and unfurled it to reveal a stone the size of a damson that had once formed part of a collection owned by Louis XIV. It was of the highest grade in both colour and clarity. The duke laid his heavy marshal's baton, hat and glass on the desk and delicately fondled the ice-cold stone. 'You really are a witch,' he laughingly told Jeanne.

Mademoiselle Toussaint was of Belgian extraction (she had grown up in Charleroi, an industrial town on the banks of the River Sambre) and her provenance was as colourful as her jacket. Growing up poor, the youngest of five children in a home where her mother, a laundress, was the only source of income, she fled to Paris as fast as she could at the age of 15, following her sister Clementine who had already made the break.

Flourishing as a *demi-mondaine* and surviving on 'a diet of wealthy admirers',[1] she became the mistress of the wealthy aristocrat Comte Pierre de Quinsonas, who took her on safari to Africa and gave her the nickname of 'PanPan' in tribute to the wild panthers they encountered. Gradually, they drifted apart as Jeanne began acquiring friends of a more artistic bent, designing handbags for Coco Chanel, collaborating with Christian Dior and attracting the attention of Louis Cartier, head of the family business.

Painted by Helleu, Boldini, Sem, Iribe and Bérard, she was courted as a style magician ('You perfume diamonds!' exclaimed her friend Princess Bibesco).[2] Cecil Beaton noted her 'almost male contempt for trivialities' and her sixth sense for what was chic and what was not, her famous '*goût Toussaint*'.[3]

In 1913, Louis Cartier commissioned the artist George Barbier to create an advertising campaign to reflect a modern, worldly woman, and Barbier naturally asked Jeanne (currently Louis's girlfriend) to model for him. She arrived wearing a fabulous full-length panther fur coat gifted to her by de Quinsonas, reputedly the first of its kind in Paris. Barbier seized on the idea and called his illustration 'Dame à la Panthère' and had Jeanne looking at the viewer with a sleek black cat sitting at her feet. The Cartier–Panthère link was thus forged.

Although Louis Cartier had a deep romantic relationship with Toussaint, he was unable to marry her because of her family background. He did the next best thing and brought her into the company to co-ordinate Cartier's accessories.

Jeanne's panther affinity made its first public appearance as a smattering of diamond and onyx spots on a 1914 wristwatch. Other examples soon followed including, in the 1920s, a Cartier greeting card featuring the sleek profile of the big cat at the feet of a woman draped in jewels.

In 1918, she was promoted to head Cartier's silver department and in 1933, Louis sensationally conferred on her full responsibility for artistic design, an area which until then he had directed himself and this made her the first woman in the fine jewellery business to be entrusted with such an important mandate. Although Jeanne's great rival, Suzanne Belperron, had been secretly appointed by Bernard Herz – a renowned Parisian dealer in pearls and precious stones operating from a private salon at 59 rue de Châteaudun – as chief designer in 1932, at the 1987 Sotheby's auction of the Duchess of Windsor's jewellery collection, only five out of sixteen Belperron pieces were correctly catalogued and credited to her.[4]

The appointment was all the more striking because, as Jeanne often told everyone, she couldn't draw. But it was this inability that fuelled her great talent. 'My inability to draw qualifies me to assess the work of others,' she said.[5]

The duke reluctantly relinquished the diamond and returned it to the velvet wrap. He had something else in mind from the house of Cartier and extracted from his tunic pocket a small pouch which he untied, tipping the contents on the blotter in front of Mademoiselle Toussaint.

Jeanne stared at the four simple art deco line bracelets with calibré-cut rubies, sapphires and emeralds, along with a necklace with diamonds.[5] She reached for a purse on the crowded desk and withdrew an onyx cigarette case decorated with a diamond and onyx panther emerging from two cypress trees, a talismanic gift from Louis Cartier following the Barbier modelling assignment. 'I'd like you to take these ordinary things and make something extraordinary for the duchess,' the duke said. 'It's her birthday on 19 June.'

'A motif?' Jeanne suggested.

'Perhaps something from up there, something modern,' the duke replied, gesturing at the exotic animals on the walls of the showroom.

In July 1940, when the Windsors arrived in Madrid following the German invasion of France, Wallis wore the Cartier flamingo brooch the duke had commissioned from Jeanne Toussaint on that March day for the first time in public. It had been a harrowing escape. Leaving their Biarritz home La Croë on 19 June, they passed many refugees on the route and were in constant danger as neither possessed diplomatic papers. Rosa Wood, who was with them, later wrote:

> I thought of Wallis and how so many people believed she cared only for clothes and jewels, and how they always pictured her against backgrounds of castles, with maids, couturiers, and hairdressers. I saw her in mud and dirt, sleeping cars, eating sardines out of tins, I saw when we were held up for hours before we could go south, when we had to sit all night long in the lobbies of little hotels. I saw her when we had no place to wash, much less do any of the things women like to do to make themselves look nicer. I saw her awaken at four o'clock in the morning and come out in the drizzle and help the Duke and my husband arrange things on the lorry, when we didn't [know] where we were going and whether we were walking into traps or whether we would be bombed. Never once did I see her cross or hear her complain or even falter except at the sight [of] the sufferings of others.[7]

On 19 December 1940, when the Windsors disembarked from the palatial yacht *Southern Cross* in Miami en route to the Bahamas, the duchess was still wearing her flamingo brooch. Greeted by Mayor Alexander

Orr Jr, it was the first time the duke (now Governor General of the Bahamas) had visited the USA in sixteen years. The duchess hadn't done so in twelve. Following their arrival, the duchess underwent a successful operation for the removal of a tooth.

The duchess adored the flamingo brooch and continued to wear it throughout her life. As extravagant as the design looks today, it was merely a daytime jewel for her. She pinned it to suit jackets and day dresses. The jewel's designer, Cartier's Peter Lemarchand,[8] made clever use of the art deco bracelets in the tail feathers. There is an arc in the setting of the tail feathers that gives the piece a sculptural and slightly naturalistic quality. The bird's plumes are set with emeralds, rubies and sapphires – forty-two of each. The legs and body are made of 102 diamonds (the provenance of the Windsor gems used is unknown, in common with most jewellery made during the Second World War). Another manufacturing detail is the hinged joint in the standing leg. It provides the piece with a bit of movement and flexibility. Although it measured about 10cm in height it looked larger on the duchess's petite frame.

On 2 April 1987, the Toussaint flamingo brooch was sold at Sotheby's in Geneva. It was reported that Elizabeth Taylor bought the jewel. She did not; she only purchased the Prince of Wales diamond brooch from the Duchess of Windsor's collection. The flamingo was purchased from the 1987 auction for £498,000, along with nineteen other items, by Mohamed Al-Fayed. This assemblage of jewels was later sold by him on 30 November 2010 at the previously mentioned Sotheby's auction in London. Estimated to sell for at least £1.5 million, it eventually fetched £1,721,250[9] and was acquired by the Cartier Collection for its historical archive of special creations, along with the Toussaint panther bracelet.

The flamingo brooch was one of the pieces Christian Lacroix, the French couturier, called 'horrible' in the 1980s, just after its Geneva auction (and let's face it, not everyone would want to wear an extravagant flamingo, even one that costs a fortune and is a masterpiece of engineering).[10] But its genesis and survival in the face of intense disregard of protocols, flouting of conventions, dubious provenance, subterfuge and dangerous circumstances is a perfect vignette of the underlying commitment that pervades the entire Windsor jewellery story, no matter what angle, conceit or thread you attempt to unravel: for Edward, Prince of Wales, King of England and Duke of Windsor, satisfying the needs, desires and obsessions of Bessie Wallis Simpson by whatever means possible was, for him, the only thing that ever truly mattered in his life. It was the only thing, in fact, that had given it meaning.

Notes

Prologue: The Duchess of Windsor's Jewels

1   Hugo Vickers, *Behind Closed Doors* (Penguin Random House, 2012) p.214.
2   *The Jewels of the Duchess of Windsor* (Sotheby's catalogue, 1987).
3   Vickers, *Behind Closed Doors*, p.216.
4   Peter Watson, *Sotheby's: Inside Story* (Bloomsbury, 1997) p.128.
5   John Culme and Nicholas Rayner, *The Jewels of the Duchess of Windsor* (The Vendome Press, 1987) p.11.
6   Ibid.
7   Watson, *Sotheby's: Inside Story* p.199.
8   Vernon Bogdanor, *The Monarchy and the Constitution* (Oxford University Press, 1997).
9   Ronald Lightbown, *The Late King's Goods: Collections, Possessions and Patronage of Charles I* (Alistair McAlpine, 1989) p.259.
10 Parliamentary Debates (Hansard), Vol. 263, United Kingdom: House of Commons, 19 July 1995, col. 1463W.
11 Andrew Roberts, *Churchill: Walking with Destiny* (Penguin Books, 2019) p.771.

Chapter 1: Hatless from the Air

1   Mary Carole McCauley, 'Timonium Woman Recalls Final Days of England's King Edward VIII', *Baltimore Sun*, 16 February 2018.
2   *The Architectural Digest*, 3 April 2018.
3   Ibid.
4   James Pope-Hennessy, *Queen Mary* (George Allen & Unwin, 1959) p.393.
5   Duff Hart-Davis (ed.), *King's Counsellor: Abdication and War: The Diaries of Sir Alan Lascelles* (Orion Publishing, 2020) p.110.
6   Ibid.

7   Ingrid Seward, *My Husband and I: The Inside Story of 70 Years of the Royal Marriage* (Simon & Schuster, 2017) p.67.

8   HRH the Duke of Windsor, *A King's Story* (Cassell & Company, 1951) p.26.

9   James Pope-Hennessy, *Queen Mary*, p.391.

10 Abbie Llewelyn, 'George V branded a "terrible father" by his son Prince Henry: "I want them frightened"' (express.co.uk, 2 April 2021).

11 Duke of Windsor, *A King's Story*, p.26.

12 Catherine Armecin, 'King Edward VIII "Furious" With Parents', *International Business Times*, 16 January 2019.

13 David Duff, *Queen Mary* (Collins, 1985) p.53.

14 James Pope-Hennessy, *The Quest for Queen Mary* (Zuleika and Hodder & Stoughton, 2018) p.243.

15 Piers Brendon and Phillip Whitehead, *The Windsors: A Dynasty Revealed* (Pimlico, 2000) p.32.

16 Pope-Hennessy, *Queen Mary*, p.524.

17 Pope-Hennessy, *The Quest for Queen Mary*, p.143.

18 Ibid.

19 Ibid., p.267.

20 Brendon and Whitehead, *The Windsors: A Dynasty Revealed*, p.29.

21 Jane Ridley, *George V: Never a Dull Moment* (Random House, 2021) p.24.

22 Alden Hatch, *The Mountbattens: The Last Royal Success Story* (Random House, 2008) p.224.

23 *Professional Security Magazine* online, 'Edward and Mrs Simpson and Bodyguards: Part One', 9 July 2020.

24 Ridley, *George V: Never a Dull Moment*, p.112.

25 Ted Powell, *King Edward VIII: An American Life* (OUP Oxford, 2018) p.203.

26 Duke of Windsor, *A King's Story*, p.186.

27 Ibid.

28 John Betjeman, *Collected Poems* (John Murray Press, 2006).

29 Duke of Windsor, *A King's Story*, p.235.

30 Christopher Warwick, *Abdication* (Sidgwick & Jackson, 1986) p.69.

31 Charles Higham, *Wallis: The Secret Lives of the Duchess of Windsor* (Sidgwick & Jackson, 1988).

32 Suzy Menkes, *The Royal Jewels* (Grafton Books, 1986) p.91.

33 Ibid.

34 Ibid., p.101.

35 Andrew Morton, *Theirs is the Kingdom: The Wealth of the Windsors* (Michael O'Mara Books, 1989) p.156.

36 Ibid.

37 Ibid.

38 Parliamentary Debates (Hansard), Vol. 263, United Kingdom: House of Commons, 19 July 1995.

39 'The Convenient Fiction of Who Owns Priceless Treasure', *The Guardian*, 30 May 2002.

40 Michael L. Nash, *Royal Wills in Britain from 1509 to 2008* (Palgrave Macmillan, 2017).

41 Greg King, *The Duchess of Windsor* (Aurum Press 2003), p.473.

42 Ibid.
43 Vickers, *Behind Closed Doors*, p.22.
44 Countess of Romanones, 'The Dear Romance', *Vanity Fair*, June 1986.
45 Alan Riding, 'The Year, 1939. The City, Paris. The House, Windsor', *New York Times*, 21 December 1939.
46 Ibid.
47 Ibid.
48 *The Washington Post*, 28 December 1989.

Chapter 2: Gangan & Co.

1   Mikey Robins, *Seven Deadly Sins and One Very Naughty Fruit* (Simon & Schuster, 2018) Chapter 2: Gluttony.
2   Hector Bolitho, *Victoria and Albert* (Bloomsbury Publishing, 2017) Chapter 35.
3   Lauren Hubbard, 'What Was Queen Victoria Like as a Mother?' (www.townandcountrymag.com, accessed 24 May 2022).
4   Ibid.
5   Ibid.
6   Jo Rowan, 'The Most Expensive Coronations in British History' (www.history.co.uk/articles/the-most-expensive-coronations-in-british-history).
7   Royal Ledger, House of Garrard, 24 Albemarle St, London, United Kingdom.
8   Ibid.
9   Jacqueline Banerjee, 'Bertie's Progress: The Prince of Wales in India, 1875–76: Part I, Bombay to Delhi' (www.victorianweb.org).
10 Menkes, *The Royal Jewels*, p.35.
11 Malcolm Forbes, 'The extraordinary gifts India gave to an English prince in 1875' (www.thenationalnews.com, 30 January 2018).
12 Ibid.
13 M.K. Agarwal, *From Bharata to India, Volume 2: The Rape of Chrysee* (iUniverse, 2012) p.127.
14 Menkes, *The Royal Jewels*, pp.39–40.
15 Andrew Graham-Dixon, 'Jewels in the crown: Inside the Royal Collection' (www.christies.com, 26 January 2018).
16 *The Private Life of the Queen, by a Member of the Royal Household* (HardPress, 2013) p.100.
17 Andy Sully, 'Queen Victoria and Britain's first Diamond Jubilee' (BBC podcast, 22 May 2012).
18 Josephine Rosenberg, 'Queen Victoria's Death and Final Arrangements' (www.thoughtco.com/queen-victoria-dies-1779176).

Chapter 3: Rubies as Big as a Pigeon's Egg

1   Alfred, Lord Tennyson, 'A Welcome to Alexandra' (1863).
2   David Duff, *Alexandra, Princess and Queen* (Collins, 1980) p.31.
3   Menkes, *The Royal Jewels* p.29.
4   Ibid., p.80.

5   Ibid., p.71.
6   Ibid., pp.71–72.
7   Royal Archives, Windsor.
8   William Clarke, *The Lost Fortune of the Tsars* (Weidenfeld & Nicolson, 1994) p.163.
9   Ibid., pp.168–70.
10 David Chavchavadze, *The Grand Dukes* (Atlantic International, 1990) p.110.
11 Albert Stopford, *Russian Diary of an Englishman, Petrograd 1915–17* (Heinemann, 1919).

Chapter 4: The Unimportance of Being Ernest

1   Papers of 1st Viscount Monckton of Brenchley, 1896–1957, Dep. Monckton Trustees, A. Correspondence and Papers, 1896–1941 (1–8) (Oxford, Balliol College).
2   Ibid.
3   Ibid.
4   Elizabeth Longford, *The Queen Mother* (Independent Publishing Group, 1985) p.61.
5   Richard Norton-Taylor and Rob Evans, 'Edward and Mrs Simpson cast in new light', *The Guardian*, 2 March 2000.
6   Ibid.
7   Duchess of Windsor, *The Heart Has Its Reasons* (Michael Joseph, 1956).
8   Papers of 1st Viscount Monckton of Brenchley, 1896–1957.
9   Powell, *King Edward VIII: An American Life*.
10 Anne de Courcy, *The Viceroy's Daughters* (Orion, 2012).
11 Anne Sebba, *That Woman: The Life of Wallis Simpson, Duchess of Windsor* (Weidenfeld & Nicolson, 2011).
12 King, *The Duchess of Windsor* (2003).
13 Sebba, *That Woman*.
14 Private papers cited by Owen Bowcott, legal affairs correspondent, *Guardian*, 22 December 2019.
15 Susanna de Vries, *Royal Mistresses of the House of Hanover-Windsor* (Port Campbell, 2014).
16 Private papers cited by Owen Bowcott.
17 Alexander Larman, *The Crown in Crisis* (St Martin's Publishing Group, 2021).
18 Private papers cited by Owen Bowcott.
19 Alexander Fury, *Financial Times*, 23 June 2020.
20 Melvyn Fairclough, *The Ripper and the Royals* (Duckbacks, 2002).
21 Nash, *Royal Wills in Britain*.
22 Higham, *Wallis: Secret Lives of the Duchess of Windsor*.

Chapter 5: The Vast Shipwreck of My Life's Esteems

1   Marion Crawford, 'The Little Princesses: The Story of the Queen's Childhood by Her Nanny, Crawfie', *Daily Mail*, 21 May 2012.
2   Higham, *Wallis: Secret Lives of the Duchess of Windsor*, p.342.
3   Hart-Davis, *King's Counsellor*.
4   Ralph G. Martin, *The Woman He Loved* (Simon & Schuster, 1974).

5   Sebba, *That Woman*, p.191.
6   Frances Donaldson, *Edward VIII: The Road to Abdication* (Weidenfeld & Nicolson, 1978) p.176.
7   Ibid., p.98.
8   Hart-Davis, *King's Counsellor*.
9   *Daily Mail*, 10 November 2021.
10 Donaldson, *Edward VIII: The Road to Abdication*, p.176.
11 Michael Bloch, *Wallis and Edward, Letters: 1931–37* (Hachette Digital, 1986).
12 Helena Normanton, *New York Times*, 31 May 1937.
13 Sebba, *That Woman*.
14 *Times Literary Supplement*, No 12 (Oxford University Press) 1 November 1974.
15 Crawford, 'The Little Princesses', *Daily Mail*, 21 May 2012.
16 King, *The Duchess of Windsor*.
17 Higham, *Wallis: Secret Lives of the Duchess of Windsor*.
18 Duchess of Windsor, *The Heart Has Its Reasons*.
19 Michael Bloch, *The Secret File of the Duke of Windsor* (Hachette Digital, 1988).
20 Higham, *Wallis: Secret Lives of the Duchess of Windsor*.
21 King, *The Duchess of Windsor*.
22 As reported in *The Age*, 4 June 1937.

Chapter 6: Bride Stripped Bare

1   HRH the Duke of Windsor, *A Family Album* (Cassell 1960) p.73.
2   Ibid.
3   Ibid.
4   Bloch, *Wallis and Edward*.
5   Aleksandar Cvetkovic, 'How To Master Morning Dress', *The Rake*, July 2016.
6   Suzy Menkes, *Harpers Bazaar*, 15 October 2010.
7   Sebba, *That Woman*.
8   As reported in *The Age*, 4 June 1937.
9   Duchess of Windsor, *The Heart Has Its Reasons*.
10 *Time*, 14 June 1937.
11 Cited in Anne de Courcy, *The Viceroy's Daughters: The Lives of the Curzon Sisters* (HarperCollins 2014).
12 Sarah Bradford, 'Lady Alexandra Metcalfe', *The Independent*, 8 August 1995.
13 de Courcy, *The Viceroy's Daughters* (2012).
14 Ibid.
15 Laura Trevelyan, BBC America, 31 March 2011.
16 www.theguardian.com/books/2009/jun/04/archive-duke-windsor-wedding.
17 Ibid.
18 Ibid.
19 de Courcy, *The Viceroy's Daughters* (2014).
20 Adrian Tinniswood, *The Long Weekend* (Vintage, 2018).

Chapter 7: An Iceberg Through the Heart

1   Hart-Davis, *King's Counsellor*, p.108.
2   Robert Rhodes James (ed.), *Chips: The Diaries of Sir Henry Channon* (Weidenfeld & Nicolson, 1967) p.63.
3 . Higham, *Wallis: The Secret Lives of the Duchess of Windsor*, p.114.
4   Rhodes James, *Chips: The Diaries of Sir Henry Channon*, p.57.
5   Susan Lowndes (ed.), *Diaries and Letters of Marie Belloc Lowndes* (Chatto & Windus, 1971) p.146.
6   *Self Portrait With Friends: The Selected Diaries of Cecil Beaton 1926–74* (Weidenfeld & Nicolson 1979) p.47.
7   Higham, *Wallis: Secret Lives of the Duchess of Windsor*, p.111.
8   Ibid.
9   Francis Watson, 'The Death of George V', *History Today*, Vol. 36 (1986) pp.21–30.
10   Duchess of Windsor, *The Heart Has Its Reasons*, p.210.
11   Hart-Davis, *King's Counsellor*, p.5.
12   Juliet Gardiner, *The Thirties* (Harper Press, 2011) p.372.
13   Ibid., p.374.
14   Ibid.
15   Ibid., p.375.
16   Hart-Davis, *King's Counsellor*, p.107.
17   Philip Ziegler, *King Edward VIII* (Harper Press, 2012) p.247.
18   Hart-Davis, *King's Counsellor*, p.108.
19   Ziegler, *King Edward VIII*, p.247.
20   Gardiner, *The Thirties*, p.376.
21   Ibid.
22   Higham, *Wallis: The Secret Lives of the Duchess of Windsor*, p.113.
23   Gardiner, *The Thirties*, p.376.
24   Higham, *Wallis: The Secret Lives of the Duchess of Windsor*, p.115.
25   *New York Daily News*, 12 December 1966.
26   Duchess of Windsor, *The Heart Has Its Reasons*, p.214.
27   Duke of Windsor, *A King's Story*, p.282.
28   Higham, *Wallis: Secret Lives of the Duchess of Windsor*, p.115.
29   Hart-Davis, *King's Counsellor*, p.108.
30   Pope-Hennessy, *Queen Mary*, p.564.
31   Duke of Windsor, *A King's Story*, p.281.
32   Crawford, 'The Little Princesses', *Daily Mail*, 21 May 2012.
33   Ibid.
34   Ibid.
35   Omid Scobie and Carolyn Durand, *Finding Freedom* (HQ HarperCollins, 2020) p.253.

Chapter 8: The Whole Bag of Tricks

1   Powell, *King Edward VIII: An American Life*, p.6.
2   King, *The Duchess of Windsor*, p.152.
3   Ziegler, *King Edward VIII*, p.261.

4   Ibid.

5   Ibid.

6   Robert Beaken (ed.), *Faithful Witness: The Confidential Diaries of Alan Don, Chaplain to the King, the Archbishop and the Speaker, 1931–1946* (SPCK Publishing, 2020).

7   Ziegler, *King Edward VIII*, p.275.

8   Ibid.

9   Sebba, *That Woman*, p.124.

10 Ziegler, *King Edward VIII*, p.280.

11 Hart-Davis, *King's Counsellor*, p.107.

12 Ibid., p.265.

13 Robert Beaken, *Cosmo Lang. Archbishop in War and Crisis* (Bloomsbury Publishing, 2012) pp.132–33.

14 John Gilbert Lockhart, *Cosmo Gordon Lang* (Hodder & Stoughton, 1949) p.393.

15 Ziegler, *King Edward VIII*, p.260.

16 Ibid., p.313.

17 Sebba, *That Woman*, p.125.

18 Ziegler, *King Edward VIII*, p.260.

19 King, *The Duchess of Windsor*, p.158.

20 Martin A. Allen, *Hidden Agenda* (Macmillan, 2000) p.27.

21 Ziegler, *King Edward VIII*, p.282.

22 *Daily Mail* online, 10 November 2021.

23 Sebba, *That Woman*, p.141.

24 Ziegler, *King Edward VIII*, p.292.

25 King, *The Duchess of Windsor*, p.199.

26 Simon Heffer (ed.), *The Diaries of Chips Channon, Vol 1: 1918–38* (Random House, 2021) p.255.

27 Ibid., pp.109–10.

28 Beaken, *Cosmo Lang*, pp.132–33.

29 Ziegler, *King Edward VIII*, p. 310.

30 King, *The Duchess of Windsor*, p.215.

31 Anna Pasternak, *Daily Mail* online, 24 February 2019.

32 Ziegler, *King Edward VIII*, p.315.

33 Ibid p.313.

34 Anna Pasternak, *The American Duchess: The Real Wallis Simpson* (Atria, 2019) p.164.

35 Sebba, *That Woman*, p.174.

36 Ziegler, *King Edward VIII*, p.326.

37 Ibid., p.327.

38 Michael Thornton, *Daily Mail* online, 8 April 2017.

39 Ziegler, *King Edward VIII*, p.327.

40 bbc.co.uk/historyofthebbc/Reith_diaries_Dec_1936_edit.pdf.

41 Hadley Hall Meares, 'Battle of the Royal Brothers', *Vanity Fair*, 22 July 2021.

42 *Daily Mail* online, 10 November 2021.

43 Hart-Davis, *King's Counsellor*, p.109.

Chapter 9: Martyr on the *Orient Express*

1   Higham, *Wallis: Secret Lives of the Duchess of Windsor*.
2   Ziegler, *King Edward VIII*, p.334.
3   Ibid.
4   *Daily Mail* online, 10 November 2021.
5   Sebba, *That Woman*, p.179.
6   *Portsmouth Evening News*, 12 December 1936.
7   Ziegler, *King Edward VIII*, p.334.
8   Sebba, *That Woman*, p.185.
9   Higham, *Wallis: Secret Lives of the Duchess of Windsor*.
10 *Professional Security Magazine* online, 'Edward and Mrs Simpson and bodyguards: part three', 9 July 2020.
11 Ibid., 'part two', 9 July 2020.
12 *Manchester Guardian*, Monday, 14 December 1936.
13 Ibid.
14 Ibid.
15 Higham, *Wallis: Secret Lives of the Duchess of Windsor*.
16 Hart-Davis, *King's Counsellor*, p.110.
17 Ibid.
18 *Time* magazine, 4 January 1937.

Chapter 10: The Adventure of Ednam Lodge

1   Ziegler, *King Edward VIII*, p.502.
2   Michael Thornton, *Daily Mail* online, 8 April 2017.
3   Ibid.
4   Andrew Roberts, *The House of Windsor* (University of California Press, 2000) p.52.
5   Michael Thornton, *Daily Mail* online, 8 April 2017.
6   Eldon King, 'It's a Royal Knockout', *The Guardian*, 2 July 2000.
7   Ziegler, *King Edward VIII*, pp.448 & 471–72.
8   Andrew Roberts, 'Hidden Diaries' (www.thesun.co.uk, 5 May 2020).
9   Ibid.
10 Bloch, *The Secret File*, p.223.
11 Pope-Hennessy, *Queen Mary*, p.614.
12 Ziegler, *King Edward VIII*, p.508.
13 Thornton, *Daily Mail* online, 8 April 2017.
14 Ziegler, *King Edward VIII*, p.511.
15 www.bbc.co.uk/bitesize/guides/zgmf2nb/revision/1.
16 *Royalty Magazine*, Vol. 21 (2009).
17 *New York Times*, 8 February 1952.
18 Andrew Alderson, *Telegraph*, 23 November 2009.
19 Ibid.
20 *Royalty Magazine*, Vol. 21 (2009).
21 Pasternak, *The American Duchess: The Real Wallis Simpson*, p.247.
22 Higham, *Wallis: Secret Lives of the Duchess of Windsor*, p.322.

23   Ibid.

24   Metropolitan Police, MEPO 2/9149 (discovery.nationalarchives.gov.uk/resultsr?q=Ednam&p=1925).

25   Ibid.

Chapter 11: The Mystery of Ednam Lodge

1   *New York Times*, 18 October 1946.
2   *Time* magazine, 28 October 1946, p.36.
3   Higham, *Wallis: Secret Lives of the Duchess of Windsor*, p.324.
4   Tori Van Orden, royalscribe@etoile.co.uk
5   Pasternak, *The American Duchess: The Real Wallis Simpson*, p.247
6   Vickers, *Behind Closed Doors*, p.339
7   Van Orden, royalscribe@etoile.co.uk
8   www.thebeaumonde.org/wallis-simpson-and-the-mystery-of-queen-alexandras-emeralds.
9   Carol Vogel, 'Jewels of Windsor', *New York Times*, 8 February 1987.
10   Higham, *Wallis: Secret Lives of the Duchess of Windsor*, p.324.
11   Ibid., p.325.
12   *Royalty Magazine*, Vol. 21 (2009).
13   Higham, *Wallis: Secret Lives of the Duchess of Windsor*, p.324.
14   Ibid.
15   Menkes, *The Windsor Style*.
16   Hans Nadelhoffer, *Cartier* (Chronicle Books, 2007) p.229.

Chapter 12: The Secret of Ednam Lodge

1   Raj Chengappa, 'The life and crimes of a master criminal Natwarlal', *India Today*, 30 November 1987.
2   Menkes, *The Windsor Style*.
3   *Sydney Morning Herald*, 30 December 2003.
4   Eloise Moss, 'The Rise of the Cat Burglar' (www.historyextra.com, 20 February 2020).
5   Charles Laurence, 'King of Cat Burglars', *Sydney Morning Herald*, 3 May 2004.
6   John Michael Hayes, *To Catch a Thief* (Paramount Pictures, 1955).
7   Moss, 'The Rise of the Cat Burglar'.
8   E.W. Hornung, *The Complete Raffles: The Ides of March* (Leonaur Limited, 2008).
9   Moss, 'The Rise of the Cat Burglar'.
10   Ibid.
11   *Daily Telegraph* (Launceston, Tasmania), 21 April 1908, p.3.
12   Ibid.
13   Caroline Elenowitz-Hess, 'How the "Queen of Thieves" Conned French Riviera Wealthy' (www.atlasobscura.com, 4 May 2021).
14   *Daily Telegraph* (Launceston, Tasmania), 21 April 1908, p.3.
15   www.bbc.com/culture/article/20140711-a-sunny-place-for-shady-people.
16   *Daily Telegraph* (Launceston, Tasmania), 21 April 1908, p.3.

17 Ibid.
18 Ibid.
19 Elenowitz-Hess, 'How the "Queen of Thieves" Conned French Riviera Wealthy'.
20 Duncan Campbell, Peter Scott obituary, *The Guardian*, 21 March 2013.
21 Ibid.
22 James Twomey, 'King of Cat Burglars' (www.mylondon.news, 4 March 2021).
23 Ibid.
24 Campbell, Peter Scott obituary, *The Guardian*, 21 March 2013.
25 Ibid.
26 Dick Kirby, *The Sweeney: The First Sixty Years of Scotland Yard's Flying Squad* (Pen & Sword Books, 2011) p.63.
27 Ibid.

Chapter 13: Auction of the Century

1   Vickers, *Behind Closed Doors*, p.228.
2   Ibid.
3   BBC *Timewatch: Windsors' War* originally broadcast 29 September 1982.
4   Countess of Romanones, 'The Dear Romance', *Vanity Fair*, June 1986.
5   Vickers, *Behind Closed Doors* (Penguin Random House, 2012) p.163.
6   Anna Pasternak, 'Life with Wallis Simpson', *Daily Telegraph*, 1 February 2020.
7   Caroline Blackwood, *The Last of the Duchess* (Pantheon Books, 1995).
8   Countess of Romanones, 'The Dear Romance', *Vanity Fair*, June 1986.
9   Ibid.
10 Ibid.
11 Ibid.
12 Hebe Dorsey, 'The Twilight of a Legend', *Washington Post*, 16 June 1979.
13 Philip Ziegler, *Mountbatten: The Official Biography* (Collins, 1985) p.679.
14 Ibid.
15 Ibid.
16 Ziegler, *Mountbatten: The Official Biography*, p.679.
17 Vickers, *Behind Closed Doors*, p.225.
18 Ziegler, *Mountbatten: The Official Biography*, p.681.
19 Vickers, *Behind Closed Doors*, p.216.
20 Menkes, *The Windsor Style*, p.100.
21 Vickers, *Behind Closed Doors*, p.214.
22 Alexander Fury, 'The Other Crown Jewels: the Wallis Simpson Collection', *Financial Times*, 23 June 2020.
23 Ibid.
24 Carol Vogel, 'Jewels of Windsor', *New York Times*, 8 February 1987.
25 Alexandre Dumas, *The Count of Monte Cristo*, Chapter 31, 'Italy: Sinbad the Sailor'.
26 Vickers, *Behind Closed Doors*, p.214.
27 Ibid., p.215.
28 Ibid., p.214.
29 Ibid.

30 Reuters cited by *New York Times*, 2 May 1986, Section A, p.22.
31 Steve Holland, 'Duchess of Windsor Leaves Fortune to Research Group', United Press International, 1 May 1986.
32 Reuters.
33 Ibid.
34 Vickers, *Behind Closed Doors*, p.216.
35 Christopher Wilson, *Daily Mail*, 2 December 2010.
36 Email correspondence with Michael Bloch, 11 & 13 February 2021.
37 Telephone interview with Aurel Bacs, 26 February 2021.
38 Ibid.
39 Watson, *Sotheby's: Inside Story*, p.149.
40 Wendell Steavenson, 'Under the Hammer', *Time* magazine, 17 March 1997, p.122.
41 Watson, *Sotheby's: Inside Story*, p.144.
42 Ibid., p.151.
43 Culme & Rayner, *The Jewels of the Duchess of Windsor*.
44 Loren Jenkins, 'For a Piece of the Windsor Glitter', *Washington Post*, 4 April 1987.
45 Ibid.
46 Ibid.
47 Francis X. Clines, *New York Times*, 3 April 1987.
48 Ibid.
49 Ibid.
50 Michael Ainslie & Richard Evans, *A Nose for Trouble* (Greenleaf Book Group Press, 2020) Chapter 12.
51 Email correspondence with Michael Bloch, 11 & 13 February 2021.
52 Loren Jenkins, 'For a Piece of the Windsor Glitter', *Washington Post*, 4 April 1987.

Chapter 14: A New York State of Mind

1   John J. Goldman, *Los Angeles Times*, 20 February 1998.
2   *Washington Post*, 28 December 1989.
3   Ibid.
4   Ibid.
5   Simon Edge, 'The Duke and Duchess of Windsor and the House of Love', *Daily Express*, 22 September 2010.
6   Ibid.
7   Ibid.
8   Ibid.
9   www.theglampad.com/2019/04/wallis-in-wonderland-the-private-rooms-and-enchanting-taste-of-the-duchess-of-windsor.
10 Ibid.
11 Ibid.
12 CNN Interactive, 'Windsors' Wares Going on Auction Block', 8 February 1998.
13 'Sotheby's Duchess of Windsor 2010 Sale Results' (thejewelleryeditor.com, 30 November 2010).
14 Ibid.

15 Enid Nemy, 'C.Z. Guest, Society Royalty, Dies at 83', *New York Times*, 9 November 2003.
16 CNN Interactive, 'Windsors' Wares Going on Auction Block', 8 February 1998.
17 Mitchell Owens, 'How the Duke and Duchess of Windsor Lived in Paris', *Architectural Digest*, 3 April 2018.
18 Joe Matthews, 'Bidding on a Royal Romance', *Baltimore Sun*, 28 February 1998.
19 Ibid.
20 Ibid.
21 Ibid.
22 Ibid.
23 John J. Goldman, 'Auction Serves Romantic Piece of Windsor History', *LA Times*, 20 February 1998.
24 *Deseret News*, 21 February 1998.
25 Bill Daley, 'Sotheby's Windsor Auction Sells Aura of Royalty', *Hartford Courant*, 26 February 1998.
26 Ibid.
27 Ibid.
28 Joe Matthews, 'Bidding on a Royal Romance', *Baltimore Sun*, 28 February 1998.
29 Ibid.

Postscript: The Only Thing That Ever Truly Mattered

1 Francesca Cartier Brickell, *The Cartiers* (Random House Publishing Group, 2019) p.89.
2 Nadelhoffer, *Cartier*, p.9.
3 Ibid.
4 Stellene Volandes, 'Battle Over Belperron', *Town & Country Magazine*, January 2012.
5 Nadelhoffer, *Cartier*, p.9.
6 Catton, 'The Duchess of Windsor's Flamingo'.
7 King, *The Duchess of Windsor*, p.337.
8 Pia Catton, 'The Duchess of Windsor's Flamingo'.
9 'Sotheby's Duchess of Windsor 2010 Sale Results', (thejewelleryeditor.com, 30 November 2010).
10 Alexander Fury, 'The Other Crown Jewels: the Wallis Simpson Collection', *Financial Times*, 23 June 2020.

Bibliography

Publications, Catalogues, Journals and Diaries

M.K. Agarwal, *From Baharata to India Volume 2: the Rape of Chrysee* (iUniverse 2012)

Michael Ainslie and Richard Evans, *A Nose for Trouble* (Greenleaf Book Group Press 2020)

Martin A. Allen, *Hidden Agenda* (Macmillan 2000)

Walter L. Arnstein, *Queen Victoria* (Palgrave Macmillan 2003)

Julia Baird, *Victoria The Queen: An Intimate Biography of the Woman Who Ruled an Empire* (Random House 2016)

Robert Beaken, *Cosmo Lang: Archbishop in War and Crisis* (Bloomsbury Publishing 2012)

Cecil Beaton, *Self Portrait with Friends: The Selected Diaries of Cecil Beaton 1926–1974* (Weidenfeld & Nicolson 1979)

Lord Beaverbrook (A.J.P. Taylor ed.) *The Abdication of King Edward VIII* (Hamish Hamilton 1966)

John Betjeman, *Collected Poems* (John Murray Press 2006)

Stephen Birmingham, *Duchess: The Story of Wallis Warfield Windsor* (Little, Brown 1981)

Caroline, Lady Blackwood, *The Last of the Duchess* (Pantheon Books 1995)

Michael Bloch, *The Duke of Windsor's War* (Weidenfeld & Nicolson 1982)

——*The Secret File of the Duke of Windsor* (Hachette Digital 1988)

——*Wallis and Edward: Letters 1931–1937* (Hachette Digital 1986)

—— *The Duchess of Windsor* (Weidenfeld & Nicolson 1996)

——*Wallis and Edward: Letters 1931–1937* (Abacus 2012)

Vernon Bogdanor, *The Monarchy and the Constitution* (Oxford University Press 1997)

Hector Bolitho, *Victoria and Albert* (Bloomsbury Publishing 2017)

Sarah Bradford, *George VI* (Weidenfeld & Nicolson 1989)

Piers Brendon, Phillip Whitehead, *The Windsors: A Dynasty Revealed* (Pimlico 2000)

Francesca Cartier Brickell, *The Cartiers* (Random House Publishing Group 2019)

Lewis Broad, *The Abdication* (Frederick Muller 1961)

Deborah Cadbury, *Queen Victoria's Matchmaking: The Royal Marriages That Shaped Europe* (Bloomsbury 2017)

Sarah Carter, *Mistress of Everything: Queen Victoria in Indigenous Worlds* (Manchester University Press 2016)

Henry Channon (Simon Heffer ed.), *The Diaries of Chips Channon Vol 1: 1918–1938* (Random House 2021)

David Chavchavadze, *The Grand Dukes* (Atlantic International 1990)

William Clarke, *The Lost Fortune of the Tsars* (Weidenfeld and Nicholson 1994)

Catrine Clay, *King, Kaiser, Tsar: Three Royal Cousins Who Led the World to War* (John Murray 2006)

Anne de Courcy, *The Viceroy's Daughters* (Orion 2012)

——*The Viceroy's Daughters: The Lives of the Curzon Sisters* (HarperCollins 2014)

John Culme and Nicholas Rayner, *The Jewels of the Duchess of Windsor* (Vendome Press 1987)

Alan Don (Robert Beaken ed.), *Faithful Witness: The Confidential Diaries of Alan Don* (SPCK Publishing 2020)

Frances Donaldson, *Edward VIII* (Weidenfeld and Nicolson 1974)

——*Edward VIII: The Road To Abdication* (Weidenfeld and Nicolson 1978)

David Duff, *Alexandra, Princess and Queen* (Collins 1980)

—— *Queen Mary* (Collins 1985)

Frank Eyck, *The Prince Consort: A Political Biography* (Chatto 1959)

Melvyn Fairclough, *The Ripper and the Royals* (Duckbacks 2002)

Juliet Gardiner, *Queen Victoria* (Collins and Brown 1997)

——*The Thirties* (Harper Press 2011)

Rupert Godfrey (ed.), *Letters From a Prince: Edward to Mrs Freda Dudley Ward 1918–1921* (Little, Brown & Co. 1998)

Alden Hatch, *The Mountbattens: The Last Royal Success Story* (Random House 2008)

Charles Higham, *Mrs Simpson* (Pan Books 2005)

——*Wallis: The Secret Lives of the Duchess of Windsor* (Sidgwick & Jackson 1988)

Margaret Homans, (Adrienne Munich ed.), *Remaking Queen Victoria* (Cambridge University Press 1997)

——*Royal Representations: Queen Victoria and British Culture, 1837–1876* (Cambridge University Press 1997)

E.W. Hornung, *The Complete Raffles* (Leonaur Limited 2008)

Richard Hough, *Victoria and Albert* (St Martin's Press 1996)

Patrick Howarth, *George VI* (Hutchinson 1987)

Robert Rhodes James: *Albert, Prince Consort: A Biography* (Hamish Hamilton 1983)

——*Chips: The Diaries of Sir Henry Channon* (Weidenfeld & Nicolson 1967)

Greg King, *The Duchess of Windsor: The Uncommon Life of Wallis Simpson* (Citadel 1999)

—— *The Duchess of Windsor* (Aurum Press 2003)

Dick Kirby, *The Sweeney: The First Sixty Years of Scotland Yard's Flying Squad* (Pen & Sword Books, 2011)

Alan Lascelles (Duff Hart-Davis ed.), *End of an Era, 1887–1920. The Letters and Journals of Sir Alan Lascelles. Vol. 1* (Hamish Hamilton 1986)

——*In Royal Service, 1920–1936. The Letters and Journals of Sir Alan Lascelles. Vol. 2* (Hamish Hamilton 1989)

———*King's Counsellor: Abdication and War: The Diaries of Sir Alan Lascelles* (Orion Publishing 2020)

Robert Lacey, *Sotheby's: Bidding For Class* (Little, Brown & Co. 1998)

Alexander Larman, *The Crown In Crisis* (St Martin's Publishing Group 2021)

Brian Learmount, *A History of the Auction* (Barnard & Learmont 1985)

Ronald Lightbown, *The Late King's Goods: Collections, Possessions and Patronage of Charles I* (Alistair McAlpine 1989)

John Gilbert Lockhart, *Cosmo Gordon Lang* (Hodder & Stoughton 1949)

Elizabeth Longford, *The Queen Mother* (Independent Publishing Group 1985)

Marie Belloc Lowndes (Susan Lowndes ed.), *Diaries and Letters of Marie Belloc Lowndes* (Chatto & Windus 1971)

Andrew Lownie, *Stalin's Englishman: Guy Burgess, the Cold War, and the Cambridge Spy Ring* (Hodder & Stoughton 2015)

———*The Mountbattens: Their Lives and Loves* (Blink Publishing 2019)

———*Traitor King: The Scandalous Exile of the Duke and Duchess of Windsor* (Bonnier Books 2021)

Ralph G. Martin, *The Woman He Loved* (Simon & Schuster 1974)

Christopher Mason, *The Art of the Steal* (Putnam 2004)

Suzy Menkes, *The Royal Jewels* (Grafton Books 1986)

———*The Windsor Style* (Grafton Books 1987)

Andrew Morton, *Theirs is the Kingdom: The Wealth of the Windsors* (Michael O'Mara Books 1989)

——— *Wallis in Love: The Untold Life of the Duchess of Windsor, the Woman Who Changed the Monarchy* (Grand Central Publishing 2018)

Diana Mosley, *The Duchess of Windsor* (Sidgwick & Jackson 1980)

Charles Loch Mowat, *Britain Between the Wars 1918–1940* (Methuen 1955)

Hans Nadelhoffer, *Cartier* (Chronicle Books 2007)

Michael L. Nash, *Royal Wills in Britain from 1509 to 2008* (Palgrave Macmillan UK 2017)

Sir Harold Nicolson, *King George the Fifth: His Life and Reign* (Constable and Co. 1952)

John Parker, *King of Fools* (St Martin's Press 1988)

Anna Pasternak, *The American Duchess: The Real Wallis Simpson* (Atria 2019)

Ben Pimlott, *The Queen: Elizabeth II and the Monarchy* (HarperCollins 2001)

James Pope-Hennessy, *Queen Mary* (George Allen and Unwin Ltd 1959)

———*The Quest for Queen Mary* (Zuleika and Hodder and Stoughton 2018)

Ted Powell, *King Edward VIII: An American Life* (Oxford University Press 2018)

Jane Ridley, *Victoria: Queen, Matriarch, Empress* (Penguin 2015)

———*George V: Never a Dull Moment* (Random House 2021)

Andrew Roberts (Antonia Fraser ed.), *The House of Windsor* (Cassell and Co. 2000)

Andrew Roberts, *The House of Windsor* (University of California Press 2000)

———*Churchill: Walking with Destiny* (Penguin Books 2019)

Mikey Robins, *Seven Deadly Sins and One Very Naughty Fruit* (Simon & Schuster Australia 2018)

Kenneth Rose, *King George V* (Weidenfeld and Nicolson 1983)

Omid Scobie and Carolyn Durand, *Finding Freedom* (HQ HarperCollins 2020)

Anne Sebba, *That Woman: The Life of Wallis Simpson, Duchess of Windsor* (Weidenfeld & Nicolson 2011)

Ingrid Seward, *My Husband and I: The Inside Story of 70 Years of the Royal Marriage* (Simon & Schuster UK 2017)

Richard René Silvin, *Noblesse Oblige: The Duchess of Windsor As I Knew Her* (Nike Publishing 2010)

David Sinclair, *Two Georges: The Making of the Modern Monarchy* (Hodder and Stoughton 1988)

Sotheby's, *The Jewels of the Duchess of Windsor* (Sotheby's 1987)

Albert Stopford, *Russian Diary of an Englishman, Petrograd 1915–1917* (Heinemann 1919)

Adrian Tinniswood, *The Long Weekend* (Vintage 2018)

Hugo Vickers, *Elizabeth, the Queen Mother* (Arrow Books 2006)

—— *Behind Closed Doors: The Tragic, Untold Story of the Duchess of Windsor* (Penguin Random House 2012)

Susanna de Vries, *Royal Mistresses of the House of Hanover-Windsor* (Port Campbell 2014)

Christopher Warwick, *Abdication* (Sidgwick & Jackson 1986)

Peter Watson, *Sotheby's: Inside Story* (Bloomsbury 1997)

Alison Weir, *Britain's Royal Families: The Complete Genealogy, Revised edition* (Random House 1995)

Sir John Wheeler-Bennett, *HRH The Duke of Windsor: A King's Story* (Cassell & Co 1951)

——*King George VI* (Macmillan 1958)

——*A Family Album* (Cassell 1960)

Susan Williams, *The People's King: The True Story of the Abdication* (Palgrave Macmillan 2004)

A.N. Wilson, *Victoria: A Life* (Atlantic Books 2014)

Christopher Wilson, *Dancing With the Devil: the Windsors and Jimmy Donahue* (HarperCollins 2001)

The Duchess of Windsor, *The Heart Has Its Reasons: The Memoirs of the Duchess of Windsor* (Michael Joseph 1956)

Philip Ziegler, *Mountbatten: The Official Biography* (Collins 1985)

——*King Edward VIII: The Official Biography* (Alfred A. Knopf 1991)

——*King Edward VIII: The Official Biography* (HarperCollins 2012)

——*King Edward VIII* (Harper Press 2012)

——'Windsor, (Bessie) Wallis, Duchess of Windsor (1896–1986)' *Oxford Dictionary of National Biography* (Oxford University Press 2004)

Newspapers, Magazines, Television Programmes and Videos

Parliamentary Debates (Hansard); *The Architectural Digest*; *International Business Times*; *Professional Security Magazine Online*; *The Guardian*; *The Washington Post*; *Vanity Fair*. *The New York Times*; *Financial Times*; *Daily Mail*; *Times Literary Supplement*; *The Melbourne Age*; *The Rake*; *Harpers Bazaar*; *Time Magazine*; *The Independent*; *BBC America*; *History Today*; *New York Daily News*; *Journal of British Studies*; *Portsmouth Evening News*; *Manchester Guardian*; *Royalty Magazine*; *UK Daily Telegraph*; *India Today*; *The Sydney Morning Herald*; *Launceston Daily Telegraph*; *BBC Timewatch*; *Reuters*; *United Press International*; *Los Angeles Times*; *UK Daily Express*; *Baltimore Sun*; *Deseret News*; *Hartford Courant*; *Town & Country Magazine*; *The Wall Street Journal*; *The Canberra Times*

Archives, Private Papers, Interviews and Collections

The National Archives; Royal Archives, Windsor; Balliol Archives: Papers of 1st Viscount Monckton of Brenchley; Michael Bloch; Aurel Bacs; Andrew Lownie; University of Cambridge: HRH the Duke of Windsor Correspondence 26 Oct 1936–5 Dec 1937; University of Cambridge: The Papers of Sir Alan Lascelles; Churchill Archives Centre; University of Southampton: Mountbatten Papers; University of Southampton: Philip Ziegler Papers; Cambridge University Library: Baldwin papers

Websites, Blogs and Online Resources

www.express.co.uk
www.townandcountrymag.com
www.victorianweb.org
www.thenationalnews.com
www.christies.com
www.theguardian.com
www.dailymail.co.uk
www.bbc.co.uk
www.thesun.co.uk
www.nationalarchives.gov.uk

royalscribe@etoile.co.uk
www.thebeaumonde.org
www.historyextra.com
www.atlasobscura.com
www.mylondon.news
www.theglampad.com
www.thejewelleryeditor.com
edition.cnn.com
www.grosvenor.com

Index

Note: *italicised* page references denote illustrations

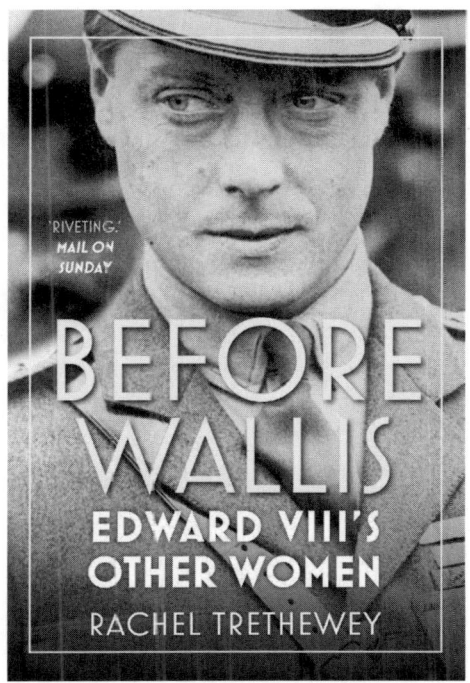

978 0 7509 9339 5

'Rachel Trethewey … discovered vast swathes of previously unpublished correspondence between Edward VIII and his mistress of 16 years … this is an extraordinary treasure-trove … it sheds new light, just when you think there's no more light to be shed, on Edward VIII.'

Christopher Wilson

You may also enjoy …

978 1 80399 011 8

Tea With Hitler is a family saga of duty, courage, wilful blindness and criminality, revealing the tragic fate of a Saxe-Coburg princess murdered as part of the Nazi euthanasia programme and the story of Queen Victoria's Jewish great-grand-daughter, rescued by her British relatives.